Check It While I Wreck It

Black Womanhood, Hip-Hop Culture, and the Public Sphere

GWENDOLYN D. POUGH

Northeastern University Press   Boston

NORTHEASTERN UNIVERSITY PRESS

"Woman Poem" from *Black Feeling, Black Talk, Black Judgment* by Nikki Giovanni, copyright © 1968, 1970 by Nikki Giovanni. Reprinted by permission of HarperCollins Publishers Inc., William Morrow.
"I'm a Hip Hop Cheerleader" by Jessica Care Moore from *Bum Rush the Page*, edited by Tony Medina and Louis Reyes Rivera, copyright © 2001 by Bone Bristle, LLC, Tony Medina, and Louis Reyes Rivera. Used by permission of Three Rivers Press, a division of Random House, Inc.
"Memorial" from *Homecoming* by Sonia Sanchez, copyright © 1970. Used by permission of Broadside Press.
"Queen of the Universe" by Sonia Sanchez from *Black Scholar*, copyright © 1970. Used by permission of *Black Scholar*.
"I've Got to Use My Imagination." Words and music by Gerry Goffin and Barry Goldberg, copyright © 1973 (Renewed 2001) Screen Gems-EMI Music Inc. All rights reserved. International copyright secured. Used by permission.

LIBRARY OF CONGRESS CATALOGING-IN-PUBLICATION DATA

Pough, Gwendolyn D., 1970–
    Check it while I wreck it : Black womanhood, hip-hop culture, and the public sphere / by Gwendolyn D. Pough.
        p.   cm.
Includes bibliographical references (p.   ) and index.
    ISBN 1–55553–608–5 (cloth : alk. paper)—
    ISBN 1–55553–607–7 (pbk. : alk. paper)
  1. African American women—Social conditions. 2. Hip-hop—United States. 3. Rap (Music)—History and criticism. 4. Popular culture—United States. I. Title.
    E185.86 .P666 2004
    305.48'896073—dc22   2003021869

Designed by Steve Kress

Composed in Bembo by Coghill Composition Company in Richmond, Virginia.
Printed and bound by Edwards Brothers, Inc., in Ann Arbor, Michigan. The paper is EB Natural, an acid-free sheet.

MANUFACTURED IN THE UNITED STATES OF AMERICA
08   07   06   05   04   5   4   3   2   1

Check It While I Wreck It

For my mother, Donna Pough

Words can never begin to express how much having you in my life has meant to me.

You are my inspiration and my main source of encouragement. I love you.

Contents

Illustrations

Acknowledgments

A lot of people in my life have helped me get to this point. A young girl from Paterson, New Jersey, does not typically make it to the point of publishing a book with an academic press, let alone getting a Ph.D. and a tenure-track position, without some help along the way. Many people have offered me encouragement and advice. And I will try to acknowledge as many of those people as I can.

First, I would like to thank God. I know that I have been blessed, and I can never give enough glory to God for shining a light on my life. I want to thank the ancestors who paved the way and whose shoulders lend me height and allow me to soar. My family has been my source of inspiration and strength throughout my life. I want to thank my husband, Cedric Bolton, for understanding when I had to write and for being my biggest cheerleader. I know that I'm loved, and I hope you know that I love you too. I want to thank my mother, Donna Pough, for modeling to me the true nature of perseverance. You raised me right, Mommy. And you did it all by yourself. If I become even half the woman you are, then I know that I'll be more than most. Jennifer Pough and Mingo Coleman, you guys are my favorite couple, and that's not just because Jennifer is my sister and we grew up together. Jennifer, we are only eleven months apart, so I cannot remember a time in my life when you were not there. Thanks for being so supportive, and I hope that I have always been as supportive to you. Cassandra Pough, Michelle Pough, and Tashina Pough are the best sisters I could ask for. We didn't grow up together, because Jennifer and I were a little older than you were. And I know you probably felt like you had three mommies growing up. But I hope you know that you are loved. My nieces Ashlee and Zaria Coleman bring joy to my life and help me to put things in perspective. I love being your auntie. I want to thank my own aunt, Deloris Reed, for being a caring and giving person. I will never forget you taking me to college freshman year and bringing my things to Boston when I started my master's program. You are a wonderful aunt and an even more wonderful person. I would also like to thank my father, John Pough, who passed away on May 4, 2003. I've always loved you more than you knew. I want to thank my in-laws, Ruby and Ervin McCloud and Priscilla Bolton. Thanks for welcoming me into your family. I also want to extend my love to family not mentioned by name but dear to my heart. Thank you to all my aunts, uncles, and cousins.

There is really nothing like good friends and colleagues, and I've had more than my fair share. There are lots of people who are not related to me but who have been like family. I want to thank the following friends and colleagues for varying degrees of support in getting me to this major milestone in my life. As this book project was extended from work begun in my dissertation, I would like to thank my dissertation co-advisors, Susan Jarratt and Cheryl Johnson. You were wonderful mentors and friends. Thank you both for your guidance and love. Jennifer and Peter Springer, words cannot begin to express how much your friendship has meant to me. Those wonderful Bajan meals helped a sister make it through graduate school. I love you guys. Lily Payne, Latisha Nwoye, Carmiele Wilkerson, Kim Dillon Shively, Tammy Kernodle, Elaine Richardson, Lisa Albrecht, Yolanda Hood, and Rod Ferguson have been wonderful friends and colleagues. I also want to thank the University of Minnesota Department of Women's Studies, especially Eden Torres, Richa Nagar, and Jigna Desai. I also want to thank the University of Minnesota Department of African American Studies, especially Keletso Atkins and Rose Brewer. The Summer Institute on Scholarship, Black Women, and Africana Studies Research Center at Cornell University was an amazing experience in the summer of 2002. I want to thank James Turner for having the vision to make that happen. And I wish to thank the New Sage Scholars Collective, which grew out of that institute. We're the next generation.

Y'all ready? I want to thank the Theta Upsilon chapter of Delta Sigma Theta Sorority Incorporated, particularly the dynamic line of nine that pledged in the spring of 1990, but most especially Kimmie Clark and Antoinette Young. I want to thank Rachel Raimist for allowing me to use her wonderful photographs. And I want to thank the people at Northeastern University Press, especially former acquisitions editor Elizabeth Swayze, for believing in this project, and current acquisitions editor Sarah Rowley for continuing to believe in the project and helping me through to the end.

The following University of Minnesota offices offered support for the completion of this project: the College of Liberal Arts, the Graduate School through the Faculty Summer Research Fellowship and McKnight Summer Fellowship, and the President's Multicultural Research Award. I want to thank Lois Williams and the Copyright Permissions Center at the University of Minnesota for helping me obtain permission to use the poetry and trying to get permissions for rap lyrics.

Finally, I want to thank Hip-Hop. Without Hip-Hop, I would not have a book to write or the mind-set to write it. Hip-Hop gave me a culture and a language. Memorizing the lyrics of my favorite songs and writing my own rhymes introduced me to literacy I could feel. In the words of Nas, "save the music y'all." Much love and peace.

Check It While I Wreck It

Introduction
Hip-Hop Is More Than Just Music to Me:
The Potential for a Movement in the Culture

In Rachel Raimist's groundbreaking film about women and Hip-Hop, *Nobody Knows My Name,* singer Leschea belts out a song about how Hip-Hop is more than just music to her. She does not just sing about Hip-Hop or even just sing over Hip-Hop beats. In the film she conveys how she lives the culture, and it is more than just music.[1] Keeping Leschea's awareness of the culture's influence in mind, there are a few fundamental things about the founding moment of Hip-Hop culture that we need to know if we want to begin to envision the possibilities for change today.[2] First and foremost, we need to understand what Hip-Hop is. To summarize, Hip-Hop started in the early to mid-1970s in the South Bronx and has since come to span the globe. It is a youth movement, a culture, and a way of life. Hip-Hop is the culture; rap is the music.

What are the implications of doing an academic analysis of Hip-Hop culture and rap music? For a long time I thought I would never write an academic piece on Hip-Hop. I loved it too much; it meant too much to me. Now I know that I love it too much not to write about it, theorize about it, look critically at it, and think about not only what needs to change but also how to make that change happen. I believe that we need to think about the whole of Hip-Hop culture in all of our interrogations in order to fully appreciate Hip-Hop as a youth movement and ultimately to recognize the political potential within it.

Rap music is a part of Hip-Hop culture, but there is more to Hip-Hop than rap. Rap music—along with graffiti writing, break dancing, and deejaying—is one of the founding elements of Hip-Hop culture. Each of these elements has had its time to shine. And each has experienced moments of co-optation and exploitation by the mainstream. In the early days of Hip-Hop the DJ reigned supreme, and soon DJs were called upon to play in posh disco clubs where most Hip-Hop kids could not even get past the velvet ropes to gain entry. Then graffiti writing became popular, and the graffiti writer was literally taken off the streets and subways, planted in art galleries, and heralded as the next big art find. This co-optation of graffiti culture happened even as the graffiti writers faced their most intense period of repression, with city officials declaring war on them and going to extreme measures to catch and punish them. Next, break dancing gained wide success. Break dancing found a higher level of exploitation because it made it all the way to the big screen, capturing the public eye in films such as *Beat Street* (1984), *Breakin'* (1984), and *Breakin' 2: Electric Boogaloo* (1985).[3] But it is rap music that found the most success as a commodified and exploited element of Hip-Hop culture. Quite frankly, rap music was easier to co-opt and exploit because the production costs of an album are far less than those of a film, and it's easier to produce and sell thousands of rap records than one piece of graffiti art on canvas. Rap—like other forms of Black music that went before it—was ready-made for capital gain.[4]

An excellent visual representation of the moment in which Hip-Hop experienced the kinds of conflicted moments of intense popularity and equally intense co-optation and commodification described above can be seen when we look at the film *Wild Style* (1982).[5] This Hip-Hop film traces the early days of Hip-Hop and shows how each element contributed to the initial founding moment. The film, set in the South Bronx, showcases the beginnings of break dancing, rapping, deejaying, and graffiti writing. It pays close attention to the art world's courting of young graffiti artists and shows the conflicted nature of this courtship. In *Wild Style* we glimpse the beginnings of Hip-Hop's dilemma: staying true to the art form inspired by the youth culture or embracing mass culture and moving on to success outside the culture. While the film portrays the graffiti world and issues of commodification, by the end of the film, in the big Hip-Hop show in the park, graffiti provides the backdrop and rap takes center stage. The film closes by suggesting that it is the rap element of Hip-Hop culture that will take the culture to the level of worldwide success.

The association between Hip-Hop and rap often results in people collapsing Hip-Hop and rap without fully realizing that Hip-Hop is the culture and rap is a form of music that comes out of Hip-Hop culture. Talking about Hip-Hop as a culture, not just in terms of its connection to rap, sets the stage for a wider understanding of Hip-Hop as a youth movement and as a cultural phenomenon that encompasses a variety of genres.

Thinking about Hip-Hop as a culture and understanding the founding elements allow us to better understand the ways in which Hip-Hop has grown and includes other elements. In fact, even the musical component of Hip-Hop has grown and encompasses more than just rap music. We can now talk about "rock/rap," "Hip-Hop soul," "rapso," and "Hip House." In terms of expanded elements of Hip-Hop, we can now talk about "raptivists" and "Hip-Hop activists," "Raptors" or Hip-Hop actors. We can also now speak of a Hip-Hop cinema, which encompasses everything from documentary to drama, comedy, and spoof. There is also Hip-Hop-inspired literature and poetry. Hip-Hop beats back the majority of the commercials shown on television. And various forms of rapping can be heard in commercials. The areas in our contemporary society touched by Hip-Hop are so vast that it is sometimes difficult to look at contemporary U.S. popular culture and distinguish between what is Hip-Hop and what is not Hip-Hop. In fact, with recent ventures such as Russell Simmons's *Def Comedy Jam* and *Def Poetry Jam*, one could joke that you could throw *def* in front of anything and see a Hip-Hop influence. Rappers are constantly coming out with new clothing lines, and "urban wear" in most circles is code for what is considered to be Hip-Hop gear. The culture has indeed permeated all aspects of society. I mention this to underline that

Hip-Hop started out as more than rap music and today is most certainly bigger than rap music. Understanding Hip-Hop culture is crucial to understanding its influence, particularly its influence on the lives of young Black women. However, I think it is also crucial that we have some understanding of the moment in which Hip-Hop culture was created.

Many scholars of rap music trace the founding of rap to African and African American oral and musical traditions, specifically African griots and storytellers, and link the rhythm of rap to the use of drums in Africa and to African American music in the United States, from slave songs and spirituals to jazz and R&B.[6] They find connections between rap music (and Hip-Hop culture more broadly) and Black nationalist traditions.[7] And they locate its origins in African American verbal traditions such as playing the dozens and signifying.[8] In *Say It Loud: The Story of Rap Music*, K. Maurice Jones traces a lineage for rap back to the "hidden messages of slave folktales; the call and response of the black church; the joy and pain of the blues; the jive talk and slang of the jockeys, hipsters, and jazz musician; the boasting of street talk; the sidesplitting wit of comedians; and the eloquence of black activists."[9] For Jones all of these African American oral traditions, including rap, can be traced back to West African oral traditions.

He notes that in traditional African societies, the spoken word and oral culture were highly evolved and included poetry, storytelling, and speaking to drumbeats. Oral culture was used to both inform and entertain. These kinds of links that flesh out the lineage and legacy of rap music are important, and we should continue to make them, highlighting the rich history of African and African American oral and musical traditions. There are several well-informed histories of rap music and Hip-Hop culture that take on the task of conveying rap's ties to the past.[10] Here, though, I am concerned with understanding the role that Hip-Hop culture plays in the larger U.S. public sphere today in order to better ascertain the role that Black women play in both that arena and Hip-Hop seen as a counter–public sphere. I equally interrogate Hip-Hop culture, the public sphere, Black womanhood, and their relationship with one another.

At the critical historical moment in which Hip-Hop culture was being created, the South Bronx and the country as a whole were suffering from postindustrial decline. Jobs were scarce, and factories and businesses were leaving urban areas. The future looked bleak, to say the least.[11] Budget woes meant that arts programs were being cut from school curriculums, and the youth who created Hip-Hop had to find alternative ways to express their creative energy. With no music class or instruments to play, they took deejaying to a new level, past simply placing a recond on a stereo and letting it play. They found ways to mix, cut, and slice records. They figured out how to keep the break beat—the part of a recording where the band breaks down—going by using two turntables and a mixer. DJ Grandmaster Flash created the scratch and turned the turntable into an instrument. Rappers built on African American oral and musical traditions and turned talk into a new art form. With no art classes, graffiti artists made the city's buildings and trains their canvas. Graffiti writing started during World War II, when "Kilroy was here" started popping up all over the place. However, no one can dispute that what the young Black and Latino writers in the South Bronx started was something new and different. Likewise, the creative form of break dancing—which started out as a way for gangs to battle without physically fighting—became a new style that other dance genres soon looked to for inspiration. When young urban Black and Latino youth were turned away from (and, indeed, turned off by) the posh, exclusive disco clubs, they had their own parties in the parks, tapping into streetlights for electricity. These young Black and Latino people in the South Bronx created something that is now a worldwide phenomenon out of nothing. They worked with the scraps they were given and developed a rich and vibrant culture and youth movement.

Understanding how young people created so much with so little makes it easier to think about how we can continue to build, expand, and improve on the culture. There are countless people who would look at the current commodified and exploited state of Hip-Hop culture, specifically rap music, and say that there is no hope. But I would point to the way in which the culture evolved and say no, that is not the case. If those youth could create such a vast and provocative culture out of nothing, surely we can begin to fashion a movement with political underpinnings based on that culture. I interrogate Hip-Hop culture and look for spaces where Black feminism, as a political project that draws on praxis (theory and practice), can make interventions and work toward change within Hip-Hop. *Check It While I Wreck It* is largely about identifying spaces where meaningful political change is possible so that we might make better use of those spaces as they occur in the future. Those of us who know about Black struggle in the United States know that what has been accomplished is largely due to the efforts of Black women. I want to explore these women's legacy and look toward how the Black women of the Hip-Hop generation can build on it.

Women's contribution to Hip-Hop culture has been lost, or rather erased. To hear some self-proclaimed Hip-Hop historians tell it, there were no significant women in Hip-Hop's history. In a section of his book *Hip Hop America*, called "Of Queens and Chickenheads," music critic Nelson George writes:

> Hip hop has produced no Bessie Smith, no Billie Holiday, no Aretha Franklin. You could make an argument that Queen Latifah has, as a symbol of female empowerment, filled Aretha's shoes for rap, though for artistic impact Latifah doesn't compare to the Queen of Soul. Similarly, you can make a case that Salt-N-Pepa's four platinum albums and clean cut sexuality mirror the Supremes' pop appeal, though neither of the two MCs or their beautiful DJ Spinderella is ever gonna be Dianna Ross. In the twenty plus years of hip hop history on record, a period that has produced black vocalists Chaka Khan, Whitney Houston, Anita Baker, Tracy Chapman, Mary J. Blige, and Erykah Badu, there are no women who have contributed profoundly to rap's artistic growth.[12]

He then goes on to name several of the women rappers who have released albums, from the early group Sequence to Foxy Brown, Missy Elliott, and Lil' Kim, and says, "Yet I would argue that if none of these female artists had ever made a record, hip hop's development would have been no different."[13] Those words have troubled me for quite some time, and I see this project as a way to correct these kinds of misguided statements. Hip-Hop may be a uniquely testosterone-filled space, but to say that women have not contributed significantly to its development is false. Women have always been a part of Hip-Hop culture and a significant part of rap music.

Consider the "Hip-Hop Cheerleaders" that Jessica Care Moore writes of, who hold it down for Hip-Hop culture and support its growth through their work and actions. Think of the early women rappers and DJs who risked getting robbed in subways trying to transport stereo equipment and crates of records to jams in other neighborhoods. Both in the beginning and now, female Hip-Hop heads are part of the crowds at shows and support rap by buying the music even when most of it is sexist and degrading to Black womanhood.[14]

Rachel Raimist's *Nobody Knows My Name* foregrounds the stories of six women—a break-dancer, a DJ, the wife of a struggling rapper, a singer, a rapper, and a rapper/spoken-word artist—intimately involved with Hip-Hop culture, women who love and are dedicated to the culture. Raimist's film grants an expanded voice to women in Hip-Hop culture that other documentary films such as *The Show* (1995) and *Rhyme & Reason* (1997) leave out.[15] The singer Leschea, rapper T-Love, and rapper/spoken-word artist Medusa are finding it hard to claim a space for themselves in the male-centered world of Hip-Hop, yet they persist because they have something to say and recognize the potential of Hip-Hop as a vehicle for that message. Listening to the stories of these women and seeing firsthand their enormous talent demonstrates clearly that George's words are not true, because without these women's voices and those of others like them, Hip-Hop would be far less than it is.

As a young woman who came of age in the era of Hip-Hop, I know that women have added tremendously to the culture. The entry of five specific female rappers into the public realm stand out in my mind as moments that signaled a shift in the culture and the music, revealing its evolution. The first was Roxanne Shante, quite possibly the best freestyle rapper to ever bless the microphone.[16]

Her MC freestyle battles are famous—we can still hear stories today about how some male rappers were scared to battle her—and she no doubt elevated the art of freestyle in rap. Shante's answer to UTFO's "Roxanne Roxanne," "Roxanne's Revenge," grabbed public attention away from the three men rappers and sparked a slew of answer raps. Would Hip-Hop be different if we had never heard of Roxanne Shante? I think it would be. Her freestyle skills elevated the art form. And while she may not have invented the answer rap, she made it a viable means of entry into the public sphere for some early female rappers.[17]

Without a Roxanne Shante first, we might not have heard the two female rappers who made up the duo Salt-N-Pepa. The wave of answer raps that Shante started paved the way for Salt-N-Pepa to record their first song, "The Showstopper," an answer to Doug E. Fresh and Slick Rick's "The Show." While George may be right in noting that Salt-N-Pepa will never be the Supremes, it's equally true that no male rap group will ever be the Temptations, and no male rapper may ever top the success and longevity of Michael Jackson. While Eminem might just be the next Elvis, I do not think any rap act to date can top that magical moment in Black and world music history that was Motown. But Salt-N-Pepa certainly improved the artistry and showmanship of Hip-Hop, showcasing a package that, in my opinion, rivaled the kind of packaged talent that came out of Motown. Everything from the way they dressed to their haircuts changed the way rap was *performed*. Their dance steps, stage presence, and performance moved the Hip-Hop show from the rough and rugged MC walking back and forth across the stage with a mike to a full-blown show. In fact, I would go so far as to say that, whatever your feelings about MC Hammer, we would not have had the kind of showmanship that Hammer exhibited if we had not had a Salt-N-Pepa first.

MC Lyte's lyrical skills and verbal prowess topped those of a lot of her male peers when she initially came out. Her flow was unique, and while some might say that we had never heard a girl rap like that before, I would venture to say that we had never heard anyone rap like that before. I cannot imagine contemporary rap music and Hip-Hop culture if MC Lyte had never performed. Her delivery was so dynamic that she elevated the rap game simply by being in it. And the fifth and latest female rapper whose impact on Hip-Hop should never be doubted is Missy "Misdemeanor" Elliott. When I first heard Missy rapping on Gina Thompson's "The Things That You Do," I knew that Hip-Hop had stepped up a notch. The way she performed her lyrics changed the way we thought about what a rapper could and could not do. Her now famous "hee, hee, hee, hee, how" had people calling her the female Busta Rhymes. But her skills as a songwriter and a producer show us that she is in a class all by herself and has made a tremendous impact on Hip-Hop. Her music videos alone changed what had become a rather predictable genre and added a touch of excitement.

What does it mean to be a woman in the Hip-Hop generation, attempting to claim a space in a culture that constantly tries to deny women voice? I am not writing a Hip-Hop history or even a history of women in Hip-Hop. Rather, I am looking at the culture and the music to see how Black women have taken a stance and how they continue to do so. I also want to call attention to the ways in which the culture inhibits their growth, denigrates Black womanhood, and endangers the lives of young Black girls, because I hope that Black feminism will take up the cause and utilize the space that Hip-Hop culture provides in order to intervene in the lives of young girls.

In Chapter One I begin by interrogating notions of the public sphere as defined by Jürgen Habermas and the Black public sphere as defined by various theorists of Black public culture in order to fully understand how intersections of race, class, gender, and sexuality further complicate understandings of the public sphere. I explore issues of spectacle, representation, and the public/private split in relation to Black public culture, and I maintain that—as a result of Black history in the United States—these concepts have to be rethought when applied to Black participation in the larger U.S. public sphere.

In Chapter Two I examine the rhetoric of Black women's expressive culture in the United States, trace the history of their participation, and document the ways Black women have simultaneously helped to shape the Black public sphere and made sure that their own voices were heard and their own needs were addressed. Understanding how Black women in the past navigated the public sphere is crucial to thinking about contemporary Black womanhood and the public sphere. In Chapter Three I examine what the role of women in Hip-Hop has been and expand on the theorization and definition of "wreck" in Hip-Hop by thinking about its uses as a rhetorical tool that builds on Black womanist traditions and a Hip-Hop present. I am concerned with the ways in which the rhetorical practices of Black women participants in Hip-Hop culture "bring wreck"—that is, moments when Black women's discourses disrupt dominant masculine discourses, break into the public sphere, and in some way impact or influence the United States imaginary.

In Chapter Four I move to the issue of women coming of age in an era of Hip-Hop and Black women claiming a public voice via Hip-Hop culture. I first look at the medium of music and probe the implications of Black women telling their own stories via rap music. I examine how these women add to the lineage of Black autobiography in America and how they use the language of the past and present to construct their identities as Black women, create a rhetoric of wreck that claims agency, and encourage self-definition not only for themselves but also for contemporary young Black women.

In Chapter Five I move to an exploration of the "ghetto girl" motif as it is represented in ghetto exploitation cinema and fiction of the late twentieth and early twenty-first century. I look specifically at the ghetto girl as a recurring element in cinema and fiction set in urban America and meant to replicate the gritty realities of life in predominantly Black and poor neighborhoods. The ghetto girl, while not always a dominant or central character in these films, is always consistently represented in caricatured ways. I problematize these representations in order to understand what they mean to the real lives of young Black women.

In Chapter Six I probe the ongoing public dialogue found in rap love songs about love and relationships between men and women. I also challenge Black feminism to look at the effect rap's constructions of masculinity and femininity have had on Black women rappers and other young Black women. Women rappers have appropriated the language used by men rappers to denigrate women and use it as a means of empowerment in their own lyrics. I maintain that if conversations and critiques of rap music and Hip-Hop culture move past merely dismissing it, we will start thinking about this particular public sphere in different ways—ways that can start to tap the potential for a more productive struggle against sexism and point the way toward meaningful disruptions of patriarchy.

In Chapter Seven I move to an examination of the pedagogical implications of rap music and third wave/Black feminist theories. I look at the classroom as a public space for dialogue and debate, and discuss what it means to ask students to think about difference using representations of Black womanhood portrayed in rap and the larger society as examples. I conclude by briefly questioning the impact that quests for "positive images" have had on the subjectivity of Black women, and offer some suggestions about the ways in which rap music and Hip-Hop culture can be used to push past positive/negative binaries.

My ultimate goal is to figure out ways to work with a culture that influences the lives of so many youth, specifically young Black women. I want to find a means to harness the energy of the youth culture and revitalize its activist beginnings, because Hip-Hop is more than just music to me. Hip-Hop is the vehicle that I hope will one day lead us to change.

Bringing Wreck:
Theorizing Race, Rap, Gender,
and the Public Sphere

Wreck: 1) fight. 2) recreation.

Wrecking Crew: 1) boast of rap groups who say one can destroy or "wreck" the other lyrically. They call themselves "wrecking crews." 2) gang of violent thugs.

Wrecking Shop: winning an MC Battle.
—Alonzo Westbrook, *Hip Hoptionary: The Dictionary of Hip-Hop Terminology*

In his 1962 text *The Structural Transformation of the Public Sphere: An Inquiry into a Category of Bourgeois Society*, Jürgen Habermas sets up an idealized model of the public sphere based on a particular historical period and context. Reflecting on the text more than thirty years later, Habermas notes not only his theoretical leanings toward a classical Marxian critique of ideology but also his quite idealized goals. Habermas writes that he felt he could move past the limitations of the worst embodiments of public opinion, publicity, and the public sphere in order to confront these ideas and change their meaning in the process of transformation from liberal to organized capitalism.[1] The idealized nature of his project cannot be neglected as we think about using his concepts to examine contemporary public cultures. It is important that we recognize what Habermas set out to accomplish because it helps us to think about how much relevance his project has for the Black public sphere. The Black Public Sphere Collective, a group of Black scholars who edited a 1994 special issue of the journal *Public Culture* and then a 1995 anthology on the Black public sphere, defines the Black public sphere as an expansion of Habermas's public sphere. It moves beyond magazines, salons, coffee shops, and highbrow tracts to include vernacular practices such as street talk, new music, radio shows, and church voices.[2] The Black public sphere "marks a wider sphere of critical practice and visionary politics, in which intellectuals can join with the energies of the street, the school, the church, and the city to constitute a challenge to the exclusionary violence of much public space in the United States."[3] This vision of a public sphere necessarily moves beyond what Habermas initially envisioned a public sphere could be.

In *The Structural Transformation of the Public Sphere*, Habermas deals with very specific terms and concepts in relation to a particular period in European society. When we think of using his concepts and terms to analyze contemporary publics, we must bear the specificity of his project in mind. For example, he acknowledges that several social issues—gender, ethnicity, class, and popular culture—have been excluded from established public spheres and so from his original analysis of them.[4] Though *The Structural Transformation of the Public Sphere* examines a particular European phenomenon at a given point in time, Habermas's model is relevant and useful because it sets up as a model a time when individuals came together, discussed issues of collective good, worked toward change, and challenged state power.

Here, I will interrogate notions of the public sphere, as defined by Jürgen Habermas, and of the Black public sphere, as defined by various theorists of Black public culture, in order to fully understand how intersections of race, class, gender, and sexuality further complicate understandings of the public sphere. I explore issues of spectacle, representation, and the public/private split in relation to Black public culture, and maintain that—as a result of Black history in the United States—these concepts have to be rethought when applied to Black participation in the larger U.S. public sphere. In order to highlight the legacy that Hip-Hop culture builds on, I provide some brief historical examples of how Blacks have negotiated and navigated the larger U.S. public sphere. I also provide examples of the ways that Black people, once they gained access to certain segments of the larger public sphere, sought to disrupt commonly held beliefs about Blacks by bringing wreck to negative images and stereotypes. They did so by claiming control of the public's gaze and a public voice for themselves. *Wreck,* as seen in the epigraph to this chapter, is a Hip-Hop term that connotes fighting, recreation, skill, boasting, or violence. The Hip-Hop concept of wreck sheds new light on the things Blacks have had to do in order to obtain and maintain a presence in the larger public sphere, namely, fight hard and bring attention to their skill and right to be in the public sphere.

Bringing wreck, for Black participants in the public sphere historically, has meant reshaping the public gaze in such a way as to be recognized as human beings—as functioning and worthwhile members of society—and not to be shut out of or pushed away from the public sphere. I make comparisons and connections between past instances of Black public culture in order to explore the implications for spectacle and representation in Hip-Hop culture and Black women involved in Hip-Hop culture. I maintain that a reworking of Habermas's concept of the public sphere is key to an expanded understanding of the political potentialities of Hip-Hop as a youth movement.

Habermas defines the bourgeois public sphere as "the sphere of private people come together as a public" who use "the public sphere regulated from above against the public authorities themselves, to engage them in a debate over the general rules governing relations in the basically privatized but publicly relevant sphere of commodity exchange and social labor."[5] Because he is describing a particular moment in eighteenth-century Europe, the "private people" Habermas describes are homogeneous in regard to race, class, and gender; there are no women or people of color represented. This does not mean that they were not there, as many scholars of color and feminist scholars have pointed out.[6] Rather, they did not have access to the public sphere in the same ways that white male property holders did.

Therefore, when we apply the notion of "commodity exchange" to Blacks in the United States (specifically Black women), the term takes on a different significance because of the history of slavery. For centuries black people themselves were a commodity, and they provided much of the labor that built the country. They are entering the public sphere after a significant period of being excluded from it; the "general rules governing relations" at one point worked to keep them out. The concept of the public sphere, as Habermas defines it, must be renegotiated in order to fit the specific needs of Black public culture in the United States.

For example, as Bruce Robbins reminds us, the current situation of identity politics and mass media will not allow us to simply reject Habermas as irrelevant for contemporary Black people because his theories are white and European-centered.[7] What Habermas has to say about how one specific group of people negotiated and navigated the public sphere in order to influence the quality of their lives can help us to see how Black people have renegotiated the public sphere in order to claim a public voice. Therefore, it is fruitful to try to flesh out the most useful aspects of his ideas. Pieces of Habermas's theory can be reworked to address the impact of Hip-Hop on the United States and the world, the phenomenon of Black women coming to voice via Hip-Hop, and women's impact on both Hip-Hop culture and the larger public sphere.

If people of color and women are to be represented in the public sphere, Habermas's model has to be altered. A variety of experiences have to be taken into consideration, and those experiences have to be open to differences between and within the various groups. For example, the idea that citizens do not carry their "particularities" into the public sphere would necessarily have to be retheorized. Black women, for example, cannot opt to leave their particularities at the door. They are physically marked as Black and female, and these are two sources of their oppression. Thus their particularities would necessarily inform their very participation in the public sphere. Particularities matter, therefore, when they work as markers that inhibit access to the public sphere. Indeed, it might be more fruitful in contemporary discussions concerning people of color and the public sphere to think in terms of multiple publics. As Nancy Fraser writes in *Justice Interruptus*, in order for a theory of the public sphere to be adequate it must encompass the multiplicity of public spheres that exist, distinguish between them, and show how some of the spheres marginalize others.[8]

Unlike Habermas's public sphere, Fraser's multiplicity of public spheres cannot be confined to a single model. She recognizes not only media and government public spheres but also everyday, informal public spheres. Fraser recognizes there is not only one way to be political; rather, multiple spheres interact with and even marginalize each other. This opens the door for a consideration of the way Hip-Hop culture functions as a counter–public sphere and the way Black women in particular experience that sphere. For example, today rappers suffer marginalization from official governmental offices—via police harassment, harsh restrictions on concert venues, censorship, and strict copyright laws that affect sampling—because of the themes that they choose to speak about in their lyrics. Some mass-media representations of Hip-Hop cast the culture in a negative light, simultaneously vilifying it and granting it a public voice. This vilification leads to moral panic and public outcry that serves to alienate the Hip-Hop generation from other members of Black communities. The alienation highlights not only the generation gap but also the class schisms that divide Black communities.

Even as the Hip-Hop generation is vilified, alienated, and marginalized, certain elements within Hip-Hop work to vilify, alienate, and marginalize others. For example, while some rappers claim to be the new voice for the marginalized group of Black youth they claim to represent, they oppress and marginalize women and homosexuals.[9] The rap lyrics that make constant references to "bitches" and "hos," "punks" and "faggots," work to create hostile environments for some women and homosexual participants in Hip-Hop culture. This hostility is evident not only in the lyrics but also in the attitudes that some rappers exhibit toward women and homosexuals, marginalizing and oppressing anyone who is not Black, straight, male, and dripping with testosterone. Even though Hip-Hop culture suffers state oppression, it can and does in certain instances act as an oppressor. Knowing and understanding this does not diminish the work members of Hip-Hop culture have to do to navigate and renegotiate the larger United States public sphere, but it does provide a glimpse of the navigation and negotiations taking place *within* the counter–public sphere of Hip-Hop.

Unlike Habermas's model, in which the bourgeoisie ideally was able to use the regulated public sphere against the public authorities that sought to suppress and squelch their public voice, today's rappers do not have access to the regulatory aspects of the public sphere in the same ways. Bearing Black history in mind, we can see a pattern in which whenever Black dissident voices enter the public space, variables of containment and severe oppression—sometimes from outside forces and sometimes from inside mistakes and misjudgments—go into play that inhibit the strength and forcefulness of their message. Examples of these kinds of dynamics can be found throughout Black history in the United States, but the most recent example prior to the explosion of Hip-Hop can be seen in how the Black Panther Party functioned as a counter–public sphere in the United States during the late 1960s and early 1970s.

The Black Panther Party used spectacle and representation in the larger U.S. public sphere to grab national attention and claim a public voice. The black leather jackets, black berets, and guns contributed to their revolutionary image. Their rhetoric of the gun—of killing and being willing to die for the people—also contributed to their ability to navigate the spectacle. Before Hip-Hop, then, we have the Black Panther Party making use of spectacle and controlling the national gaze. However, unlike what we find in most of contemporary Hip-Hop, the Black Panther Party used spectacle and representation with a social and political goal: power for the people. In this way, the Black Panther Party and Black groups that came before and after them renegotiated the public sphere in order to claim power for themselves.[10]

Examinations of Black history in the United States show that while Habermas's model can be useful, it has to be reconfigured to fit Black experiences. Habermas begs to be reread with the lens of inclusion and difference firmly in place and with a special emphasis on race, class, gender, and sexuality. Because the space for such difference does not exist in Habermas's original work—due to the period in which he wrote it and the specific historical period he deals with—one has to be created through a method of reinterpretation. I find a useful model for reinterpretation in the feudal period, which Habermas also addresses.

For example, *representative publicity* is a term that needs to be looked at in terms of race, class, gender, and sexuality. Representative publicity and the "publicness" of lords is characteristic of the period prior to the development of the public sphere, in Habermas's model. Habermas describes the publicness of lords, kings, and noblemen as a display or embodiment that presented them as a higher power—higher than the people they presented themselves to. He goes on to suggest that such representation is an aura—something that pretends to make something invisible visible. It is something staged and "wedded to personal attributes such as insignia (badges and arms), dress (clothing and coiffure), demeanor (form of greeting and poise), and rhetoric (form of address and formal discourse in general)—in a word, to a strict code of noble conduct."[11] For Habermas, representative publicity, because of the power arrangements of the era, is something that is placed before the people, a form of spectatorship that lacks political possibilities because there is no participation. However, when one moves forward to the late-twentieth-century United States and considers a minority group that historically has not had access to the public sphere, spectacle takes on an entirely different role.

For Black people in the United States specifically, their role has historically been one of invisibility. This invisibility in the eyes of the governing body and the society at large—represented by creative minds such as Ralph Ellison in *Invisible Man* and theorists such as Michele Wallace in *Invisibility Blues: From Pop to Theory*—calls for a certain amount of spectacle on many levels. This invisibility is one reason Habermas needs to be reread to fit Black experiences in the U.S. public sphere. The spectacle becomes the key; one has to be seen before one can be heard. Spectacle and cultural representation (when more direct political access is not available) are the first steps in creating a disruption, the first steps in bringing wreck. When Black bodies and Black voices lay claim to public spaces previously denied to them, that space necessarily changes on some level due to their very presence.

When representation becomes possible, it takes on a new role in that minority leaders are often called on to represent the race. Kobena Mercer calls the phenomenon of one Black person who has managed to obtain a public presence being constantly called upon by the larger society and the communities from which he or she comes to represent the entire race the "burden of representation."[12] Although he discusses it predominantly in terms of Black artists and artistic freedom, the concept is relevant for any Black person who enters a place of prominence in the larger public sphere. As Mercer notes, the task of speaking for an entire marginalized group is impossible, and creates in the representation a sense of urgency because the call to speak for and represent is itself a cultural reproduction of a racism that requires regulation of Black visibility in the public sphere.[13] Mercer's views on the burden of representation illuminate the ways representations and representatives of the race function as tools of a racist society bent on gatekeeping and allowing only a few marginalized voices a public presence. However, the question of representation and representatives needs to be broadened in order to consider the strategic and political uses of representation by marginalized voices.

Systemic regulation and exclusion force the minority to go to great lengths to claim public space—even if it means becoming a representative. At least as representatives, they have access to a public voice. In fact, some use their role as representative to correct wrongs and replace stereotyped representations of Blacks in the United States with more positive images. They use their position as representative to bring wreck and counter stereotypes. For example, the image of the illiterate, untrainable Black brute is challenged by the intelligent, well-spoken Black public intellectual poised to represent the race. Also, for some Blacks—both historically and currently—their role as representative is not viewed as a burden. They pride themselves on being the voice of the people.

Some historical examples of this kind of representation are evident in the examination of early-twentieth-century African American clubwomen, W. E. B. Du Bois's "talented tenth," and the Black

Panther Party. African American clubwomen in the late 1800s and early 1900s sought to influence the images of Black womanhood prevalent in the larger U.S. public sphere. They used literacy and social outreach projects to reshape and combat negative images of Black womanhood. African American clubwomen saw themselves as "race women" and viewed the work they did as "race work." They also saw themselves as working toward women's progress.[14] As Angela Davis notes in *Women, Culture, and Politics,* the club-women's motto, "Lifting as We Climb," highlighted their dedication to a tradition of struggle and politically linked them to crucial progressive causes.[15] For the clubwomen of the day, this meant influencing the ways Black womanhood was represented in the larger public. They made use of both spectacle and representation to accomplish their goals. They carried themselves with the utmost respectability and subscribed to middle-class virtues of womanhood. Thus they enacted a form of spectacle that surfaced, for example, in the shroud of silence surrounding Black women's sexuality. In order to combat stereotyped public images of Black women as sexually promiscuous, some Black women developed what Darlene Clark Hine calls a "culture of dissemblance" surrounding sexuality.[16] This silencing was a spectacle in that they consciously decided what they would show of themselves in public and crafted the presentable and respectable public image of Black womanhood.

They also thought it was their duty not only to help Black women of the lower classes but also to speak for them and represent their needs to the larger public. This form of representation surfaced in what Hazel Carby calls the "policing of the Black woman's body."[17] The clubwomen were vigilant in their efforts to control the public images of Black womanhood—so much so that they sought to control recent Black women immigrants in the North, who were seen as a threat to both the progress of the race and the "establishment of a respectable urban black middle class."[18] As proper race women, the clubwomen used their own visibility and action in the public sphere to ensure that Black womanhood was represented in ways that uplifted the race. I will say more about the ways in which clubwomen navigated the public sphere in the following chapter; however, it is important to note here the interaction of spectacle and representation exhibited by the clubwomen. Their use of spectacle and representation helped them to combat negative images of Black womanhood. And on some level, their very presence in the public sphere as speakers, activists, and writers brought wreck to commonly held beliefs not only about Black women's capabilities but also about the proper place in the public sphere for women in general. They used their position as race women to advocate for the race and to show the larger society all that the race could accomplish given the right opportunities. Similar interactions can be seen in Du Bois's concept of the "talented tenth."

W. E. B. Du Bois coined the phrase "talented tenth" in his 1903 essay by the same title and maintained that Black people should be led by "exceptional men"—"the best of their time." He wrote that "the Talented Tenth of the Negro race must be made leaders of thought and missionaries of culture among their people. No others can do this work and Negro colleges must train men for it. The Negro race, like all other races, is going to be saved by its exceptional men."[19] What is perhaps most interesting about Du Bois's concept is the way it took shape within Black communities. He sets up a tradition—from slavery until the time he wrote—of stellar men and stellar acts. But it is his call for a talented tenth, his urging, that brings forth a kind of representation that some would say continues today.

The talented tenth—groomed for leadership and deemed proper—is also the group allowed to speak for the race. Like the clubwomen, this group too felt it knew what was best (an attitude that continues to exist today). There is also a certain element of spectacle, a spectacle that exudes a certain sense of class and by extension a certain element of respectability. It is not simply enough to be educated. It is just as important to appear educated—one would be no good without the other. The talented tenth, as it became embodied in Black communities, represented the best foot forward. They represent the best and brightest and therefore the ones allowed to have a public presence and voice in matters concerning the race. Even though Du Bois renounced the concept years later, it had already taken root. Traces of it can be seen in certain aspects of the civil rights movement and even today's public intellectual displays, showcased on CNN and elsewhere, with huge panels at all-day symposiums devoted to the best and brightest of Black America, whose participants are prepared to talk about and give advice to Black Americans.

During the civil rights movement, Black people created a form of spectacle in order to gain entry into the public sphere and attract the media. Men marched in suits and ties. Women marched in dresses, stockings, and high heels. They were a vision of respectability— marching and singing, not rioting and shouting. They wanted main-stream America to see that they were good people, respectable citizens who deserved civil rights. Their clothing and the manner in which they conducted themselves showcased this attempt at respect-ability and no doubt encouraged many mainstream white Americans to join the struggle, but it did not stop the firehoses and dogs.[20]

The exceptional-men mentality and the notion of a talented tenth will no doubt continue.[21] But it was reshaped and altered for a brief moment with certain elements of the Black Power movement, specifically the Black Panther Party.

The Black Panther Party had to attract the attention of the media before it could be given any serious consideration. While the Black Panther Party did consider itself to be the vanguard of the revolu-tion, its members did not feel that they were sent to lead the people in the same ways as the talented tenth was meant to. They insisted instead that they were taking their lead from the people. Their use of spectacle was twofold: their uniform of black beret, black leather jacket, and gun was meant not only to capture the mainstream American imagination but also to attract the masses of Black people, specifically the brothers on the block. They too used spectacle and representation to control gaze and as such bring wreck to what the larger public thought it knew about Black people. The Black Pan-ther Party, instead of taking its cue from a talented Black elite, felt that the revolution would come from a group that the larger U.S. public had all but written off. In trying to move the masses of Black people, the Panthers went a step beyond standard Marxism's notion of the proletariat rising to power. They attempted to move the Black *lumpenproletariat*. Former Panther leader Elaine Brown writes:

> The Black "lumpen proletariat," unlike Marx's working class, had absolutely no stake in industrial America. They existed at the bottom level of society in America, outside the capitalist system that was the basis for oppression of Black people. . . . At their lowest level, at the core, they were the gang members and the gangsters, the pimps and the prostitutes, the drug users and dealers, the common thieves and murderers.[22]

The Panthers wanted the lumpen proletariat to rise. They have in fact been criticized for celebrating and idealizing the lumpen.[23] In this regard, some comparisons can be made between Hip-Hop culture's glamorization of the ghetto and their reinterpretations of 1970s blaxploitation cult figures such as gangsters, pimps, and big-time drug dealers. Even Hip-Hop's fascination with Glocks and Uzis can be connected to the Black Panther Party's rhetoric of the gun and ultimately their celebration of the lumpen and glamorizing of the ghetto. Before Hip-Hop, the Black Panther Party gave the United States its greatest nightmare. Although there was always a strain of the fear of Blackness running through the country, the Black Panther Party boldly reconfigured the nightmare's gaze. Where the United States once had its lies and stereotypes about Black brutes given by films such as *The Birth of a Nation* (1915), the country now had to contend with a gaze controlled by the spectacle.[24] The Black Panthers not only presented a menacing picture themselves, but—speaking for the people, as representatives of the people—promised to ignite the lumpen proletariat, thus increasing the Panthers' numbers and by extension their threat. The Black Panther Party offers, then, a twentieth-century example of Black rage and a less-than-respectable representation in the larger U.S. public sphere. They set the stage for what we would see later in Hip-Hop culture.

Hip-Hop as a youth movement grew out of the rubble of a dying Black Power movement. Just as the Black Power movement was taking its last breath in the mid-1970s in America's inner cities, Hip-Hop was being created by Black and Latino youth in the South Bronx. It is therefore not much of a leap to see the Hip-Hop generation as direct descendants of the legacy left by Black Power groups such as the Black Panther Party. Certain segments of the Hip-Hop generation, in fact, can be seen as bringing to fruition the Black Panther Party's hopes of giving those voiceless members of the masses of Black people a voice. Rap music and Hip-Hop culture bring elements of spectacle and representation to higher levels in the larger U.S. public sphere than many aspects of Black public culture did in the past. Hip-Hop journalist Bakari Kitwana concurs: "Rap marked a turning point, a shift from practically no public voice for young Blacks—or at best an extremely marginalized one—to Black youth culture as the rage in mainstream popular culture. And more than just increasing Black youth visibility, rap articulated publicly and on a mass scale many of the generation's beliefs, relatively unfiltered by the corporate structures that carried it."[25] Rap music and Hip-Hop culture offer a space in the public sphere and a chance to voice the concerns of this generation.

For example, in response to the public outrage and debate caused by accusations that some rap promotes and glorifies violence, many rappers have spoken out against the blame society places on rap music by claiming to be the voices of the Black people in America's inner cities. In interview after interview, rappers can be counted on to claim that they are "representin'" for the Black people left behind in their respective neighborhoods.[26] Many rappers argue that they bring the stark reality of life in American ghettos to public attention. The fact is, some of the most humanizing and accurate accounts of life in impoverished ghettos come from rap songs and not the network news. Thus rappers bring wreck: they disrupt their way into and make themselves visible in the public sphere with the goal of not only speaking for disenfranchised Black people but also claiming both a voice and a living for themselves in a society bereft of opportunity for them. In making these disruptions, the rappers and other participants in Hip-Hop culture bring wreck to the common (mis)representations of Black youth. Much like the Black Panther Party did in the 1970s, these youths bring wreck by redirecting the gaze and controlling the images the larger public sees. In this they are representing the exact opposite of late-nineteenth- and early-twentieth-century notions of Black respectability.

They do so by making use of spectacle in ways that tell—in public—the stories that were once hidden from the larger public. Rap lyrics display gritty descriptions of sexual acts that the early club-women would no doubt disapprove of, especially coming from the mouths of women rappers barely out of their teens. Depictions of Black-on-Black crime, drug deals, drive-bys, and pimping are not necessarily the leadership of Blackness that the talented tenth wanted to foster and highlight. However, contemporary rappers are not shying away from the starker realities of life in America's inner cities. Rap music and Hip-Hop culture provide a spectacle of Black manhood not seen since the Black Power movement. The Hip-Hop generation has captured the American imagination, and that of the world. They have done so by making creative use of spectacle.

Rappers, with their bold use of language and dress, also use image and spectacle as their initial entry into the public sphere. In this instance, spectacle functions dually as both style and a plea to be heard, to be allowed to represent. They view representation or "representin' "—speaking for the people and voicing their concerns—as their role. In a talk given at Brown University titled "Material Witness: Race, Identity and the Politics of Gangsta Rap," Michael Eric Dyson describes the Hip-Hop generation's use of representation:

> At their best rappers shape the torturous twist of urban fate into lyrical elegies. The act of representing that is much ballyhooed in hip-hop is the witness of those left to tell the afflicted's story. They represent lives swallowed by too little love or opportunity. They represent themselves and their peers with aggrandizing anthems that boast of ingenuity and luck in surviving.[27]

Although Dyson's view that rappers are speaking for the people may sound a bit naive to some, he no doubt arrives at this stance by taking into consideration the numerous rappers who have gone on record in interviews as saying that they are the voice of their respective "hoods." Whether they actually perform this task or not can be disputed; the same argument can be made in relation to the

Black Panther Party and the impact it had on the Black community. Some felt that the Panthers were self-serving in the same ways that rappers are seen as self-serving—due to the money they receive and their manipulation of media attention.[28] Rappers do bring issues and concerns, via their lyrics, to public attention that might not otherwise be heard. For example, while the government and the media pay a certain amount of lip service to the rising unemployment rate and the impact of poverty and crime on Black communities, rappers give narrations of Black experiences with these issues and so represent the concerns of some segments of their communities. For rappers, speaking for the people means representing the people. They are self-designated tellers of the people's suffering. But unlike the representative publicity of nobility and lords prior to the development of the public sphere Habermas describes, they are not simply a show placed in front of the people. And they do not have power already.

The show, the spectacle, is the first step toward change—the first part of getting heard. For a historically marginalized and invisible group, the spectacle is what allows them a point of entry into a public space that has proved to be violent and exclusionary. In fact, when we take into consideration the many marches, protests, and demonstrations—all grand displays of spectacle—that the Black public cultures prior to the Hip-Hop movement had to develop in order to gain civil rights, the necessity of spectacle to Black political action becomes clear. As stated earlier in relation to the civil rights movement, after a legacy of slavery and being labeled as three-fifths human, Blacks had to create a spectacle that allowed them to be seen as respectable citizens. And when that display was met with violence and exclusion, the logical next step would necessarily be the types of spectacle created by the Black Power movement, with guns, rage, and riots. All of these attempts are ways in which Blacks have tried to negotiate their freedom with the tools and power allowed them in this racist country. And while some methods worked better than others, when we move to the present and see how the gains of these past movements are being taken away one by one and how society as a whole has regressed in terms of race issues, should we be surprised that Black youths involved in Hip-Hop find themselves left with spectacle yet again as a way to gain entry into the public sphere? What has really changed?

Before Hip-Hop grabbed the national imagination, the Black and Latino youth who created it were neglected and unseen except for token guest spots in the nightly news as the criminal threat. With Hip-Hop culture sweeping the country and the world, these same youth now enjoy a form of publicity once denied to them. Spectacle, however, becomes a double-edged sword, because while without it rappers would have no vehicle to represent to the public at large or themselves, with only spectacle and no semblance of the political projects inherent in other forms of Black public culture the rappers risk becoming stuck in forms of publicity that have limited usefulness. Spectacle is limited because it works only as long as the group attempting to impact the public sphere controls the gaze. As soon as the spectacle is co-opted, it ceases to be effective. For example, while guns and menacing public images catapulted the Black Panther Party into the larger public sphere, once the media took control of the images and the U.S. government used them to launch an all-out attack on the Black Panther Party, the group not only suffered repression but also lost the support of the masses they had hoped to lead to revolution.

While exceptional representations of Blackness, as seen with the talented tenth and Black clubwomen, initially gave the larger U.S. public sphere images of Blackness that contradicted negative stereotyped images, these failed when they became co-opted by the larger public sphere. The exceptional few stand out as just that, leaving the rest of the group in the same position—marginalized and invisible—that they previously held. Representation is limited in similar ways: even though the person or group doing the representing is voicing the genuine needs of the community, they can represent the entire community to only a limited extent. Someone's needs will always be left out. Yet even with the limited usefulness of representation and spectacle, the gains made by the Black public sphere could not have happened without them.

Another way in which Habermas's model can be reread in order to accommodate the specific situation of U.S. Black culture occurs with his reading of the public/private split. In Habermas's view, citizens get all the basic things they need—the things that sustain and nurture them—in the private sphere. And by having their basic needs met in the private space, citizens are then able to participate fully in the public sphere. Historically, Blacks have been in the public sphere fighting for the basic rights that Habermas suggests one should receive in the private sphere. Not to mention the fact that it was Black labor and industriousness that provided the economic basis for the comforts and necessities enjoyed by the white male propertied class. As Patricia Hill Collins notes, "Race not only shaped African American participation in the institutionalized racism organized via slavery but also influenced the new nation-state's distinctly American notions of its public and private spheres."[29] While some of the things Blacks struggled for—freedom, justice, and peace—are indeed concerns of Habermas's eighteenth-century public sphere, the very basic needs that Habermas leaves to the private domain become the goal of Blacks for achieving public power, the guiding hope influencing public participation and action. To this notion I would add the very real concept of second-class citizenship to which many Blacks in the United States feel they are relegated when it comes to the distribution of rights and quality of life. And, as I will discuss later, when Hip-Hop culture and rap music are taken into consideration, even the basic element of love becomes a part of the public debate—something that has to be fought for in the public sphere.

For Habermas, ideas about freedom and love grew out of the experiences of the traditional patriarchal conjugal family's private sphere. However, the legacy of slavery and oppression seriously impedes the development among African Americans of this type of family, which Habermas notes is an eighteenth-century phenomenon. Thus, the private spaces in which subjectivity and the private/individual self is formed do not exist in the same way for American Blacks today. For Habermas, the comfort and stability of the patriarchal conjugal family were what allowed the individuals who constituted the public to make use of their reason, appropriate the state-governed public sphere, critique public authority, and convert the public sphere that already existed in the world of letters into forums for discussion.[30] In short, when you are not worried about where your next meal is going to come from, you can think about gaining a public voice and maintaining public power.

Yet for U.S. Blacks participating in the public sphere, this comfort and stability could not be taken as a given. They had to make a way out of no way from the time when their very freedom was denied until their freedom was supposedly granted. Blacks historically have had to continually create spaces of opportunity in the larger U.S. public sphere. For Black people in the contemporary United States, appropriating the state-governed public sphere is not an easy task. The public is not simply an extension or larger version of the private. The two are not conjoined in the same way as they are in the European model described by Habermas. Rather, they are related for Black publics in that entrance into and disruption of the public domain become necessary to gain the basic necessities of private life. Habermas does not describe different types of families or experiences that differ from those in bourgeois society. But when we start to expand Habermas's model and make space for difference, we can begin to account for other experiences.

For example, Black experiences with containment and surveillance become crucial to understanding Black experiences with the so-called split between public and private. Patricia Hill Collins notes that containment keeps Blacks in certain spaces, such as the legally segregated communities of the past and the de facto segregated communities of today.[31] Surveillance takes the form of police repression or suppression and the policies and practices of other government agencies, such as welfare and social services, that act to police specific members of the community as well as the group as a whole. The surveillance also comes from within when certain members of the community are suppressed and denied voice in order to show only the exceptional, or when Black male voices are privileged over Black female voices.[32] Surveillance and containment also work effectively to silence potentially powerful and highly visible members of the community. As discussed earlier, there is always a risk in making use of various forms of spectacle and being visible in the larger United States public sphere. Also, changing meanings of and attitudes toward the terms *public* and *private* in the United States influence not only Black experiences of the public and the private but also their experiences with containment and surveillance.[33] Is it any surprise, for example, that once Blacks gain access to the public sphere and take steps toward making the country accountable for providing their private needs by securing public government jobs, there has been a national push toward the privatization of these kinds of jobs?[34] Even the once valorized public has become devalued, and privacy itself—especially access to it— becomes the marker of real privilege. Now anyone who cannot escape the public sphere or public spaces of containment and surveillance is marked as less than a citizen.[35]

Therefore, when one takes into account Black experiences in the United States, different connections need to be made; different questions need to be asked. For example, in the foreword to Oskar Negt and Alexander Kluge's *Public Sphere and Experience: Toward an Analysis of the Bourgeois and Proletarian Public Sphere*, Miriam Hansen asks, "How do African-Americans negotiate the multiple rifts between their diasporic cultural heritages, white appropriations of them (in music, fashion, language), and a dominant media culture that still renders them stereotyped or marginalized, barring them from anything but exceptional, spectacularized authorship, self representation, and power?"[36] While Hansen sees this as a limitation, I see it as an opening—a space in which to view exactly how Blacks have negotiated these rifts, appropriations, stereotypes, and marginalization. I think that the "spectacularized authorship, self-representation, and power" that Blacks historically and presently are left with have the potential to become political tools.

To Make a Public Black and Bid It Change

> Many of the institutions that constitute the Black Public Sphere have been invaluable to the transmission of communal values, traditions of resistance, and aesthetic sensibilities.[37]

As discussed previously, Blacks historically navigated and negotiated the larger public sphere (and currently do so) by using what was available to them, namely, spectacle, representation, and the re-negotiation of concepts such as the public/private split. In doing so, they helped to shape (and continue to shape) a Black public sphere that aims to evoke change in the larger public sphere. The change sought has taken a variety of forms throughout Black history in the United States. However, the consistent factors have always been collective struggles and the greater good for the Black community writ large. The 1995 release of *The Black Public Sphere: A Public Culture Book* also marked a resurgence of interest in the ways Black people have negotiated a public space and a public voice.

The theorists represented in *The Black Public Sphere: A Public Culture Book* extend and complicate the bourgeois public sphere Habermas describes by including Black men and women. They make these inclusions not for the mere sake of including, but rather to document the ways in which Blacks have made a difference and to further explore how they might continue to evoke change. The Black public sphere as a counterpublic, more often than not, has been about the business of making change—both change in the larger U.S. public sphere and change that would benefit the lives of people in Black counterpublics. The Black public sphere is defined as "one critical space where new democratic forms and emergent diasporic movements can enrich and question one another."[38] The Black public sphere represents a looser and more expansive public space than the one Jürgen Habermas sets up. The Black public sphere does not represent a monolithic Blackness but rather shows variety and multiplicity. Thus the Black alternative and counterpublics, while not entirely rejecting Habermas's bourgeois public sphere, extend and expand Habermas in order to create a more relevant discussion that prevents exclusion, encourages intersections, and evokes change. Careful examination and consideration of the Black public sphere highlights how politics and culture work together within Black publics and their interactions with the larger public.

The topics of inquiry addressed in *The Black Public Sphere: A Public Culture Book* range from newly freed Blacks in Virginia to Martin Luther King Jr., from the civil rights movement and Malcolm X to Blacks in Brazil and rap music and Hip-Hop culture. The essays cover events as distant as Reconstruction and as recent as the Rodney King beating. As varied as the topics and events discussed in these essays are, they share a goal of questioning and critiquing both Black public spheres and the existing order. They start a much-needed conversation that combines the various spheres of Black life and values the political potential in all of them. They are useful in situating the public spaces in which conversations occur about how race, class, gender, and sexuality intersect with and influence one another. Part of this situating takes place by naming the Black public sphere and theorizing its place in relation to governing spheres. Some Black public sphere theorists, following Nancy Fraser, state that Black public spheres are subaltern counterpublics or simply counterpublics.

Fraser coined the term *subaltern counterpublic* and defines it as "parallel discursive arenas where members of subordinated social groups invent and circulate counterdiscourses, so as to formulate oppositional interpretations of their identities, and needs."[39] Michael Hanchard, making a distinction between the middle and working classes, prefers the term *micro-public sphere,* defined as "spheres of public articulation that were not limited to, but dominated by the idioms, norms and desires of working-class women and men."[40] By complicating and further nuancing the notion of subaltern counterpublic spheres, we are able to break apart notions of a monolithic Black community that has one set of goals and one set of means by which to obtain those goals. We are able to see not only difference within Black communities but also the ways in which various factions of Black communities sometimes oppress one another.

Research on the Black public sphere is also making meaningful connections and distinctions among race, class, gender, and sexuality. For example, Michael Dawson's essay "A Black Counterpublic? Economic Earthquakes, Racial Agendas, and Black Politics" traces lines of class and gender in order to highlight that there is no such thing as a unified set of Black interests.[41] He surmises that there is currently no Black public sphere or even a counterpublic, yet argues that one existed in the early 1970s. He also argues that there is a possibility for one to exist again, and offers the following starting points: the growing and intersecting movements of people of color and environmental movements, and rap music's oppositional standpoint, which provides media that are somewhat controlled by members of the Hip-Hop community and thus can offer critique and open up discussions on a variety of subjects in the Black community, including sexism. He does note one qualification, however: that no mass-based Black counterpublic is possible if Black women are not allowed a public voice and the dignity of their humanity.[42] Dawson's starting points and qualification are fruitful in rethinking the Black public sphere, specifically as it relates to rap music's prominence and ability to bring social issues into the larger public sphere and to the necessity of validating Black women's voices and contributions. However, it is necessary to rethink even some of the ways that theorists of the Black public sphere have begun to think about Black public culture.

In his book *What the Music Said: Black Popular Music and Black Public Culture,* Mark Anthony Neal establishes a timeline for the Black public sphere that begins after slavery. Only after emancipation was it possible for a true Black public sphere with an active and recognized citizenship—albeit a marginalized citizenship—to be formed. However, that citizenship was extended only to men. Thus Neal finds that the traditional Black public sphere was dominated by Black male discourse. He further notes two early public spheres that were crucial to the establishment of a functioning Black public sphere: the Black church and the blues. According to Neal, the Black church was the more visible and produced and distributed the majority of Black critical discourse. The blues, "as the primary musical text of informal public institutions like the jook, rent parties, and after-hours clubs," became a second source for the dissemination of Black critical discourse.[43] Neal complicates the notion of the Black public sphere by extending its space to include not only expressive culture but also the public spaces that celebrate the culture. By including the counterpublic spaces of the jook joint and the rent party, he is moving away from liberal bourgeois notions of what constitutes a public sphere. He recognizes that Black critical discourse can take place in a variety of media, including Black music. This recognition is especially fruitful as we move to the Hip-Hop generation and begin to think about the political and cultural relevance of Hip-Hop culture and the possibilities it creates for changes in the larger public sphere.

Neal also recognizes that women were present in these public spaces. He notes the centrality of Black female voices in the blues and references Elsa Barkley Brown and Evelyn Brooks Higginbotham's work on the ways in which Black communities—both men and women—used the church to debate, discuss, and disseminate information. Likewise, Houston Baker, in *Critical Memory: Public Sphere, African American Writing, and Black Fathers and Sons in America,* articulates the fact that women were always present in the Black public sphere, using as an example his own mother's activities. His mother co-led the campaign to raise funds for the hospital of which his father was superintendent, wrote speeches for his father, and was the financial consultant for the campaign. Baker views his mother's actions as continuing the legacy of Black womanist activism.[44] He knows that his mother and women like her contributed to the building of Black institutions. And even though the focus of his project is the work and presence of Black men in the Black public sphere, he does make mention of notable women such as his mother. In fact, after a lengthy discussion of all that Black men have done, he posits a rhetorical question: "but by now, you are surely asking: 'Have the mothers, sisters, daughters, nieces, no part in all of this?' And the answer is, of course they do."[45] Of course they do. They always have and they always will.

In ways that we have yet to fully recognize and acknowledge, Black women have helped to shape and build the Black public sphere as we know it. They have shaped the public sphere so much that I would add the caveat that we can no longer simply say that the women were present. We need to articulate fuller accounts of their voices and their work. It is no longer acceptable to note Black male dominance in public discourse in ways that dismiss or write off any detailed discussion of women. We need to extend our interrogations and discussions in ways that validate not only the presence of women in the Black public sphere but women's roles in shaping that sphere. Instead of commenting on the strength of the Black male presence in the public discourse, we need to ask what Black women were doing to enable that presence. We will no doubt find women like Baker's mother writing speeches, raising funds, and building institutions. Instead of simply noting the dominance of the Black church as a public sphere and attributing this to the charismatic leadership of Black men preachers, we need to look at the women who make up the majority of the congregation members in the Black churches of today and of the past. As Alice Walker rightly notes when reflecting on the civil rights movement in the documentary *A Place of Rage,* if it were not for the Black church, then the civil rights movement as we know it could not have happened. And if it were not for the women, then the Black church would not have been able to support the movement, because they made up the majority of church members. These kinds of realizations push our interrogations further than "the women were also present." We already know that women were there. What we need to explore is how they used their influence and how they shaped the Black public sphere.

I maintain that we will not know exactly what the Black public sphere is or what it can be until we fully examine Black women's roles in it. For example, even when Black women were disenfranchised, they had a say in where the Black vote went. Elsa Barkley Brown documents such women in her study of Black Richmonders in the 1800s. These women saw Black men's votes as community property. They gathered in Black churches with Black men and children to discuss major issues, and here everyone voted.[46] Brown maintains that "in Richmond and throughout the South exclusion from legal enfranchisement did not prevent African American women from shaping the vote and the political decisions."[47] The Richmond women that Brown writes of guarded guns in order to keep the meetings safe. They took Election Day off from work in order to have large groups of Black people attend the polls together. By contributing to the numbers, they hoped to ensure that Black men would not be turned away and that they would be able to protect the voters and each other. Brown highlights the ways the Black women of Richmond helped to shape the Black public sphere in that city and by extension effect change in the larger public sphere. No doubt there are countless stories throughout history of women like those in Richmond, Houston Baker's mother, and the Black churchwomen and blues women that Mark Anthony Neal mentions. However, we will not hear their stories or know how they influenced and shaped the Black public sphere if we do not begin to rethink the Black public sphere. As Brown states:

> African American collective memory in the late twentieth century often appears partial, distorted, and dismembered. The definitions and issues of political struggle which can come from that partial memory are limited. Before we can construct truly participatory discussions around a fully democratic agenda where the struggles of women and men are raised as issues of general interest necessary to the liberation of all, we have some powerful lot of rerememembering to do.[48]

Half stories and half histories are no longer satisfactory, not if we want to realize the fullness of the Black public sphere's potential. We can start by noting that the discourse of the Black public sphere has historically and currently been dominated by the voices of Black men. But if we truly want to know what the political struggle has been and what the possibilities for freedom are, we must look at the women surrounding the men. When we simply say the women were there, we miss the full account. They were there shaping and molding the public in ways that ensured that we would have a Black public sphere to speak of.

The rerememembering of Black historical events Brown mentions needs to occur. However, we also need a whole lot of reenvisioning of contemporary happenings as well. Like the Black women of Richmond, Black women took part in the Black public sphere throughout history and continue to do so today. Black women were major players through Reconstruction, the civil rights movement, and the Black Power movement. They were also very present and very active in the founding of the Hip-Hop movement. Refusing to explore the ways in which Black women contributed and continue to contribute gives us at best partial pictures of the Black public sphere. Understanding women's involvement and learning from and duplicating what worked for them, however, might just help us to enact change today. And as Black public sphere scholars have noted, if the Black public sphere is not ultimately about the business of evoking change, then we are wasting time.

My Cipher Keeps Movin' Like a Rollin' Stone: Black Women's Expressive Cultures and Black Feminist Legacies

Gaining political rights and protections as first-class citizens involved acquiring formal citizenship and exercising It in the public sphere. Black women participated in shaping and running this Black public sphere from its inception.

—Patricia Hill Collins, *Fighting Words: Black Women and the Search for Justice*

The story of African American women in public arenas, then, is a story of passion—a passion for the acquisition of literacy and for the opportunity to develop one's talents and abilities fully, to demonstrate one's potential and to commit oneself to the betterment both of self and of the race.

—Jacqueline Jones Royster, *Southern Horrors and Other Writings: The Anti-Lynching Campaign of Ida B. Wells, 1892–1900*

Black women have participated in the Black public sphere in numerous ways, simultaneously helping to shape that sphere and making sure that their own voices were heard and their own needs were addressed. To explore the ways Black women have used expressive culture to claim a voice in the public sphere—to, as Erykah Badu belts in the song "On and On," "gotdamit, sing their songs"—I start with the Hip-Hop concept of a cipher as a place where people gather to create knowledge and exchange information. *To cipher* means to understand, to figure out. In Hip-Hop the cipher is built when people shape and build knowledge together. The cipher is in constant motion, created throughout U.S. history whenever Black women—whether expressing themselves through writing, public oratory, music, or club activities—come together to discuss issues of importance to themselves and the Black community.

The cipher is both a space that Black women create for themselves and a space in which they question themselves about what it means to be both Black and woman in the larger U.S. public sphere. Black women have historically found ways to make their voices heard and to claim a space for themselves in the public sphere. To claim any of these early women as feminist is foolhardy. However, not to recognize the ways in which contemporary Black feminist thought builds on their legacy is doubly so. Examining the lineage of Black women's expressive culture is a way to unearth the beginnings of the Black women's empowerment that enabled and fostered contemporary Black feminist thought.

Scholars are tracing Black women's rhetorical contributions and building a historical legacy for Black women's literacy, public speaking, and writing.[1] Scholars are also pushing the boundaries of Black feminist thought by not only establishing a Black feminist legacy but also trying to learn from the positive and negative aspects of that legacy in order to evoke change today.[2] All of the work that is taking place in the ever-growing and evolving field of Black women's studies is important and needs to continue. However, in order for us to truly make these kinds of inquiries meaningful for future generations of Black women scholars and activists, we need to tap into the potential of Hip-Hop culture.

There are links that can be made, for example, between the Black women thinkers and activists of the past and Black women participating in Hip-Hop culture today. Both groups have struggled with some of the same issues, such as sexuality, identity, and dedication to uplifting Black communities. They have met with the same obstacles, namely, resistance from some members of their own communities and repression from the controlling public sphere. However, they have persisted and persevered. They have helped to create a strong and vital Black public sphere and made use of the larger U.S. public sphere whenever possible to bring wreck and gain access.

They have done so not only for themselves but also for the entire Black community. They have seen their literacy practices, for example, as a way to combat the negative images that society places on Black womanhood and to have a say in the ways in which those images are reshaped. In " 'To Protect and Serve': African American Female Literacies," Elaine Richardson develops a concept that speaks to the ways Black women have had to cope in a larger society socialized to discriminate based on race, class, gender, and sexuality. She maintains that Black women developed special skills and ways of knowing and acting, and used expressive arts and crafts in order to overcome, to advance, and to protect themselves, their loved ones, and the Black community.[3] For Richardson,

> African American females communicate these literacies through storytelling, conscious manipulation of silence and speech, code/style shifting and signifying, among other verbal and nonverbal practices. Performance arts such as singing, dancing, acting, steppin, and stylin, as well as crafts such as quilting and use of other technologies are also exploited to these purposes.[4]

What Richardson recognizes is that Black women have historically used whatever means available to them to express themselves, not just for the sake of self-expression but to have an impact on the larger public sphere and to further the race. This adaptability is a strength of Black women's expressive culture, which can also be seen in the way Black women make use of multiple genres in order to get their messages across.

Writers such as Alice Walker and June Jordan, for example, make skillful use of poetry and essay. Walker even uses the novel form when necessary. If Ntozake Shange cannot say what she has to say in a play, she will write a novel. Toni Morrison not only writes novels but theorizes the field through her writings on literary criticism. Women such as Ida B. Wells Barnett wrote pamphlets, essays, letters to the editor, and speeches. Frances Ellen Watkins Harper wrote novels, short stories, essays, and speeches. Most of these women have also been staunch activists committed to social justice. Before

Black women enjoyed their current access to the public sphere, they were expressing themselves in the beautiful gardens and quilts that Alice Walker talks about in the essay "In Search of Our Mother's Gardens."

Today, women rappers find themselves producing not only rap songs but also autobiographies, books of poetry, and novels, and they lend their talents to the silver screen via various forms of Hip-Hop cinema. Because of Black women's successful navigation of the Black public sphere in the past, we can today have a Queen Latifah, who is a rapper, actress, talk show host, businesswoman, and writer. This listing of the multiple ways that Black women have made use of their expressive talents is not an attempt to glorify Black women but rather an effort to showcase the ways Black women make use of whatever medium or genre is at their disposal and best conveys the issues they want to address. They keep their cipher moving through time in this way because the message can be enclosed in any kind of venue, be it enclosed in a quilt, submerged in a story, or conveyed with that certain look or expression that Black women have made an art form. When we find Black women shaping the Black public sphere, knowing that they make use of a variety of expressive venues helps us to see how they work those venues to the benefit of themselves and the race—how they have historically used expressive culture to bring wreck.

A starting point for recognizing the impact Black women have had on both the Black public sphere and the larger U.S. public sphere surfaces when examining Maria Pia Lara's reinterpretation of "illocutionary force." Her ideas dovetail with my thoughts on how Black participants in the larger sphere have brought wreck using the tools of spectacle and representation. Her focus on the women's movement in the United States does not complicate issues of race, class, gender, and sexuality significantly and therefore hinders her project's usefulness for Black women's studies. However, just as we find in Habermas, there are seeds in the work that lend themselves to reinterpretation and expansion in ways that help us to view Black women's specific contributions to the Black public sphere and the larger United States public sphere more clearly.

In *Moral Textures: Feminist Narratives in the Public Sphere,* Lara notes that in order for two parties to obtain consensus and mutual understanding in the larger U.S. public sphere they must make use of powerful and imaginative speech to attract attention, create possibilities, gain recognition, and form solidarity between both groups. After an illocutionary act has successfully taken place, no party remains the same. All are changed by the force and significance of the illocutionary act. The action in turn makes new meanings in the public sphere, redraws the boundaries between justice and the good life, and deconstructs liberal understandings of public and private.[5]

Although Lara deals specifically with the history of the (white) women's movement in the United States and its impact, at the end of her project she also gives a nod to how her concept of illocutionary force fits with Black struggles for recognition and liberation in the United States. She notes that Blacks had to be creative in their approach to traditional U.S. democratic culture and institutions; this led to an aesthetic creativity that in turn allowed them to achieve illocutionary force. She maintains, "Black Americans were drawn to the possibilities of structurally and affectively transforming the founding notion of the bourgeois public sphere into an expressive and empowering self-fashioning."[6] Lara's references to the ways Blacks have made use of illocutionary force in order to re-shape the larger public sphere are useful as we begin to think about the ways Black women specifically have had to approach both the larger U.S. public sphere and the Black public sphere. However, interrogations of the Black public sphere lead us to see that Black women's approach to the Black public sphere was and is often complicated by a sense of belonging and a dedication to the improvement of the race.

Black women have historically made use of illocutionary force to have their voices heard and to impact the larger society. What is missing, more often than not, is the recognition. Even feminist revisionist work such as Lara's sometimes stops short of recognizing the multifaceted contributions of Black women. Throughout history, we can see Black women's influence on feminist struggle and feminist consciousness in the United States. In fact, it is not too big a statement to say that because of the critique and urging of Black women, the feminist movement has turned out as self-reflective as it is. In the nineteenth century, Sojourner Truth's very presence in the struggle for women's enfranchisement no doubt made suffragists reflect on what they meant by the term *woman*. In the late nineteenth and early twentieth centuries women such as Ida B. Wells Barnett advocated for women's rights while also challenging white women's racism. Black women thinkers and activists in the 1970s helped to shape the renewed women's liberation movement. It was the voices of Black women, lesbians, and Black lesbians, such as those of the Combahee River Collective and Barbara Smith, that spoke out against the rampant racism and homophobia in the women's movement. These same voices soon after were joined by poor and working-class women who began to speak out against the decidedly middle-class orientation of the public face of the women's liberation movement. Without these dissident and disrupting voices feminism today would look a whole lot different. Feminism would not make the attempts toward inclusiveness that it currently does. Keeping Black women's contributions in mind then becomes just as important when we address the United States women's movement as it is when we address the Black public sphere.

When tracing and contextualizing Black women's expressive culture and Black feminist legacies, it is helpful to separate the activities in much the same way that we tend to explore feminist movements and struggle in the United States. The use of the term *waves* signifies the periods in U.S. history with specific and recorded levels of women's rights activities. The first wave denotes the suffrage movement. The second wave denotes the women's liberation movement, which began in the late 1960s and early 1970s and is still going on today. There is also an up-and-coming third wave of feminism, which consists of women and men who grew up with feminism and the privileges that the feminist movement has gained. This is not to say that feminist struggles follow any specific pattern or lineage, or even to say with absolute certainty that Black women's expressive culture—especially expressive culture linked to struggle and resistance—would fit neatly into such a lineage or pattern. Indeed, much has been written suggesting that Black women have a legacy of resistance and an active presence in the public sphere that predates captivity and enslavement in the United States. Therefore it predates the suffrage movement, which usually marks the beginning of feminist activism in the United States.[7]

Scholarship tracing Black women's place in precolonial African society and the impact that the legacy of these women had on African American women enslaved in the United States and their descendants highlights kinship systems, shared belief systems, and related senses of obligation and responsibility that move across time and space to inform Black women's advocacy and activism.[8] The history and legacy of Black women's participation in the public sphere—across continents, time, and throughout the diaspora—is rich and interesting. However, for the sake of clarity and organization it helps to focus on Black women's participation in the waves that we have come to see as pivotal points of feminist struggle in the United States. But, just as it is not so easy to demarcate waves of feminist struggle, with their overlappings and continuations, with Black women's expressive cultures it is also not easy to draw lines between periods, as the struggle in many instances remains the same and the lineage and legacy are continued—albeit in different ways—throughout the generations.

Nineteenth and Early Twentieth Centuries: Black Women's Intellectual Traditions and Activism

Early Black women's intellectual traditions and activism offer a significant starting point for understanding the ways Black women made use of a variety of expressive cultures and in doing so laid the groundwork for a Black feminist tradition. Some nineteenth-century Black women found ways to be vocal and active and to voice their opinions on the most pressing issues of the day. They also sought to shape the ways Black women were viewed in the larger U.S. public sphere. They were working against the early misconceptions surrounding Black womanhood—misconceptions that were being created even as they vigorously worked to defend the virtue of Black womanhood. These women worked against the images of the mammy, the seductress, and the tragic mulatto, all created to justify first their enslavement and subsequently an oppression that would linger until this very day. They voiced their opinions about the times they lived in. Both free Black women and women who reclaimed their freedom by escaping spoke out against the enslavement of Black people. Black women also spoke out against the lynching of Black people, the unfair practice of segregation, and the importance of the Black vote.

These women made use of a variety of expressive tools. They wrote essays, speeches, autobiographies, slave narratives, poems, and songs. They also spoke out, sang out, and at times cried out against injustice. Some of these women who set the foundation for all that Black women's expressive culture would become in the future were Mary Ann Shadd Cary, Frances Harper, Harriet Jacobs, and Maria Stewart, to name only a few. They were more than merely present. They were women such as Sojourner Truth, Anna Julia Cooper, and Ida B. Wells Barnett, and without them the women's movement in the United States would not look the same. Black women such as Zora Neale Hurston, Ma Rainey, Bessie Smith, and Billie Holiday were also active participants in the Harlem Renaissance and in early blues and jazz cultures, and without them certain Black cultural movements would look very different. They contributed immensely to what Black expressive culture, Black struggles for liberation, and feminist thought and struggle were and what they would (and could) eventually become.

Some of these women used rhetorical tools such as writing essays and editorials as well as making speeches to a variety of audiences. They saw the spoken and written word as preambles to making change in the larger society. They saw themselves as representatives of not only Black womanhood but also the race. These women articulated resistance against stereotyped images of both Black women and the Black race, navigating the written and spoken word in order to achieve their goals. They made style of strategy by omitting, displacing, falsifying, and—when the need arose—accommodating. They carved out spaces for themselves and demanded that they be heard. Not only did they voice their individual experience, but they voiced experiences that symbolically stood for the collective whole.[9]

A few specific examples of how Black women made use of expressive culture during this time period help us to see the lineage and legacy of Black women's expressive culture and its common themes: Black women's sexuality, the vindication of Black womanhood, and concern for the Black community. It is not surprising, for example, that these themes surfaced during the enslavement of African peoples in the United States, in the speeches of Maria Stewart, the writings of Frances Ellen Watkins Harper and Pauline E. Hopkins, and the narratives and autobiographies of Harriet Jacobs, Harriet E. Wilson, and Elizabeth Keckley. An early example of Black women's expressive culture that encompasses all three themes is the narrative of Harriet Jacobs, *Incidents in the Life of a Slave Girl*.

Harriet Jacobs was an enslaved Black woman who struggled against unwanted sexual advances and liberated herself by escaping to the North. She had a hard life, and she wrote about it because she wanted to help ensure that no other Black woman experienced what she had. Jacobs makes use of the Black woman's rhetorical trope of sass in order to survive the many hardships she endured as both an enslaved Black woman and a free Black woman. For theorists such as Joanne Braxton, sass is a rhetorical weapon of self-defense used to preserve self-esteem and develop a safe distance between oneself and those who would seek to do one harm.[10] The image of the Black woman with her hand on her hip in outrage is evoked to visualize the sassy Black woman.[11] For theorists such as Sandra Mayo, sassy Black women are strong and assertive, with a "strong sense of somebodyness."[12] They know their worth and their significance. For poets such as Maya Angelou, a Black woman's sassiness is enough to offend those who oppose her; it causes her to walk like she's "got oil wells pumping in [her] living room."[13] For myself, sassiness is the precursor to bringing wreck for Black women and a large part of the lineage in the Black women's expressive culture that Black women rappers build on as they cause their own disruptions in the public sphere.

Jacobs's *Incidents in the Life of a Slave Girl* is read by many as a subversive text.[14] It is precisely its subversive nature that allows it to strike such a mighty blow for Black womanhood and ultimately for all Black people still enslaved. Throughout, she maintains an aura of politeness and respectability; however, the careful reader notes her ripping away the structures that would seek to destroy her. Even her respectability itself is a sassy act, for she realizes that "nothing annoys them [white southerners] so much as to see colored people living in comfort and respectability."[15]

Jacobs's narrative is just as interesting for what it does not say about Black women's sexuality as what it does say. Indeed, much has been written about the gaps in *Incidents in the Life of a Slave Girl*. Many scholars feel that Jacobs conceals certain incidents in her life because of some sort of shame or guilt.[16] I am inclined to read the silences and gaps as a purposeful move, a sassy act that is also a method of self-protection. Her silence functions more as a precursor to the "culture of dissemblance" that Darlene Clark Hine finds in her study of nineteenth-century midwestern Black women. The culture of dissemblance is the cloak of silence that Black women have used to cover any semblance of a sexual identity. Because of the negative stereotypes surrounding Black women's sexuality, they felt it best not to lay claim to a sexual identity; above all, one should not speak of anything sexual in public.[17] The culture of dissemblance functioned as a way to protect Black women from the negative stereotypes about them.

Jacobs has to conceal some parts of her life for her continued protection. Not only did she have to worry about the actual physical sexual harassment that she suffered at the hands of her owner, Dr. Flint, but she also had to be concerned that the people she told her story to—both the people she spoke to and the readers of her text— would think ill of her and consider her a woman without morals. I would add that her silence is a sassy tool that, simply put, does not allow the reader the luxury of knowing all of Jacobs's personal business. She tells the reader about the slave master, Dr. Flint, and his unwanted advances, but she does not reveal the who, when, where, what, and how of her sexual relationship with Mr. Sands, the father of her two children. The vivid descriptions of Dr. Flint's relentless pursuit help to make her case about the harmful impact of slavery on Black womanhood. Her relationship with Mr. Sands is none of our business. Jacobs concludes, "God alone knows how I have suffered; and He, I trust, will forgive me."[18]

Jacobs also defended Black womanhood by critiquing the injustices that many Black women were subjected to during the enslavement of African peoples. Contextualizing her own experiences, she writes:

> The influences of slavery had had the same effects on me that they had on other young girls; they had made me prematurely knowing, concerning the evil ways of the world. . . . But, O, ye happy women, whose purity has been sheltered from childhood, who have been free to choose the objects of your affection, whose homes are protected by law, do not judge the poor desolate slave girl too severely.[19]

She continues:

> Pity me, and pardon me, O virtuous reader! You never knew what it is to be a slave; to be totally unprotected by law or custom; to have the laws reduce you to the condition of chattel, entirely subject to the will of another.[20]

Jacobs is breaking apart stereotypes, exploding misconceptions, disproving the way people had begun to think about Black women. While she does not touch her own sexual endeavors, she does make it known that Black women like herself were victims, not the sexual predators they were painted to be. She plays on society's desire to protect the young by noting that the women enslaved were too young to have known of the things they were made to know. She also tackles the double standards that Black womanhood calls forth, noting that Black women are not protected like other women. And even as she asks for pity, in pointing out the double standard her text hints of sarcasm.

Also in a tradition of activism and social uplift that would continue in Black women's expressive culture, Jacobs wrote her narrative to help further the cause of all Black people, specifically those still enslaved. Her narrative had an activist project and goal and highlighted her earnest desire "to arouse the women of the North to a realizing sense of the condition of two millions [*sic*] of women at the South still in bondage, suffering what [she] suffered, and most of them far worse."[21] She saw her work as her "imperfect effort in behalf of [her] persecuted people."[22]

Women of the Black clubwomen's tradition similarly approached themes of Black women's sexuality, vindication of Black womanhood, and concern for the Black community. In the late 1800s and the early 1900s Black women found themselves trying to create a space for themselves in the public sphere that not only validated their voices but even more so their very being. Faced with the exclusionary racism of white women suffragists and the slanderous and stereotyped images of Black womanhood that existed during that time, the clubwomen gathered together in the spirit of social uplift. Clubwomen truly believed that African Americans were judged by the larger society as a group, and in order for them to be treated with respect they had to personally see to it that all Black women were equally worthy.[23] Their attempts to realize the goal that all Black women be treated with respect in turn provided the Black community with all its social services.[24]

Because the clubwomen's ultimate goal was to uplift the race in general and all Black women specifically, they often found themselves subscribing to certain white middle-class values. These values and standards led them to discount and dismiss any deviations in Black womanhood that did not fit these standards. Their values also led them to take part in what Hazel Carby has called "the policing of black women's bodies" and also what Darlene Clark Hine calls the "culture of dissemblance." Each phrase highlights extreme responses to the sexually stereotyped attitudes surrounding Black womanhood. Carby's policing highlights the amount of control exerted on the lives of young Black women so that they would not become wayward women who fit all the negative stereotypes. Hine's culture of dissemblance highlights the self-policing that Black women during this time participated in as a mode of self-protection; it prohibited any public displays of sexuality. As Darlene Clark Hine and Kathleen Thompson put it, "Because of the intense desire to contradict the image of immorality with which Black women had been burdened, the clubwomen put their feet on the straight and narrow path and expected everyone else to do the same."[25] These kinds of restrictions set the tone for what was allowed to count as "proper" Black womanhood and what had to be left out or silenced. They also established a pattern for Black women's intellectual traditions and Black feminist struggles that would continue for years to come.

Two women in particular who personified the goals of clubwomen addressed the themes of sexuality, Black womanhood, and Black community, and left a significant body of expressive work were Ida B. Wells Barnett and Anna Julia Cooper. Cooper's *A Voice from the South* is often cited as the first Black feminist treatise. In this work she encompasses Black feminist thought, activism, and visions for change, all in one project. Cooper was a race woman who helped to organize the Colored Women's League in Washington, D.C. She was both an educator and a public speaker, and she spoke out frequently on the progress of Black women. She believed that women were vital to the advancement of the race, and she vigilantly defended and advocated for Black womanhood. She saw herself as a representative for Black women, someone equipped to speak for her less fortunate sisters.[26]

Cooper's *A Voice from the South* simultaneously defends Black women's sexuality and vindicates Black womanhood with the understanding that doing so would in turn uplift the entire Black community. Her writing is deeply tied to Christianity. She recognizes "the necessity of the church training, protecting, and uplifting our colored womanhood is indispensable to the evangelization of the race."[27] She had high hopes for Black womanhood and was known to give speeches about the needs of Black women at churches and to groups of ministers. She writes:

> [M]y plea for Colored Girls of the South: the large, bright, promising fatally beautiful class that stand shivering like a delicate plant left before the fury of tempestuous elements, so full of promise and possibility, yet so sure of destruction . . . oh save them, help them, shield, train, develop, teach, inspire them . . . there is material in them well worth your

while, the hope in a germ of a staunch, helpful, regenerating womanhood on which, primarily rests the foundation stones of our future race.[28]

She truly believed that the future of the race rested with Black women: "only the Black woman can say 'when and where I enter, in the quiet undisputed dignity of my womanhood, without violence and without suing or special patronage, then and there the whole Negro race enters with me.'"[29]

Ida B. Wells Barnett also represents the Black woman's early use of expressive culture to further the race. She was an activist for women's rights and against the lynching of Black people. She struggled with white women for the inclusion of Black women in early women's rights battles. And while she subscribed to nineteenth-century values of proper ladyhood, she took her place in the male-dominated public sphere by writing and speaking.[30] She wrote and spoke vigilantly to dismantle stereotypes about race and gender. And she did not limit her scope to stereotypes about Black people; she also sought to tell the truth about the culpability of white men and women. She wrote now famous lines that questioned the purity and vulnerability of white womanhood and white men's desire to protect it.

> Nobody in this section of the country believes the old threadbare lie that Negro men rape white women. If Southern white men are not careful, they will over-reach themselves and public sentiment will have a reaction; a conclusion will then be reached which will be very damaging to the moral reputation of their women.[31]

She was not afraid to tell the truth as she saw it, and she willingly and publicly entered into discussion on the hypocrisy of lynching and the laws that governed the South.

> The miscegenation laws of the South only operate against the legitimate union of the races; they leave the white man free to seduce all the colored girls he can, but it is death to

the colored man who yields to the force and advances of a similar attraction in white women. White men lynch the offending Afro-American, not because he is a despoiler of virtue, but because he succumbs to the smiles of white women.[32]

She was ahead of her time in her boldness and direct nature. She fought with both Blacks and whites to have her voice heard, and many tried to silence her and deny her access to the public sphere. Long before the Black Panther Party started telling Blacks in America to pick up the gun, Ida B. Wells Barnett declared, "[T]he lesson this teaches and which every Afro-American should ponder well, is that a Winchester rifle should have a place of honor in every Black home, and it should be used for that protection which the law refuses to give."[33]

Even the leading race man of the time, Frederick Douglass, acknowledged Wells Barnett's strength as a race woman, her contributions to the Black public sphere, and her influence on the larger United States public sphere. When she published her first pamphlet against lynching he commended her:

> Brave woman! You have done your people and mine a service which can neither be weighed nor measured. If the American conscience were only half alive, if the American church and clergy were only half Christianized, if American moral sensibility were not hardened by persistent infliction of outrage and crime against colored people, a scream of horror, shame, and indignation would rise to the Heaven wherever your pamphlet shall be read.[34]

Douglass's words of praise ring loudly today as we recognize the greatness of Ida B. Wells Barnett and how she pioneered and fashioned a Black women's tradition in the public sphere that was bold and unafraid of telling the truth. Her uncompromising dedication to the survival of the whole race, male and female, made her a prototype for what Alice Walker would later come to call womanism.

Although we most often hear of Frederick Douglass's *Narrative of*

the Life of Frederick Douglass, an American Slave, Written by Himself as
the seminal slave narrative, and he is more often than not touted as
the leading African American thinker and speaker of the time, he
was also in dialogue with and at times on the same panels as women
such as Sojourner Truth and Frances Ellen Watkins Harper, to name
only two. Black women were there, and Douglass's praise of Ida B.
Wells Barnett speaks volumes to the central truth that Black women
also helped to shape the public discourse and the Black public
sphere. Although we often hear about the great debate between
Booker T. Washington and W. E. B. Du Bois as a critical moment
in the shaping of Black intellectual thought, we do not often hear
what the African American clubwomen were doing and saying
around this time. They had just as much to say, and they used a
variety of media to do so. In addition to being thinkers and shapers,
these women were also activists. Most linked their intellectual ideas
with actual projects such as group homes for newly migrated Black
women from the South. The clubwomen's activist projects and the
way they tackled the themes of defending Black women's sexuality,
vindicating Black womanhood, and uplifting the race make them
the foremothers to contemporary Black feminist thought, even
though some of them would have never claimed such a title for
themselves, considering themselves first and foremost race women.
However, their dedication to the survival of the race laid the foundation for womanist traditions.

Continued Legacies of Uplift and Vindication: From Blues Women to Civil Rights

The fact that there was indeed a continued Black women's activism
and advocacy throughout and beyond what has been traditionally
thought of as the first wave of feminist struggles leads us to the
complications implicit in categorization.[35] Categories and groupings
resist the kinds of overlappings and continuations that exist in the
intellectual and expressive traditions of Black women in the United
States. These overlappings and continuations become extremely

relevant when we look at women and blues culture in the United States. In terms of overlappings, it is important to note that the African American clubwoman movement discussed above was very much active and present for the birth of the blues. Women like these continued their legacy by participating in the civil rights movement, and many of the organizations they founded and created are still in existence.

Classical blues and civil rights represent two distinctly Black public spheres in which it can truly be said that if it were not for Black women, they would not have come into being in the way that they did. Black women were the first to put the blues on wax, and they made up the majority of the early blues singers, thus laying the foundation for blues culture. Black women were also the majority of the workers in the civil rights struggle, even if they were not in the spotlight. And without Rosa Parks the Montgomery bus boycott would not have happened when it did, and the civil rights movement would not have gotten started when it did.

Scholars such as Hazel Carby, Angela Davis, and Tammy Kernodle are currently reexamining the blues women for their feminist undertones. What was once dismissed as sad, sappy women crying over their lost loves is now being granted the critical eye of feminist readings. These readings do not simply celebrate the blues women but rather critically interrogate them by taking into consideration the entirety of the Black public sphere and the larger United States public sphere in which the blues women traveled and sang. The blues women exhibited an empowered presence by making the sexuality of Black working-class women a part of the dominant discourse. Their empowered presence becomes even more pronounced when we take into consideration that they were singing against conflicting stereotyped notions of the asexual Black woman as mammy and the hypersexual Black woman. The early blues women also traversed certain borders of sexuality that had not been crossed to date (in fact, many have yet to be crossed in popular black music to the same extent). (For example, Ma Rainey and Bessie Smith's recording of "Prove It on Me Blues" broached the subject of lesbianism, and these were also questions in the public discourse surrounding their sexuality.[36] By singing so freely about their sexual urges and desires, the blues women worked against the policing of Black women's bodies and the culture of dissemblance. They also complicated the very classed notions surrounding who was best suited to represent the race by singing about the very real and basic desires of a large part of the Black masses. The Black public sphere of classical blues became a space that Black women blues singers dominated—a place where they essentially controlled the public discourse in ways that, quite frankly, we have yet to see again.

The blues women were in a privileged space in that they not only dominated the Black public sphere that was blues culture but also had a very public presence in the larger public sphere. As such, they established an alternative public persona for Black woman-hood, a persona that went against popular images of the Black domestic worker, for example.[37] These women offered the count-erimage of the beautiful black dame. They were dressed in furs, dia-monds, sequined gowns, and gold. Nothing about them suggested that they were there to clean house. The blues women used their lyrics to complicate the meanings of Black women's sexuality by (1) publicly claiming that they indeed had sexuality, (2) blurring the lines of sexuality by claiming female dominance and in some cases lesbianism, (3) laying claim to female desire, and (4) disrupting pop-ular and classed notions of love and sexuality.

When we move to the issue of Black women and civil rights, we find that, similar to the case of the blues, if it had not been for Black women and the roles they played, this particular Black public sphere would have come about quite differently. The Black women involved with the struggle for civil rights in the United States are seldom lauded for all that they contributed. When we think of the civil rights movement, we usually think about the great men lead-ers. Visions of Dr. Martin Luther King Jr., Jesse Jackson, Stokely Carmichael, and Medgar Evers come to mind. It is only in recent times—as we begin to rethink the movement and all that happened within it—that we come to see the real significance of Black wom-en's contributions, mostly because some of these women are finally speaking and writing their memoirs and making their stories a part of the larger public discourse surrounding the Black struggle for civil rights in the United States. Historians are also rethinking the movement and acknowledging that prior to and in the early years of the movement there were more women than men working toward civil rights.[38] When we take what we know about the club-women and all they did in the name of uplift and improvement, it is not hard to envision Black women working in such large numbers and in such active roles.

If we think of the Montgomery bus boycott as jump-starting the official civil rights movement in the United States, then it is hard not to recognize Rosa Parks as the woman without whom there would not be a movement.[39] We are taught in most history classes that Rosa Parks was a poor, tired, and downtrodden Black woman who just could not get up and move to the back of the bus. The truth of the matter is, she was an activist who was deeply involved with the National Association for the Advancement of Colored People (NAACP) and the struggle for civil rights. And she was only forty-two years old. She could have easily walked to the back of the bus; she did not want to. She notes herself that "the only tired [she] was, was tired of giving in."[40] It was also women who initially took up the cause of Rosa Parks and initiated the first boycott of the buses. News of her arrest spread by word of mouth because one Black woman saw her being escorted off the bus and called other women. Jo Ann Robinson and other women in the Women's Political Council called for the boycott that took place on December 5, 1955. They sent out the initial flyers from which other flyers would excerpt and abbreviate.[41] When we think about the grand display of Black determination that the bus boycotts exhibited, it is crucial that we not neglect Black women's roles in that. They were the first to say "Enough is enough" in a way that spearheaded mass action.

However, by the time we come to the end of the civil rights movement—particularly to the March on Washington—we see Black women and their deeds effectively moved to the background. Even though the attendance at most civil rights events was largely women and youth, "nothing that women said or did broke the impasse blocking their participation."[42] When women such as Dorothy Height questioned why women were not represented among the speakers at the march, they were told that women were indeed represented because they belonged to the labor groups and churches who sent speakers.[43] And Mahalia Jackson's performance was given as an example of women's participation. Dorothy Height remembers:

> To address the issue, the organizers gave a number of us prominent seats on the platform. We were seated. In all the March on Washington pictures, we're right there on the platform. There were several women who just refused to do anything. Some were so angry that they didn't really want to take part. The women represented a cross section of organizations, including labor, religion, and social welfare groups. What actually happened was so disappointing, because actually women were an active part of the whole effort. Indeed, women were the backbone of the movement. A look at the pictures gives the impression that we were intimately involved.[44]

Dorothy Height's comment reflects how Black women were systematically silenced even while they did a lot of the work and provided the foundation for the movement. This speaks volumes about how Black women's shaping of the Black public sphere has been handled historically and currently. And whenever we see the shining Black spokesman commanding the public sphere and dominating Black public discourse, her statement reminds us to look for the women seated or standing in the background. They are the reason the Black prince is able to shine. When we really look at Black women's participation in the public sphere, we are forced to—as Dorothy Height remembers—"recognize that, traditionally, Black women, through their unstinting support of race movements and their willingness to play frequently unquestioned subordinate roles, and to put the men out front" gave us what we now call the Black public sphere.[45]

The 1970s: Black Power, Blaxploitation, and Women's Liberation

During the 1970s, while working to end oppression for all Black people in groups such as the Black Panther Party, the Student Nonviolent Coordinating Committee (SNCC), and the Black Liberation Army, some Black women found that the movement they thought was supposed to free them all was centered on freeing Black masculinity and establishing a Black patriarchy. They also found that, like their foremothers in the late 1800s and early 1900s, they had to struggle against stereotyped representations of Black womanhood and Black women's sexuality. The major difference, however, was that some of the images and representations they opposed came from the Black men they were fighting for freedom with. They found themselves struggling to claim a place in a movement that told them the only position for them was "prone," while encouraging them to use their "pussy power."[46] These women began to address issues of gender, and found that the women's liberation movement was too focused on the issues of white, middle-class women to seriously engage their specific issues and needs. Thus the title of Gloria T. Hull, Patricia Bell-Scott, and Barbara Smith's anthology, *All the Women Are White, All the Blacks Are Men, but Some of Us Are Brave,* becomes a fitting description of the ways Black women were marginalized in both race-based and gender-based movements. Out of this generation of writers and thinkers the lineage of Black women's expressive culture is extended by the works of Ntozake Shange, Alice Walker, Toni Morrison, Angela Davis, Millie Jackson, Carolyn Rogers, Sonia Sanchez, and Nikki Giovanni, to name only a few. These women were so successful in creating a space from which to voice their issues that they ushered in a whole new era in which Black women's expressive works take center stage. Their work has been taken up by the academy and has become canonized in what Ann DuCille calls the "occult of true Black womanhood," which highlights once again the problems underlying spectacle and representation: that the expressive and creative works of Black women that represent Black culture in specific ways are welcomed in spaces where the actual physical bodies of Black women are still marginalized.

The Black Arts movement was the literary arm of the Black Power movement, and as such it functioned as a space in which many of the ideas about Blackness and struggle began to take shape. It was common to attend a rally and hear several political poems or songs performed, or attend a poetry reading and come away with political knowledge. The participants in the Black Arts movement believed in art for people's sake, not art for art's sake. Thus they wrote speeches, songs, poems, and plays—things that would touch mass audiences at their initial hearing. The genres they chose spoke to the immediacy of the moment. Their mission was to combat the negative images of Blackness and replace them with positive ones.

Although the militant writers of the Black Arts movement in the sixties saw the destruction of images and misconceptions that degraded Black people as the ultimate goal of the movement, they left intact some of the most damaging misconceptions and images and created and fostered others—images of the Black woman as subservient and emasculating, as baby maker and sex object. Most of the work completed during the Black Arts movement held tightly to the sexism inherent in the Western society they sought to distinguish themselves from. Yet even as the Black Arts movement itself failed to show concern for women's issues, the women poets of the Black Arts movement spoke out in voices that were sometimes silenced but nonetheless clear.

The women poets of the Black Arts movement share what could be called the "double-consciousness" of Black feminism.[47] That is to say, their devotion to Black people—male and female—was a major concern in their polemics. However, being a woman led to concerns that proved to be just as important after the demise of the movement. These women used their poetry to destroy historical misconceptions about Black womanhood and build on the legacy and foundations of Black women's intellectual and expressive traditions by vindicating Black womanhood, defending Black women's sexuality, and showing concern for the Black community. Poet Nikki Giovanni contextualizes the significance of this lineage in her reference to Black women writers such as herself belonging to "not just the continuum of Black women writers, but the continuum of Black women."[48]

The poetry by the women of the Black Arts movement highlights the dual struggles of race and gender, and often Black women's sexuality becomes the starting point for a variety of critiques. Poets such as Sonia Sanchez and Nikki Giovanni protested the blatant degradation of Black women's sexuality in the Black Power movement. In her poem "Memorial," Sonia Sanchez attacks the ideology of communal sex and "pussy power" that urged Black women to drop their panties for any revolutionary brother and have little (boy) children in order to ensure an uninterrupted supply of soldiers for the revolution. Sanchez's answer to pussy power is: "that ain't no revolutionary / thing com / munal fuck / ing / ain't nothing political / bout fucking."[49] These women poets also questioned sexist notions about their place in the movement. They were the descendants of Sojourner Truth, Ida B. Wells Barnett, and Fannie Lou Hamer, and they knew very well their position was neither prone nor five steps behind their men. Kay Lindsey's "Poem," published in Toni Cade Bambara's landmark 1971 collection *The Black Woman*, highlights the irony of the woman's place question. Lindsey compares the racism that the Black community has fought so vehemently against with the sexism that still prevailed in the Black community. She compares the position forced on Black women by Black Power movement with the racism forced on Black society by white laws of segregation. This paradox can be seen throughout the lineage of Black women's expressive culture and intellectual traditions. Although most Black women poets of the Black Arts movement claimed early allegiances to race, they found it hard to be Black and a woman and not address the conflicting misconceptions about Black women's place in the movement. Through writing poetry and voicing protest in Black Power organizations in the name of sisterhood, they fought to secure a place for women in the movement.

They also sought to combat the misconceptions about Black womanhood that were placed on Black women by the larger society and internalized by the Black community. The Black matriarch is one such misconception, and Black women poets let politicians such as Daniel P. Moynihan and misguided Black revolutionaries who felt Black women should step back and let Black men lead know how they felt about this misrepresentation of Black womanhood.[50] The demonization of Black women who stood strong as backbones to Black families and worked inside and outside of the home infuriated the Black women poets and prompted June Jordan to title an essay "Don't Talk About My Momma." In the poem "Queen of the Universe," Sonia Sanchez correctly takes the blame away from Black women and places it where it belongs:

blk/menNNN & blk/woooomen have a history of alienation
in this country the cracker done superimposed on our
minds myths bout our selves.
     we be busy callen
each other matriarch or no good bums
     cuz the cracker done identified us as such.[51]

She plays on the quest for self-definition that prevailed in the Black conscious minds of this time by daring them to reject *all* misrepresentations of Blackness fostered by white racism.

Nikki Giovanni also tackles the misconception of the matriarch in "Woman Poem":

it's having a job
they won't let you work
or having no job at all
castrating me
(yes it happens to women too)
it's a sex object if you're pretty
and no love
or love and no sex if you're fat
get back fat black woman be a mother
grandmother strong thing but not woman[52]

Thus poets such as Sonia Sanchez and Nikki Giovanni questioned these caricatured representations of Black womanhood through their work. They questioned the contradictions in these representations and sought to redefine Black womanhood in a way that confronted the lies and began to name the truth.

The Black Arts movement was such an important time for Black expressive culture in general because Black people had access to numerous publishing houses; several Black presses were formed as well. However, even with the enormous amount of work that was produced in this period, the academy is just starting to show critical attention and interest. The current rise in Hip-Hop culture and the renewed interest in spoken-word poetry that stemmed from Hip-Hop no doubt had a lot to do with the new popular interest in the Black Arts movement. Russell Simmons's *Def Poetry Jam* on HBO, which often mixes contemporary spoken-word artists with rap artists and elder poets such as Nikki Giovanni, Amira Baraka, and Sonia Sanchez, offers one example. Still, lesser-known women poets of the Black Arts movement are difficult to find these days. Only the most popular poets, such as Nikki Giovanni, Mari Evans, and Sonia Sanchez, are widely anthologized. And if the woman poet is anthologized in anthologies edited by Black men, more often than not those poems are either pro–Black or pro–Black man. For example, Nikki Giovanni's "Beautiful Black Men (with compliments and apologies to all not mentioned by name)" can be found in all of the anthologies edited by men. Other women writers are few and far between. In *Black Fire: An Anthology of Afro-American Writing*, Larry Neal and Amira Baraka (LeRoi Jones) included just seven women out of over sixty featured writers. Women wrote only three of the essays in Addison Gayle's *The Black Aesthetic*. If it were not for anthologies such as Toni Cade Bambara's *The Black Woman*, Erlene Stetson's *Black Sister*, and special journal issues such as *Conditions Five*, much of the Black women's voice of the late 1960s and early 1970s would have been lost.

The 1970s also gave the Black public sphere its first Black female superhero in the form of Blaxploitation actresses such as Pam Grier and Tamara Dobson. Films such as *Coffy, Foxy Brown,* and *Cleopatra Jones* presented Black female action heroines to go along with the Sweet Sweetbacks and the Shafts. These films with women leads were just as concerned with the theme of revenge against white oppression as the rest of the genre. However, they added issues of gender to the mix and so finessed the borders between blaxploitation and Black Power, female objectification and women's liberation. They worked in and against the very limiting stereotypes of Black womanhood, leaving some in place while subverting and rearranging others. The blaxploitation movies essentially represent the larger public sphere's (represented by Hollywood) attempt to co-opt the

Black Power movement in order to stabilize and depoliticize it. Hollywood saw Black America thirsting for images of themselves and tried to quench the thirst with new stereotyped images, or revamped versions of the old ones. With Black women as the leads in films such as these, Hollywood found a way to exploit not only the Black Power movement but also the women's liberation movement.

The women leads in the blaxploitation films become Black superwomen or, as film critic Donald Bogle calls them, "superbadd super mamas." They become a hybrid of all the stereotypes of Black womanhood, such as the mammy and mulatto. They protect the community from inside and outside foes, nurture, kick butt, and look good doing it.[53] The super-bad action heroine takes all the good qualities from the other stereotypes. She has the nurturing nature of the mammy without her asexual status. She has the so-called beauty of the tragic mulatto without the tragedy. In the movie *Foxy Brown* (1974), for example, Pam Grier embodies the Black superwoman; she takes on an entire drug ring singlehandedly. She is portrayed as beautiful, sexy, and exotic. Even the theme song for the film aptly describes the all-encompassing superwoman: "Foxy, hey Foxy, yeah Foxy Brown. You're cute and sweet, no but you don't mess around. . . . Oh but please don't make Foxy mad or you'll find out the lady is super bad."

The film *Foxy Brown* also uses stereotypical images to subvert and rearrange them. This comes across in the way it deals with Foxy's sex life, which is practically nonexistent compared to those of her men hero counterparts in the genre. While promiscuity is prevalent in movies such as *Sweet Sweetback's Badass Song, Shaft,* and *Superfly,* it has no place in *Foxy Brown, Coffy,* and *Cleopatra Jones.* This silencing of Black women's actual sex lives while playing on their sexuality to objectify them works as a complication of the previous generation's way of dealing with misconceptions about Black women's sexuality. The Black women that these heroines represent are not hiding behind a culture of dissemblance or policing their bodies, but they are not having a whole lot of sex either. They use their sexy bodies to seduce and trap bad guys, and they have sex with specific purposes in mind. For the most part sexuality is just another tool for revenge.

By having sexy and desirable Black women as the leads, the films also countered the stereotype of the desirable white woman. The white women in the films can never compete with the leading ladies, and that leads to the films tackling the issue of white men's desire for Black women. The white men who harass or otherwise lust after Black women in these films—unlike Harriet Jacobs's Dr. Flint—are subjected to harsh punishment. In *Foxy Brown* a white judge is belittled: "I heard of a meat shortage but this is ridiculous; I can't find it. Talk about assault with an undeadly weapon, and I mean talk about your blunt instruments." Steve, the boyfriend of Foxy's archenemy in the film, is castrated, thereby signifying on the very real castrations of the Black men accused of raping white women (and written about by Ida B. Wells Barnett in her campaigns against lynching).

There are several implications for the Black audience these images were aimed at entertaining. While there is no doubt that Hollywood used the images they felt Black audiences wanted to see in order to draw them into the theaters, the images served dual purposes. On one hand, they exploited old stereotypes about Blackness and used them in superficial ways. On the other hand, they worked in some instances to subvert and rearrange negative stereotypes, sometimes complicating commonly held beliefs in ways that were neither positive nor negative. While the women heroines in the film were shown as liberated, they still fit the traditional goals of working for the community and vindicating Black womanhood. Even though they presented a very sexual public image, they were not indiscriminately having sex, thus highlighting the continued struggle against the image of the promiscuous Black woman. Their bodies were exploited in a variety of ways because of their objectification in the films.

The clearest example of this exploitation is seen in both *Coffy* (1973) and *Foxy Brown* when we get various shots of Pam Grier's breasts for reasons not particularly significant to the plot. In an era when women were mythically burning their bras, Hollywood gives us Pam Grier's breasts. By exploiting Black women's bodies, the blaxploitation movies fall short of offering fulfilling and complete images of empowerment for Black women. However, the films do offer some interesting subversions and complications. If we really begin to critique and explore the genre, we can see the ways Black women such as Pam Grier have participated in cultural processes of gender construction for Black women and turned some of those processes completely around. We will also be able to explore and critique contemporary reclamation of Grier's characters such as the ones offered by women rappers Foxy Brown and Lil' Kim. They are bringing the big bad Black supermamas into the new millennium and using them to construct contemporary Black women's gender and sexuality. Critiquing and understanding the originals helps us to fully appreciate and critique the new; just as we cannot totally discount the complicated and conflicted Black Arts movement and blaxploitation era, we cannot totally cast aside the conflicted and complicated representations of Black womanhood in Hip-Hop culture or sexually explicit women rappers such as Lil' Kim and Foxy Brown.

A Third Wave? Black Feminism to Hip-Hop Feminism and Why We Need to Take It There

Black feminist theory has reached a point where it can strategically and wholly critique itself. These strategic critiques work as reconsiderations of Black feminism aimed at learning from the past and present to evoke change in the future. They interrogate Black feminism, ask hard questions, document the good work that has been done, acknowledge the missteps, and look toward a renewed Black feminism. New Black feminist criticism reenvisions Black history in the United States and notes Black women's contributions to not only the Black public sphere but also the larger United States public sphere. Black feminist critics are claiming militant Black feminist foremothers, naming them as warriors, and finding the seeds of radical Black feminism. This is no small task, given—as we have seen—the way Black women's voices have been systematically silenced. They are daring to question the ways in which Black feminism itself functions as a form of spectacle, and pushing the political implications of its usefulness in that form. They even question the space that Black feminist thought currently holds in the public sphere and the amount of control Black women actually have over that space and their own images and representations. They question and critique each other in an attempt to form a dialogue that builds on and is true to the legacies of change left by Black women in the past. However, even as Black feminist critics build on these legacies, they question the holds and limitations of some of the ideas that dominated the earlier projects. For example, they critique the project of respectability that dominated much of early Black women's activism and find that it was limiting and exclusionary. They also find that respectability—like spectacle and representation—is double-edged. However, more than anything else, recent Black feminist interventions seek to convey that Black feminist thought is a serious body of work that should be viewed critically.[54]

Valerie Smith's understanding of Black feminist theories and the ways they can be used by readers is very helpful when thinking about the expanded possibilities of a Black feminist critique. In *Not Just Race, Not Just Gender: Black Feminist Readings,* Smith combats the myth that Black feminist theory should be used only to talk about Black women. In fact, she questions the notion that only Black women can *do* Black feminist theory. Smith finds Black feminist theory more useful when it is detached from the positionality of the critic and is a site of critique that challenges all monolithic notions, including notions of Americanness, woman, Blackness, and Black woman.[55] She offers the descriptor "theorizing Black feminisms" as opposed to a Black feminist theory, since the latter hints that there is only one way to do Black feminism.[56] Following Kimberle Crenshaw, Smith offers a method of intersectionality—reading at the intersections of the constructions of race, gender, class, and sexuality and looking for the interconnections among them.[57] This methodology leads her to the understanding that Black feminism, as reading intersectionality, allows for a historical and contextualized understanding of the ways racism, misogyny, homophobia, and class discrimination function, and how they subordinate oppressed people and reinforce one another.[58] Black feminism as a way of theorizing encompasses more than just race and gender.

The majority of studies on Black popular culture largely focus on the work and texts of men and pay minimal attention to issues of gender except for very specific explorations of the construction of Black masculinity. With the exception of critics such as bell hooks, most of these scholars do not find a way to combine the study of Black popular culture with a Black feminist agenda. The studies are also very limited in the aspects of Black culture they address. Critics of Black popular culture have also neglected the Black woman rapper. In a political climate overly concerned with gangsta rap, Black cultural critics are producing numerous articles and books to quench the thirst of America's obsession with this genre of rap, thus leaving others unaddressed. Black cultural critics who focus on rap are therefore limited to the construction of Black male images. While I have no problem with using popular culture to evaluate and critique constructions of gender, I do not believe we should do so by continuously neglecting Black women's cultural texts. Recent studies and texts on Black popular cultures, especially those dealing with rap music, have yet to pay serious attention to issues of gender.[59] Even in areas such as popular literature, where Black women writers such as Terry McMillan helped to create a multibillion-dollar market, there have not been many critical interrogations devoted to these Black women's texts. In fact, there is no substantial body of critical work on the phenomenon of Black women's popular fiction.

Connections need to be made in an effort to include all aspects of Black popular culture. Perhaps the most enlightening critical text on Black popular culture that explores not only Black women's texts but Black women's subject matter is Jacqueline Bobo's *Black Women as Cultural Readers*. Bobo sets up a space for Black women as cultural critics, values the influences they have in making the texts of other Black women successful, and sees the political potential in the Black woman's stance as cultural critic. She constructs a model of Black women's interpretive community and notes the activist nature of this community. She writes, "Black women's challenge to cultural domination is part of an activist movement that works to improve the conditions of their lives. Included in the movement are Black female cultural producers, critics, and scholars, and cultural consumers."[60] For Bobo, as for me, cultural elements are intrinsically linked to political and activist concerns. She sees the Black women's interpretive community as a part of Black women's historical resistance to oppression and cultural domination. Bobo brings to studies on Black popular culture the Black feminist voice that is desperately needed and provides an example of the ways the two can be patched together.

Several Black and third-wave feminists have started to approach in their writing the tenuous relationship among rap music, Hip-Hop culture, and feminism. They offer a variety of different feminist perspectives on rap, rappers, and Black women. Some condemn the sexism in rap and encourage others to do the same. Others offer complicated analyses that critique the larger societal issues that contribute to rap's sexism, production, and consumption. Some offer third-wave feminist critiques that ask how one can be a child of the Hip-Hop generation, love the music, and still critique and actively speak out against the sexism. They all offer examples of how Black feminists have begun to deal with, think about, and write about rap music and Hip-Hop culture.

For example, bell hooks's "Gangsta Culture—Sexism and Misogyny: Who Will Take the Rap?" explores society's inconsistent response to sexism and misogyny, noting that when the sexism and misogyny is found in Black youth cultural forms there is more public outcry than when it is found in white media forms. She also notes that gangsta culture is as American as apple pie and baseball, and young Black men rappers are not social deviants but true purveyors of the society's culture. In fact, the rappers become grunt workers for the patriarchy: they sow the field of misogyny for the patriarchy and provide the labor necessary to keep it in operation, much as Black men and women provided the free and exploited labor that built the United States. Rightly, hooks also notes that if it were not for the fact that young middle-class white men are becoming rap's biggest consumers and using it to ape Blackness and disrupt middle-class sensibilities and decorum, there would not be such intense outcry and outrage.

While hooks finds that it is the "white supremacist capitalist patriarchy" that needs to be changed, she also cautions that Black women should always speak out when Black men are oppressive toward Black womanhood. For hooks a critique of rap music is meaningless without a critique of the larger society. She realizes that rap is not created in a social and cultural vacuum and that it shares many of the larger society's faults, even doing its dirty work. However, hooks does not let Black men rappers off because they are pawns of the system. She maintains that they should be critiqued, but the critique should include the entire problem.[61] Similarly, Michele Wallace's "When Black Feminism Faces the Music, and the Music Is Rap" links the critique of rap to a critique of the larger society. Wallace, like hooks, finds rap's sexism and misogyny no big surprise given the society we live in. She also notes that although Black feminist critique is seen as divisive in Black communities, Black women rappers and Black women in general must offer more feminist critiques of rap. Like hooks, she encourages Black women to speak out. And, like hooks, Wallace offers a second-wave Black feminist perspective.[62]

Third-wave feminist Eisa Davis, in her article "Sexism and the Art of Feminist Hip-Hop Maintenance," takes up the need for dialogue expressed by Wallace. This is especially crucial to her because she grew up with the music and it provided the sound track to her life. Davis, like many third-wave Black feminists, has a need to salvage the music; thus she even goes as far as to question the harm misogynist lyrics can do. For Davis, true dialogue across the sexes would lead to the recognition that negative internalized representations are false, get rid of self-hate, and lead to a more productive battle against sexism.[63] Likewise, third-wave, self-proclaimed Hip-Hop feminists such as Shani Jamila, dream hampton, Eisa Nefertari Ulen, Tara Roberts, and Joan Morgan are tackling the precarious relationship among Black women, Hip-Hop, and feminism.[64]

Each of the works discussed above offer varying views and critiques of rap music, specifically rap music performed by Black men rappers. And each discusses the need for a steady, unflinching critique of the music and the culture. The works vary in the ways in which they make connections between rap and the larger society.

They also vary in their discussion of the impact of class and economic issues on rap and rappers. These kinds of links between feminism and rap will and should continue. However, what I would like to see occur would take as a topic of inquiry the work of Black women rappers. I maintain that the work of women rappers offers a productive and seldom-utilized platform for the work of feminism and the struggle against sexism. Much of the work currently being done by Black feminists and feminists on rap focuses on the sexism and misogyny of Black men rappers. With the exception of the studies of Murray Forman, Kyra Gaunt, Nancy Guevara, Cheryl Keyes, Robin Roberts, and to some extent Tricia Rose, the work of women rappers is being ignored.[65] This is unfortunate, because Black feminist criticism and theory can also tell us significant things about women rappers. For example, in *Reconstructing Womanhood: The Emergence of the Afro-American Woman Novelist,* Hazel Carby argues that nineteenth century Black women writers reconstructed Black womanhood against the "cult of true womanhood." This argument can be extended and applied to Black women rappers today who continue to reconstruct Black womanhood by embracing their sexuality and challenging society's norms and stereotypes. An expanded Black feminist theory is needed to contribute to the work of the Black public intellectual, especially the public intellectual dealing with Black popular cultures.

The one thing that most of the Black women of the Hip-Hop generation have in common is that they all came of age in the post–Black Power era. As such, they share several commonalities with their Black Power, Black Arts, and blaxploitation foremothers. These commonalities are evident in the Hip-Hop generation's openly stated connection to the Black Power movement. In a sense, the women of the Hip-Hop generation are building a home for themselves on ground that was cleared by the Black women thinkers, writers, and activists of the late 1800s and the early to mid-1900s and broken by those of the 1970s. The head start made by earlier Black women has made claiming a space from which to speak somewhat easier; however, Black women today are still plagued with some of the same issues. For example, the issues of sexual stereotypes that plagued the clubwomen also confront the women that came after them. But the Hip-Hop generation, like Black women in the 1970s, find these sexual stereotypes combined with images coming from Black men. Today, in addition to the old images of the sexually promiscuous Black woman, and the prone pussy-power-wielding women of the recent past, we have the bitches, hos, stunts, skeezers, hoochies, pigeons, chickenheads, and baby mamas put forth by Black men rappers. The need to struggle against stereotyped images is still present. Black women of the Hip-Hop generation have found ways to deal with these issues within the larger public sphere and the counter–public sphere of Hip-Hop by bringing wreck to stereotyped images through their continued use of expressive cultures.

1. MC Lyte
Reproduced by permission
of Rachel Raimist

2. Queen Latifah
Reproduced by permission
of Rachel Raimist

3. MC Lyte and Queen Latifah
Reproduced by permission of Rachel Raimist

4. Missy "Misdemeanor" Elliott
Reproduced by permission of Rachel Raimist

5. Foxy Brown
Reproduced by permission of Rachel Raimist

6. Monie Love
Reproduced by permission of Rachel Raimist

7. Trina
Reproduced by permission
of Rachel Raimist

8. The Inc. (left to right: Ja Rule, Charlie Baltimore, Ashanti, and Irv Gotti)
Reproduced by permission of Rachel Raimist

I Bring Wreck to Those
Who Disrespect Me Like a Dame:
Women, Rap, and the Rhetoric of Wreck

Women of the Hip-Hop generation, like the Black women who went before them, find themselves in a similar position of trying to navigate a space for themselves in a Black-male-dominated public discourse. While we cannot say women of the Hip-Hop generation hold the same spaces in the public sphere as their foremothers, we can say with some degree of certainty that the way Black women of the past navigated the public sphere has had a direct effect on the way Black women of the Hip-Hop generation feel they can move within this sphere. Quite frankly, by the time we reach the Hip-Hop era, Black women have generations of conditioning to stay in the background while Black men claim the limelight. We also have a history of seldom speaking out against Black manhood even when it poses a direct threat to Black womanhood. We also have, however, glimmers of Black female outspokenness that grabs public attention and disrupts the Black male dominance of the Black public sphere. Examples of these instances surfaced when Michele Wallace wrote *Black Macho and the Myth of the Superwoman* and had the nerve to go on TV and defend her ideas; when Ntozake Shange wrote *For Colored Girls Who Have Considered Suicide* and the play made it all the way to Broadway; when Alice Walker wrote the novel *The Color Purple* and it was adapted as a feature film; when

Terry McMillan wrote the novel *Waiting to Exhale* and it too was adapted as a feature film. Each of these instances of Black female outspokenness was met with tremendous outcry from the Black public sphere. They were lambasted by Black men and even some Black women for portraying negative images of Black manhood or showing Black men in a negative light. Some people even accused them of the classic "airing dirty laundry."

It is these legacies—both those of the Black women who were outspoken and those of the women who allowed Black men to shine in the Black public sphere—that I believe the women of the Hip-Hop generation build on. While women of the Hip-Hop generation do not dominate the movement by doing the majority of the work to ensure the movement's success, as the Black women in the civil rights and Black Power movements did, if we look carefully, they are the ones doing the meaningful work. They are the activists, the ones trying to use Hip-Hop to create meaningful change. I expand on the theorization and definition of wreck in Hip-Hop by thinking about its uses as a rhetorical tool that builds on Black womanist traditions and a Hip-Hop present. I am concerned with the ways the rhetorical practices of Black women participants in Hip-Hop culture bring wreck—that is, moments when Black women's discourses disrupt dominant masculine discourses, break into the public sphere, and in some way impact or influence the U.S. imaginary, even if that influence is fleeting. While bringing wreck may not change the world in drastic or even long-lasting ways, it is my hope that by shedding light on those crucial moments in Hip-Hop culture where Black women have brought wreck, we will be able to make more meaningful use of future moments of wreck.

Exploring various theoretical texts and histories of women in Hip-Hop provides a sense of the space that has been allowed to them and serves as an opening to think about how they use that space to create a rhetoric of wreck that allows them to combat the factors that hindered their foremothers. I am not so much concerned with writing women into Hip-Hop history; I assume their presence. Neither am I concerned with documenting the work of every female rapper or every woman involved with Hip-Hop culture. Rather, I am more concerned with documenting the ways Black women of the Hip-Hop generation intervene in the public sphere and the ways they bring wreck to it.

Rhetoric of Wreck

So far, I have examined the historical lineage of bringing wreck as it pertained to Black people throughout U.S. history and their intervention in the larger U.S. public sphere. I have explored wreck as disruptions that somehow shifted the way Black people were viewed in the society at large. Bringing wreck does not always change the world, but it is capable of making small and meaningful differences. As a way of thinking specifically about the potential inherent in Black feminist change, bringing wreck offers new possibilities for the potential of Black women's speech and action.

The phrase "bringing wreck" is used in Hip-Hop typically to signify skill and greatness: the rapper is so good, has so much skill, that he or she wrecks the microphone. Or, the break dancer can bring wreck by outdancing all other competitors and making others afraid to approach the dance floor because they cannot compete. Often, bringing wreck is used in a boastful manner, such as Queen Latifah's refrain "Check it while I wreck it, sing it while I bring it." She is telling the crowd to pay attention to her because her rapping skills are so good that she can do damage with her very words. It is also used as a form of praise. After rapping, deejaying, or breakdancing very well, one could be told something like: "You brought wreck! Your style is nice! You wrecked it!" In short, when a member of the Hip-Hop generation is really good at what he or she does, that person is praised for bringing wreck.

Bringing wreck is also used to connote damage already done. A member of the Hip-Hop generation may marvel, for example, over the aftermath of a twister, hurricane, flood, or tropical storm by saying, "Damn, Mother Nature brought wreck!" It can also connote anger and a desire or intent to do real damage. For example, the woman who caught her partner cheating might say, "Oh, no he didn't. He don't know who he's messing with. I will bring wreck" before she breaks a car windshield or trashes an apartment. All of these shades of bringing wreck contribute to the kinds of wreck Black women participants in Hip-Hop culture exhibit. However, the wreck that I want to focus on can best be described as a rhetorical act that can be written, spoken, or acted out in a way that shows resistance. Bringing wreck, as the term is used here, is a rhetorical act that has close ties to various other speech acts that are often linked to Black womanhood: talking back, going off, turning it out, having a niggerbitchfit, or being a diva. Each of these actions has simultaneously been embraced by some Black women as a marker of unique Black womanhood and renounced as the stereotypical Black woman stance by others. For example, while most Black women would relish the fact that they can tell people off, put them in their place, and leave them speechless, they do not embrace the stereotype of the neck-moving, eye-rolling, loud, hand-on-hip, Sapphire-like Black woman throughout the popular and dominant cultures. Serious attention is beginning to be paid to this gift of gab that seems to represent Black women, and critics are coming up with descriptive names for talking that talk.

Black women's speech acts—what they say, and how and where they say it—are garnering some critical attention. The ways Black women come into and develop language have been taken up by linguists, cultural critics, and well-known writers who offer their own accounts of coming into language and voice. In these accounts and inquiries into Black women's language use, we get the beginnings of an understanding of the potential inherent in Black women's speech and action. Linguists such as Denise Troutman-Robinson and Geneva Smitherman are already laying out the importance of Black women's speech for sustained resistance against oppression. Troutman-Robinson notes that due to the systemic nature of oppression in the United States, Black women have had to develop and pass on to future generations of Black women a form of verbal and nonverbal expression that combines politeness with assertiveness.[1] It is necessary, in a society that harshly stereotypes your womanhood and seeks to render you invisible, to assert yourself and make yourself visible. However, it is also necessary to maintain a degree of civility and politeness while being assertive.

Smitherman maintains that we must develop a womanist language for the twenty-first century that "speaks the truth to the people."[2] According to her, we must build on the legacy of our foremothers and draw on their linguistic leadership.[3] "Is the African American Verbal Tradition the purview of Black men only? What are the discourse options available to Black women? Who is the Black woman, and how *do* a Black woman sound?"[4] Smitherman finds that Black women do indeed lay claim to the African American verbal tradition: they signify, play the dozens, and "talk shit."[5] For her, and for myself, the challenge lies in channeling Black women's use of language toward meaningful change. Part of harnessing the power and potential of Black women's speech and expressive culture is recognizing how Black women come into language and examining the spaces in which that speech and expressive culture occurs. The spaces that have been found thus far are the kitchen and the garden.

Black women's speech and expressive culture have been limited in the public sphere due in part to circumstances discussed earlier in this work, such as maintaining community, promoting Black manhood at the expense of Black womanhood, and constantly vindicating Black womanhood against misrepresentation. They have also been limited because the places in which they have been allowed to thrive have been devalued. It is only recently that we have begun to reclaim the legacy of Black women's language and expressive culture as it is found in the everyday spaces of their lives. Writer Alice Walker finds these legacies in the gardens of women like her mother, who found a way to express their creativity through magnificent gardens and splendid quilts in spite of the oppressive and repressive states of their lives.[6] Writer Paule Marshall reclaims these legacies from the poets in the kitchen, women like her own mother, an immigrant from Barbados, and her friends, who sat in the kitchen and talked with one another about everything from child rearing to politics to the economy to war. Their response to being made to feel invisible was to take their mouths and make them into guns. Amongst each other, in the kitchen they were heard; they were validated.[7] Black feminist cultural critic bell hooks also remembers her mother and other Black women talking in the kitchen, and it is from them that she learned how to talk back, even as she, like the young Paule Marshall, was not allowed to join in on grown-folk conversation.

The concept of "talking back" as a Black women's rhetorical stance is crucial as we move from a discussion of the what and where of Black women's speech and expressive culture to a discussion of the potential and possibility inherent in bringing wreck. Bell hooks notes that talking back is more than expressing one's creative power. Talking back is a challenging political gesture of resistance to forces that render Black women nameless, voiceless, and invisible. Talking back is "a gesture of defiance that heals . . . that is no mere gesture of empty words, that is the expression of our movement from object to subject—the liberated voice."[8] Bringing wreck draws on Black women's speech patterns such as talking back in that it too is concerned with resistance and liberation. However, it also builds on a legacy of Hip-Hop in which a more stylized rhetorical presence is used, drawing on grander elements of show and spectacle than talking back.

Bringing wreck also builds on and moves past other Black women's speech acts such as going off, which writers Faye Childs and Noreen Palmer describe as the Black woman's unique way of dealing with anger and frustration. For them, going off is an unhealthy way of dealing with anger—and it feeds the stereotypes of Black womanhood. They identify two levels of going off, the "sista sass level" and the "Sapphire level." The sista sass level is "the type of angry response that include[s] slanted eyes, angled body posture, titled heads, and sashaying on about our business when finished speaking our minds."[9] The Sapphire level is "an escalated angry response that takes an argument to the extreme."[10] The Sapphire sister loses perspective, can become abusive, and uses violent tactics. Some aspects of going off are clearly present in bringing wreck; if we think of bringing wreck as the Hip-Hop continuation of Black women's rhetorical traditions, then the connections become all the more expected.

For Childs and Palmer, going off is a direct effect of the "invincible Black woman syndrome."[11] They argue that Black women struggle to maintain an appearance of strength while denying their limitations and sometimes their weaknesses. They believe that Black women are so used to denying their own needs, anger, and hurt that it often builds up, and the end result is going off.[12] This uncontrolled/uncontrollable state is where going off and bringing wreck part ways. Bringing wreck is a decided act, not an unavoidable breaking point. While there is a level of being fed up involved, the women of the Hip-Hop generation who enact a rhetoric of wreck do so after making a conscious decision to speak out. They are bringing wreck in order to create change.

Similar to going off, turning it out is another speech act that is linked to Black women. Linguist Karla Holloway sees turning it out as the Black woman's response to being made to feel less than a grown woman, like a mindless person with no character, integrity, or common sense. Black women are usually treated this way when others buy into the stereotypes surrounding Black womanhood. For Holloway, turning it out could mean "handing over to our adversary our version of the stereotype that motivates their disrespect to us—just to prove to them that they could no better handle the stereotype than they can determine or control our character."[13] Turning it out coincides with bringing wreck more than going off does, because it is a conscious act. One decides to turn it out; one does not just snap after constant abuse or neglect. At the moment when the Black woman realizes that she has been disrespected, she proceeds to turn it out in a willful act, in the spiritual tradition of "I shall not be moved."

Similarly, the niggerbitchfit is a stance that some would place in the realm of stereotyped representations of Black womanhood. For writer Jill Nelson, the niggerbitchfit is a powerful rhetorical tool for change, "what happens when a nice colored girl, having exhausted all possibility of compromise, communication, and peaceful conflict resolution, turns into everyone's worst nightmare, a visible grown-up Black woman mad as hell and with nothing to lose, and opens her mouth."[14] It is the embodiment of righteous anger and rage, a response to being fed up. Or, in the oft-quoted words of Fannie Lou Hamer, the niggerbitchfit surfaces when one is "sick and tired of being sick and tired." Nelson sees it as a revolutionary act that is an expression of rage against attacks on Black womanhood from just about all aspects of society. To qualify as a niggerbitchfit, the act has to be a public display. Nelson believes that the best niggerbitchfits are those that are strategic and collective, when Black women speak out loudly together in righteous anger and outrage against disrespect that impacts all our lives: "At its best it is a tool for uniting, organizing, channeling rage into collective power, and that collective power into the ability to effect change."[15] It is the potential for collective niggerbitchfits that becomes appealing when thinking about the possibilities for Hip-Hop feminism bringing wreck in Hip-Hop culture. If we could envision ways to harness the collective power for bringing wreck within the Hip-Hop generation in order to combat the sexism and misogyny within it and outside of it, then we would no doubt be able to use this power to effect meaningful change.

Diva is another term that has been used to describe Black women's public speech acts. Lisa Jones's "bulletproof diva" is the Black woman who recognizes her own beauty and strength because she realizes that the larger society will never validate her or even be able to comprehend her true worth. For Jones, the bulletproof diva is not "the emasculating black bitch too hard for love or piety. It's safe to assume that a Bulletproof diva is whoever you make her— corporate girl, teen mom, or the combination—as long as she has the lip and nerve to raise up herself and the world."[16] The bulletproof diva as a construct of the third wave of Black feminism, which Lisa Jones represents, is crucial to understanding the concept and ultimately the potential of bringing wreck. The definition of the bulletproof diva has within it implied activism. In order to qualify, one must be linked to the tradition of community uplift. However, this Hip-Hop version of uplift expands further than the Negro communities of old. The bulletproof diva potentially raises both herself and the world.

The possibilities for the bulletproof diva having an impact on the world becomes evident when we read her in conversation with Lauren Berlant's notion of "diva citizenship," which provides the framework for an understanding of how the diva and subsequently bringing wreck can be used in the counter–public sphere of Hip-Hop and the larger public sphere to evoke change. Berlant writes, "Diva citizenship does not change the world. It is a moment of emergence that marks unrealized potentials for subaltern political activity. Diva citizenship occurs when a person stages a dramatic coup in a public sphere in which she does not have privilege."[17] Although diva citizenship does not have world-altering strength, Berlant recognizes it as a moment when the normally unprivileged diva is able to grab the public, captivate the public, and subvert attention away from the dominant story line. She ceases to be invisible, reinscribes herself into the public space, and provides a retelling of the dominant history. While holding the larger public captive and telling her story, the diva bids others to not only acknowledge her suffering but identify with it. The diva's retelling and reinscribing become pedagogical moments for the larger public and compel them to want to change and be better human beings. Ultimately it is these pedagogical implications that bringing wreck is most concerned with. When a woman of the Hip-Hop generation is able to build on the legacy of Black women's activism, expressive culture, and speech acts and grabs hold of the public sphere by bringing wreck, there must be the potential for change. Ultimately, the moment of bringing wreck should bring those who witness it to a different understanding of Black womanhood, even if only momentarily.

Women, Rap, Wreck

Most examinations of rap music and Hip-Hop culture critique rap as a masculine discursive space and seldom look at Black women's experiences within this space. With the exception of critiques of misogyny and sexism in rap music and Hip-Hop culture, how rap music and Hip-Hop culture influence Black womanhood goes unexplored. Several Hip-Hop scholars have begun to take on the task of writing women into the history of Hip-Hop and validating the creative contributions of women to the field. They have written revisionist histories that document the women who were involved during the early days of Hip-Hop culture. And they are giving critical attention and consideration to women rap lyricists and the interventions their lyrics and presence have made in the counter–public sphere that is Hip-Hop culture.

The work of Nancy Guevara and Cristina Veran can best be classified as revisionist histories. They find that women have always been a part of the culture, even in the early days. Guevara finds that while women's participation has been distorted, women have been involved creatively in Hip-Hop culture via rap, graffiti writing, and break dancing. She reinserts these women by using the personal stories of women participants: graffiti artist Lady Pink, female rap group US Girls, female rapper Roxanne Shante, and break-dancer Baby Love. She finds that the dismissal of women in historical accounts of the development of minority cultures is quite deliberate and "serves to impede any progressive artistic or social development by women that might threaten male hegemony in the sphere of cultural production."[18]

Likewise, Cristina Veran traces women's early histories in rap by documenting the women rappers of the 1970s and 1980s. She notes the early vision of women such as Sugar Hill Records label owner Sylvia Robinson, who had the foresight to sign up-and-coming young rappers and produce many of the early rap albums. Veran notes that there were many women actively involved in the shaping of Hip-Hop culture in the early days—women who started their own businesses, organized parties, and created new styles from dance to music.[19] It would be too easy to ask why we do not hear more about these early women Hip-Hop innovators. They have no doubt fallen victim to the same erasure that provokes us to reenvision history in all aspects of society. Veran notes that a love for the culture of Hip-Hop motivated many of the women involved in the early days. And I would add that a simple love for the culture—not a desire to become rich and famous—could be the reason that many of the early women in Hip-Hop were more inclined to play the background, much like the Black women who wanted simply to improve the Black community and not become race spokespeople.

The women rappers—the female MCs—that Guevara and Veran

uncover are all women that I remember hearing as a young Hip-Hop head. I remember seeing and hearing US Girls in the movie *Beat Street* (1984). Even then, their refrain "US Girls can boogie too" let me know that there could potentially be a space for me in the culture that I loved. The group consisted of Lisa Lee, Sha Rock, and Debbi Dee, and they held it down for women in Hip-Hop in the film. But before I ever heard of US Girls, I was already jamming to the Sugar Hill Records female group Sequence. I knew all their lyrics, and I even bit some of Cheryl the Pearl's rhymes in my own burgeoning baby raps. These early women could rap just as well as the men who were rapping during that time. More female MCs, such as the Mercedes Ladies, who boasted of being the first all-female crew with a woman DJ and MC, followed them, as would female rap groups such as Finesse and Sequence, Salt-N-Pepa, BWP, JJ Fad, and Sweet Tee and Jazzy Joyce; solo artists such as Dimples Dee, Sparky D, Roxanne Shante, the Real Roxanne, Pebblee Poo, Sweet Tee, MC Lyte, Queen Latifah, Yo Yo, Boss, and Da Brat; and the Trinas, Eves, Lil' Kims, Foxy Browns, and Missy Elliotts that grace the airwaves today. While the number of re-corded women rappers in no way surpasses that of men, their presence in the rap game speaks volumes. As the most visible element of Hip-Hop culture currently, rap sets the tone for a lot of what the dominant society recognizes as Hip-Hop culture. Having women's voices represented via Hip-Hop in the larger public sphere opens the door for a wealth of possibilities in terms of the validation of the Black female voice and Black women's agency.

Scholars such as Venise T. Berry, Yvonne Bynoe, Cheryl Keyes, Murray Forman, Kyra D. Gaunt, Wanda Renee Porter, Robin Roberts, Tricia Rose, and Eric King Watts have all explored the various aspects of Black women's agency via rap music. They address the ways Black women use Hip-Hop culture to grapple with and create images.[20] They discuss the ways Black women use rap to negotiate body politics and sexual politics.[21] They explore the Black feminist aspects of some Black women rappers.[22] They link lineages of Black women's expressive cultures, from double dutch to girls' games to Hip-Hop.[23] And they also examine issues of Black female empowerment via Hip-Hop.[24] The growing body of scholarship on women and rap music provides a rich starting ground for explorations into the ways Black women use the whole of Hip-Hop culture to not only assert agency, claim voice, grapple with and create images, negotiate sexual and body politics, evoke Black feminism, continue lineages, and empower themselves, but also lay claim to the public sphere and subvert stereotypes and domination by bringing wreck.

Cheryl Keyes argues strongly for the centrality of women's voices in rap music, noting that they are not incidental and have added significantly to the genre of music. Her essays " 'We're More Than a Novelty, Boys': Strategies of Female Rappers in the Rap Music Tradition" and "Empowering Self, Making Choices, Creating Spaces: Black Female Identity Via Rap Music Performance" place the artistry of female rappers on the map and lend credence to their skills. She notes that early women rappers, while shedding light on the female perspective of life in urban America, often employed strategies such as appropriating male performance behavior and directly contradicting male standards as a way to gain recognition.[25] And she shows that their co-opting of b-boy stances did not stop them from borrowing from foremothers such as comedienne Jackie "Moms" Mabley and song stylist Millie Jackson.[26] Like the revisionist historians discussed earlier, Keyes firmly locates women in the rap continuum. She also places female rappers in four categories: the queen mother, the fly girl, the sista with attitude, and the lesbian.[27] For my own purposes, categorization of women rappers is not beneficial, since lines blur and identities constantly intersect. I am more interested in the ways women rappers resist easy categorization in defining their own identity and negotiating representations of Black womanhood. Therefore, the way they grapple with images and deal with sexual politics becomes crucial.

Venise T. Berry, Tricia Rose, Eric King Watts, and Kyra Gaunt have begun to think about the ways women rappers deal with conflicting female images and sexual politics in Hip-Hop. Berry explores the development of a Black feminist voice in rap music via a struggle for positive images and Black female identity construction.[28] She also examines the way women rappers resist stereotypes. Rose sees women rappers as a part of the dialogic process in rap and notes that there are three dominant themes in women's rap songs: "heterosexual courtship, the importance of female voice and mastery in women's rap and black female public displays of physical and sexual freedom."[29] Watts notes the potential for an empowering eroticism of the female voice in Hip-Hop. He examines the power of the erotic to lend women control over their own representation and by extension the entire rap game itself.[30] And Gaunt finds that there is a direct lineage between the games that Black women grow up playing and their contributions to Black expressive cultures.[31] All of the research that has been completed on Black women in rap is crucial and sets the foundation for further study. Frankly, compared to what has been written about men, there has not been enough of a focus on women and rap. Therefore, what currently exists becomes crucial for further studies. I find that these early works formulate not only a history of women in rap but also the beginnings of a theoretical body of work aimed at understanding women's participation and the societal elements that influence and/ or inhibit that participation.

Rap music and Hip-Hop culture, as an example of a youth movement that crosses gender, sexuality, race, and class, becomes an excellent example of public displays of intersections and contact zones, providing an ideal space to examine the way difference is simultaneously constructed and navigated. The ways Black women find a voice and establish a presence in this arena further nuances the ways difference is negotiated in this particular youth movement. What happens when Black womanhood enters Hip-Hop culture? How does that presence bring wreck to commonly held ideas about gender and difference? And what impact does this wreck have on the larger societal public sphere?

I believe that Black women participants in Hip-Hop culture have developed key survival skills and formulated various ways to bring wreck to the stereotypes and marginalization that inhibit their interaction in the larger public sphere. Through Hip-Hop culture, a generation of Black women is coming to voice and bringing wreck. These women are attacking the stereotypes and misconceptions that influenced their lives and the lives of their foremothers. And they are maintaining a public presence while they counter the negative representations of Black womanhood that exist within Hip-Hop culture. Usually when they are able to grab public attention by bringing wreck, these moments become instances when everyone pays attention. Queen Latifah's "U.N.I.T.Y." presents one such instance.

"U.N.I.T.Y.," which won a Grammy in 1993, presents the perfect starting example of a Black woman bringing wreck in Hip-Hop in a way that has implications for change both within the counter-public sphere of Hip-Hop and the society at large. In this song, Queen Latifah builds on the legacy of promoting and fostering community and vindicating Black womanhood left by her Black womanist foremothers by calling for unity. Love of the Black community is evident in the song's refrains: she chants that Black men and women should be loved "from infinity to infinity." The song is also an instance of outspokenness in that she calls attention to sexual harassment, domestic violence, and the influence negative images of Black womanhood have on young Black women.

The first verse of the song is a critique of society that calls into question beliefs about "proper" dress and being able to walk on the streets free from harassment. Queen Latifah's story of walking down the street in cutoff shorts on a hot day and being groped by an unknown man carries with it the experiences of millions of women who walk down the street and receive catcalls from strangers and the millions of women who suffer more than verbal abuse, the women who are attacked or raped. Queen Latifah's story is the in-between, in that she is not raped but she is touched in addition to the verbal harassment of being called a bitch. Because it is in-between, it serves as a pedagogical moment in the diva sense of bringing wreck. It has the power to call into question not only what happened to Queen Latifah but also all of the variations, such as what could have happened to her and what has happened to many women. As we listen to Queen Latifah, we realize that no matter how short the pun-pun shorts a woman is wearing, it is not okay for a man to make lewd comments. And it is definitely not okay for a man to touch, fondle, rape, or otherwise invade the sanctity of her body and her personal space. Queen Latifah's lyrics make us call into question a variety of acts that occur daily in the objectification of women, from catcalls to physical harassment and rape. And by doing so she brings wreck not only to "those who disrespect [her] like a dame," but also to notions of what is acceptable in our society in regard to women and their bodies. While this form of wreck does not go past the initial moment when the song was released and constantly played on the airwaves, it does represent a moment when the masses of people were thinking about these issues collectively.

Queen Latifah's strong message has feminist undertones, even if Queen Latifah herself does not identify as a feminist. When asked if she was a feminist, Queen Latifah balked: "I don't even adhere to that shit. All that shit is bullshit! I know that at the end of the day, I'm a Black woman in this world and I gotta get mine. I want to see the rise of the Black male in personal strength and power. I wanna see the creation of a new Black community for ourselves and respect from others."[32] Queen Latifah, then, appears to be a Hip-Hop embodiment—minus the cursing of course—of the Black clubwomen who went before her. She has definite goals that do not include the label "feminist," but her agenda, because she is a Black woman, certainly overlaps with feminist causes such as harassment and domestic violence. However, the vindication of Black womanhood is a trait she shares most strongly with the Black women who went before her.

Queen Latifah also tackles the impact that negative representations of Black womanhood found in rap lyrics have on the young Black women who listen to it. In addition to letting the listener know that she is neither a bitch nor a ho, she also challenges the image of the gangsta bitch popularized in the rap lyrics of some men rappers and questions the usefulness of this image to young Black women. This critique is important because often young women listen to these lyrics minus any real critique, and they emulate the kind of woman that the men rap about. The gangsta bitch, in an era of gangsta rap, becomes the epitome of Black womanhood; she is what young women strive to be in order to gain acceptance from the men. Queen Latifah brings the reality of this kind of lifestyle into focus when she cautions young would-be gangster girls about the possibilities of being shot or having their face sliced with a knife by another gangster girl.[33] Her words of advice are an example of bringing wreck because she actively seeks to uplift and create change. Queen Latifah is reaching out to a younger generation of Black women in order to teach them the reality of trying to emulate the kind of woman some rappers—in this instance her own friend rapper Apache—rap about as the ideal woman. The reality for the gangsta bitch is she could be shot and killed, or she can be scarred for life with one slice of the knife. This image is a very different image than the "ride or die chicks" that most men rappers paint in their lyrics, the down-for-whatever, hard-core shortys who will do anything for their men. Queen Latifah offers the reality, and by doing so she brings wreck.

In the second stanza, Queen Latifah calls attention to domestic violence and represents a woman who has had enough and finally leaves the abuser. She paints the picture of a woman who has come to the realization that love does not come with physical pain. Queen Latifah's lyrics are forceful and empowering. She lays out the facts and suggests actions that the woman can take. Even though she tells the story in the first person, the message, the pedagogical moment, comes as a stated fact that is directed at the listener: "A man don't really love you if he hits ya." This well-placed statement broadens the implication of bringing wreck further. It makes the story bigger than the teller and includes the millions of abused women suffering around the world. Queen Latifah brings wreck by bringing the issue of women's abuse into focus for the society at large and causing us to question both the abuse against women and our own action or inaction against it.

Similarly, Eve's "Love Is Blind" brings the issue of domestic violence into both the counter–public sphere of Hip-Hop and the larger public sphere. Eve, however, does not take on the persona of the battered woman, as Queen Latifah does in "U.N.I.T.Y." She instead takes on the persona of the vengeful best friend. She threatens the abuser with murder throughout the song, which ends with her killing the abuser. Similar to Queen Latifah's "U.N.I.T.Y.," Eve uses the song as a pedagogical moment. However, it is a lesson aimed not only at the women who suffer abuse but also at the men who abuse. For the men, the message is clear: keep beating up on women and you might catch a bullet and die. For the women, the message is similar to the one found in Queen Latifah's lyrics: men who really love you do not hit you. Eve makes use of rhetorical questions throughout the song to highlight her point by essentially asking if a man who really loves a woman would give her a black eye, make her cry every night, and ultimately cause her to wish for his death.[34] Eve is bringing wreck not only by rapping the lyrics and posing these questions. She also expands on the activist elements of bringing wreck by building institutions aimed at combating the problem. She started the Love Is Blind foundation to address do-mestic violence issues in more significant ways than a song could.[35] She too has a mission of uplift similar to that of her Black foremoth-ers, and she would like to see a collective effort of women in the Hip-Hop generation uplifting each other. She notes, "A lot of women tell me I uplift them. . . . We gotta do it collectively. . . . I see how a lot of women disrespect themselves. When we change our actions, men will change their minds. I think a lot of women get tired of hearing that shit. I'm glad that women feel like I can uplift them."[36] While Eve's words may seem a bit naive in terms of the exact amount of influence women's actions have on the men rappers who use the words *bitch* and *ho*, she is on to something in her desire for the collective action of Black women. This collective action could take the form of the collective niggerbitchfit that Jill Nelson encourages. Or it could be as simple as Black women col-lectively deciding not to deal with men who do not respect Black womanhood, as Rebecca Walker recommends in "Becoming the Third Wave."[37] The important point is that songs such as "Love Is Blind" and "U.N.I.T.Y." inspire the desire for collective action. Eve's "Love Is Blind" and the second stanza of Queen Latifah's "U.N.I.T.Y." build on the diva qualities of bringing wreck in that they offer testimonies aimed at changing the world, or at least the way we think about women's place in it.

Within each rapper's delivery and style of rap there are other ele-ments of bringing wreck. These are most evident in the music vid-eos of these songs. In the "U.N.I.T.Y." video, for example, Queen Latifah raps the lyrics from a telephone booth, and she is yelling into the phone in a manner that can best be classified as turning it out or going off. In the video for "Love Is Blind" Eve represents the calculated and thought-out stance of a woman ready to turn it out or, better yet, navigate a niggerbitchfit. She studies the situation; throughout the video, she is on the side examining the scene. The video, unlike the lyrics, does not end with her killing the abuser. She does use the gun to threaten him, but the event culminates in a bright beam of lights and doves flying into the air and him on the ground alive. The video version, more than the song alone, serves as a pedagogical moment. Both songs' lyrics and videos offer examples of the ways Black women have used rap music to bring wreck.

"She Used to Be My Girl": Hip-Hop As Woman and the Issue of Representation

As S. Craig Watkins notes in *Representing: Hip-Hop Culture and the Production of Black Cinema*, Black youth view representation practices as important and vital for both the political aspects and the pleasurable aspects of their lives. They use both aspects in combination with representation to respond to a world that is becoming increasingly saturated with communications media. Representing, as Black youth in the Hip-Hop generation see it, expands far beyond the common definitions of the word. They have created a culture of representing that includes "a complex set of practices, styles, and innovation."[38] The spectacle of representation then becomes a stylized manner of conveying to the world—via the various media available through Hip-Hop—the plight of the Hip-Hop generation as they see it. For this historically marginalized and invisible group, the spectacle is what allows them a point of entry in the public space that has proved to be violent and exclusionary. As Watkins notes, "For many Black youth, the sphere of popular culture has become a crucial location for expressing their ideas and viewpoints about the contradictory world in which they live."[39] The counter–public sphere of Hip-Hop allows them the space and tools to voice their views on the world and their own lives, to represent in ways that only they can.

A common form of representing that occurs in Hip-Hop is men rappers representing Black women and Black womanhood. This representing plays out in a variety of ways, but the most often noted is the representation of Black women as bitches, hos, stunts, skeezers, hoochies, and chickenheads. All of these derogatory representations have been the subject of much feminist criticism of rap. Likewise, there has been a lot of focus on representations of Black women as strong Black mothers or dear mamas (not to be confused with baby mamas and their drama) and Black queens. These are the more positive representations that serve as the flip side to the bitches, hos, and so on. These kinds of representations help remix the classic madonna/whore split. These are also the representations that Black women rappers seek to bring wreck to by countering the lyrics and adding their own stories and voices. Such representations of Black womanhood garner the most attention, both from the women rappers who speak out and from the feminist thinkers who offer critiques. Other representations that are just as problematic but perhaps a bit more complicated do not receive as much critique or outcry. One such representation is that of Hip-Hop gendered feminine.

A representation that can be read as at the same time positive and negative is that of Hip-Hop itself being represented as a woman. The use of woman as a symbol for Hip-Hop can be compared to historical uses of woman as symbols of both nation and virtue throughout time. These kinds of representations of Black women in rap can be compared to early American representations of women's place in the public. Theorist Mary P. Ryan writes of early American women who were not allowed to speak publicly but inspired public speaking. These women were the center of toasts and honored at civic celebrations, but they were not allowed to command the public space and speak. These women were also used as public symbols: they stood for and represented liberty and civic virtue and served either as outcasts or ornaments but never as wanted and validated public speakers.[40] So, basically, we can have a woman Statue of Liberty and a statue of the goddess of justice each representing the key virtues of our public sphere, but women were not free to formally get up and argue a case for liberty and justice in the public realm. These national symbols and virtues can be compared to the practice of gendering Hip-Hop feminine.

Perhaps the most widely recognized version of this particular form of representation of woman as symbol in Hip-Hop is found in Common's "I Used to Love H.E.R." The song breaks down the history of rap music and Hip-Hop culture, representing Hip-Hop as a woman that Common loves. He first met her when he was ten. He takes us on through Hip-Hop's Afrocentric and pro-Black stages and is quite upset when she goes to Los Angeles and becomes too commodified. He mourns the mainstream's co-optation of Hip-Hop, blaming commercialization and a wave of gangsta rap for ruining the pure Hip-Hop he used to know, but he vows to save her.[41]

The video for Common's "I Used to Love H.E.R." offers the visual image of the story he tells in the lyrics. We see him as a youngster in his room listening to Hip-Hop music. We also see a young, beautiful Black woman dressed in old-school Hip-Hop gear. Although we rarely see her face, we see lots of her body. The video follows this young woman, the female embodiment of Hip-Hop, through various stages. The clothing she wears and the situations she is placed in represent the key stages of Hip-Hop culture. However, Hip-Hop gendered feminine has no agency. She is something men rappers love, something they do. She does not act; she is acted upon. She does not do; she is done. This is evident in the video when we see how helpless the female embodiment of Hip-Hop is in the face of the forces that would seek to destroy her, such as capitalist exploitation, commodification, and gangsta culture. No matter how positive the image of Hip-Hop as a woman seems, as a symbol, it does nothing to encourage women's agency and participation in Hip-Hop. As a symbol, the woman is never as strong as the men who possess her and use her for their own ends.

Common's rendering of Hip-Hop as a woman inspired others to offer their own gendered representations of Hip-Hop. One example is the Roots song "Act Too (The Love of . . .)";[42] another is in the Tribe Called Quest song "Bonita Applebum."[43] Other, recent representations that seek to gender Hip-Hop masculine have also surfaced. In addition to the letter to Hip-Hop written by feminist journalist Joan Morgan in her book *When Chickenheads Come Home to Roost*, in which Hip-Hop is not only gendered masculine but represented as a once loving partner who has lost his way and became abusive, a recent film and a song from its sound track also seek to represent Hip-Hop in the masculine. *Brown Sugar* and a song from its sound track by Erykah Badu titled "Love of My Life (Ode to Hip-Hop)" both rely heavily on the Common song and fall short of fully bringing wreck to the gendered representations of Hip-Hop as feminine. Although Badu sings of her love for Hip-Hop and genders Hip-Hop masculine in her lyrics, she (re)presents a different version in the video, in which she herself embodies Hip-Hop. She becomes like the beautiful Black woman in the Common video and goes through all the various stages of Hip-Hop. She even wears a variety of colorful T-shirts that are clearly marked "Hip-Hop." Even though Erykah Badu's video flips back to representing Hip-Hop as a woman, she at least has agency and is represented as fully active in the video. We see her face as well as her body. She is break-dancing, deejaying, and rapping. She acts. She has agency and in this way brings wreck to the representation that Common offers of the female Hip-Hop.

The film *Brown Sugar* at first glance appears to gender Hip-Hop as masculine. Written by Rick Famuyiwa (who also—along with Todd Boyd—wrote the Hip-Hop-inspired coming-of-age story *The Wood*) and Michael Elliot, the film remixes the romantic comedy genre for the Hip-Hop generation. Famuyiwa also directs the film, and Sanaa Lathan and Taye Diggs play the lead characters, Sidney Shaw and Andre "Dre" Ellis. Hip-Hop symbolizes a multitude of things in this film. It represents the friendship and growing romantic feelings between Sidney and Dre, and it also represents each to the other. For example, throughout the film, Sidney is working on a book that she titles *I Used to Love Him*. The book is a letter to Hip-Hop that documents and traces its growth. It is also a letter to Dre that conveys how Sidney really feels about him. Similarly, Sidney represents all that is true and pure about Hip-Hop for Dre.

While these embodiments of Hip-Hop appear to move us away

from the typical representations of Hip-Hop gendered feminine, the film cannot sidetrack this *common* trap. The references and images in the film clearly show that here, just as in the Common song and the Erykah Badu video, Hip-Hop is gendered feminine. The character of Sidney overwhelmingly and consistently represents Hip-Hop throughout the film. From the signature delicate gold nameplate she wears in every scene except those in which she is formally dressed to the way she acts as the barometer for what is real Hip-Hop, Sidney, more than any other character in the film— even the MC Cabby, played by Mos Def—represents Hip-Hop in this film.

A constant refrain in the film is the question that Sidney asks each of the rappers she interviews: "So, when did you fall in love with Hip-Hop?" The film starts out with a series of men rappers, DJs, and well-known rap record label owners contemplating that question. Rappers such as Method Man and Black Thought, DJs such as Pete Rock, and record label owners such as Russell Simmons and Jermaine Dupre all recollect the songs and artists that made them fall in love with Hip-Hop. Not surprisingly, all of these men name other men and songs by other men. While this initial framing of men naming and listing other men as the sparks that ignited their love for Hip-Hop may seem to effectively gender Hip-Hop masculine, we need to look at the scene more carefully to get the true meaning. It is Sidney who poses the question each time. It is she they seek to impress with their answers. She might just as well be saying, "So, when did you first fall in love with me?"

Likewise, even though Dre represents Hip-Hop to Sidney in that her letter to Hip-Hop doubles as a love letter to him, Sidney also represents Hip-Hop to Dre. It is her validation that he seeks and craves throughout, both through the music reviews she writes and through the look in her eyes, to let him know if he is remaining true to real Hip-Hop. In proving himself worthy of Hip-Hop, Dre is ultimately trying to prove himself worthy of Sidney. Sidney is also, for Dre, the woman who is *like* Hip-Hop. In a New Year's Eve toast, it is Sidney, not his wife, who receives the ultimate praise and compliment. Dre toasts Sidney by likening her to "the perfect verse over a tight beat." And he closes the toast by adding, "To

Hip-Hop." By likening Sidney to what is quintessentially Hip-Hop—the perfect verse over a tight beat—and collapsing Sidney and Hip-Hop, Dre effectively one-ups Tribe Called Quest's praise in "Bonita Applebum." Sidney is more than a Hip-Hop song; she *is* Hip-Hop.

There are several other subtle instances in the film that work to place Sidney in the role of Hip-Hop and that gender Hip-Hop feminine. The last instance that I will discuss here stems from the film's title, which also represents Dre's dream girl in the movie. "Brown sugar," according to Dre, stands for the woman who is "definitely wifey material, fine, smart, classy, but not a snob, hella hella sexy, but not a ho." The fact that the screenwriters chose to title the entire movie based on this one statement by Dre effectively exhibits the film's ultimate gendering of Hip-Hop as feminine in the movie. Not only is Hip-Hop at its purest considered brown sugar, so is Sidney.

These kinds of complicated representations in which women are meant to stand for all that is good and pure give way to the kinds of conflicted representations to which women of the Hip-Hop generation have a hard time bringing wreck. Like the early American women, women of the Hip-Hop generation are used to represent symbolically and are discouraged from claiming a public voice and representing for themselves. The struggle to claim a space in the masculine sphere of Hip-Hop leaves women fighting not only the historical stereotypes that plague Black women but also the negative images and misconceptions attributed to Black women in Hip-Hop culture. In an effort to claim a space for themselves, Black women involved with Hip-Hop culture must continuously bring wreck.

Bringing Wreck: Confronting and Changing Images and Representations

Black women of the Hip-Hop generation are not content just to be a symbol of Hip-Hop; in acts of resisting and renegotiating the images that men rappers have used to represent women within Hip-Hop, they have sought to bring wreck to the images. The most widely quoted and recognized example of this kind of wreck comes from Queen Latifah with songs such as "U.N.I.T.Y." and "Ladies First." Women rappers from Queen Latifah to Salt-N-Pepa, Yo-Yo to Missy Elliott, and Roxanne Shante to Eve bring wreck to misrepresentations of Black womanhood in Hip-Hop culture and rap music by their very presence in this counter–public sphere. Their physical presence as real women, not symbols, helps to shake up notions of "a woman's place." The fact that they use their lyrics to bring women's issues to the forefront of rap music and Hip-Hop culture further disrupts the commonly held misconceptions and misrepresentations of Black women in Hip-Hop. This wreck and disruption take place on a variety of levels, two of which I'll mention here.

The first disruption I explore takes place in what some have called the sister of Hip-Hop: spoken word. Two spoken-word artists who speak out and bring wreck to the negative images of Black womanhood that exist in Hip-Hop culture are Jessica Care Moore and Sarah Jones. Both women have a stage presence that can easily be labeled Hip-Hop. They also infuse their poetry with sentiments and images familiar to the Hip-Hop generation. And both poems that I will discuss here were performed on the show that blends spoken word with rap, *Def Poetry Jam*.

Jessica Care Moore says, "I'm a Hip-Hop cheerleader / carrying hand grenades / and blood red pom poms / screaming from the sidelines of a stage I built."[44] These words not only flip the script on the stereotypical image of woman as cheerleader, but also bring into focus the lineage of Black women standing on the sidelines cheering Black men on and working diligently to build and shape the Black public sphere. Moore's words effectively add herself and women of the Hip-Hop generation to that lineage. Throughout the poem, she complicates notions of women's place in Hip-Hop by bringing to the surface women's significance to the growth of the Hip-Hop movement. She also criticizes the negative images and messages that come out in the music. Moore writes:

> I'm a Hip-Hop cheerleader
> I buy all your records
> Despite the misogyny
> Not looking for the blond in me. . .
> I'll be your number one fan
> I'll scream the HAY's
> I'll tolerate all your hoes
> I'm a Hip Hop cheerleader[45]

Moore uses spoken word both to claim a voice and to bring Hip-Hop to task. She incorporates and signifies on Hip-Hop phrases such as "hey, ho" and uses them to question and critique misogyny. She uses the poem ultimately to explore the larger relationship between Black men and women.

Sarah Jones seeks to disrupt the images of Black women as sexually promiscuous and the limiting of Black women's worth to their vaginas. Her poem "Your Revolution" has the mantra-like refrain "Your revolution will not happen between these thighs," signifying on Black Power movement ideas about "pussy power" through its remix of Gil Scott Heron's classic "The Revolution Will Not Be Televised" and also signifies on Hip-Hop's constant references to sex that end up objectifying Black women. Jones flips the script and uses the rappers' own words to disrupt their objectifying narratives. In front of each of the men rappers' lyrics Jones adds the refrain "Your revolution will not."[46]

Of course, the rappers who make booty songs are not thinking about revolution. Jones is, however, and by doing so she is more than building on the militant poet foremothers of the Black Arts movement. Beneath the repetitive refrains is the hidden question that brings wreck to the booty-focused factions of Hip-Hop: "Why are you not thinking about revolution instead of being obsessed with sex?" This critique brings the reader to question why indeed rap music does not have more uplifting and powerful messages to give us.

Sarah Jones's "Your Revolution" for a while was played on the same radio stations that played the rap music she critiqued. As a result of her taking the rappers' own lyrics and using them in her poem, the Federal Communications Commission labeled "Your Revolution" indecent and fined Portland radio station KBOO seven thousand dollars. The fact that she had to fight to get the FCC to reverse its decision and clear her poem of the indecent label exemplifies the very real repression that can occur when Black women speak out and bring wreck. Jones notes, "Hip-Hop is the most important tool our generation has in terms of expressing the different layers of our reality. . . . It's fine if rappers want to be ballers, but just because I'm a woman doesn't mean that I'm nothing but body parts in a song. . . . My words were meant to tell everyone from Jay-Z to Biggie, I love your skills, but here's what I would love to hear contributed to the conversation."[47] The controversy of the FCC's 1999 decision and Jones's subsequent fighting of that decision has made an impact on the larger public, with numerous articles appearing in various media. She has the public attention, and this allows her to bring wreck in the diva sense because this moment is a pedagogical one that we will look back on and think about in terms of not only free speech but also the objectification of women in rap music.

The second level of disruption I will focus on here moves from the genre of spoken word to that of rap and takes into consideration a rapper who most people would not credit with combating stereotypes. Foxy Brown, with her hypersexual persona, at first glance would appear to epitomize the hos and bitches that men rappers rap about and spoken-word artists such as Jessica Care Moore and Sarah Jones speak out against. Foxy Brown, in fact, often claims these labels for herself. The reclamation of terms once considered derogatory is widely debated, but I will not enter that debate at the present time. I will offer, however, that rappers such as Foxy Brown, Trina, Khia, and Lil' Kim can showcase the double standards that have plagued women throughout the ages. For example, in "My Life" Foxy Brown raps about the double standards that exist for men and women rappers. She raps about the fact that if she is unpleasant, people call her either a bitch or rude. However, they find the same behavior in men amusing. She also notes that men who have multiple partners are called macks, while women are called whores.[48] Foxy Brown brings wreck to age-old double standards and claims a space for herself as a woman in the sphere of rap. She is also claiming her right to be who she wants to be in that sphere, whether she is considered rude or sexually promiscuous. She also notably addresses the misconception that men are involved with rap for the love of it. Examples such as Common's "I Used to Love H.E.R." and The Root's "Hip Hop You the Love of My Life" highlight widely held beliefs that only men can have "real" love for Hip-Hop, just like only men can have "real" rapping skills. All others are in it for the money. Foxy Brown brings wreck to claims that she is in it for the money by asking, "What the fuck he in it for?" She also calls men rappers to task for the way they collapse women into categories of bitch and ho based solely on gender.

Foxy Brown's "My Life" offers but one example of the kind of wreck that Black women rappers bring to the counter–public sphere of Hip-Hop. Eve's "Love Is Blind" and Queen Latifah's "U.N.I.T.Y.," both discussed earlier, are others. Missy "Misdemeanor" Elliott's celebration of her right to an attitude in "I'ma Bitch" is yet another. The list of Black women bringing wreck and thereby controlling their own representations in the counter–public sphere of Hip-Hop and the larger society is long and continues to grow each time a woman picks up a mike and wrecks it. It also grows when women involved in Hip-Hop begin to share their own experiences and stories, as Foxy Brown does in "My Life." The power of autobiographical accounts and life stories in the disruption of negative representations of Black womanhood and Black women coming to voice is also used by women of the Hip-Hop generation to bring wreck to the negative images and stereotypes that influence their lives.

(Re)reconstructing Womanhood:
Black Women's Narratives
in Hip-Hop Culture

The autobiography has always served multiple purposes for African Americans granted the resources and capabilities to tell their stories. As far back as the slave narratives African Americans have used the autobiography not only to tell their life stories and document their own personal truths, but also as vehicles for social justice and social change. Scholar V. P. Franklin notes that autobiographies helped individual Blacks claim and proclaim a selfhood in a society that denied the existence of their realities.[1] Thus autobiographies became a platform from which the self could be acknowledged as well as a space from which to secure a public voice. Black feminist scholar Joanne Braxton notes that for Black women in particular, the act of writing autobiography is inextricably linked to the act of claiming a place in society.[2]

Slave narratives and later autobiographies granted African Americans the space to validate their own lives and in turn to validate the lives of other African Americans with similar experiences. Autobiographies worked as rallying documents that called attention to the status of Africans in America. In this regard, they were also political and exhibited illocutionary force in that they were often emancipatory and sought change. Maria Pia Lara notes that women's narratives exhibited illocutionary force through their transformative goals of justice and democracy, which surfaced in the telling of one's story in order to project change in the future.[3] Illocutionary force redraws understandings of justice and the good life and deconstructs the liberal understanding of the public/private split.[4] In short, illocutionary force flips the script and brings wreck using personal narrative and life stories to effect change. It forces us to acknowledge different ways of being in the world and in doing so to recognize the prejudice and biases that typically inform the public sphere. This acknowledgment and recognition often lead to some kind of change. For example, the slave narratives illustrated illocutionary force, as did the autobiographies linked to political struggle both prior to and after the civil rights and Black Power movements in the United States. W. E. B. Du Bois's *The Souls of Black Folk,* Malcolm X's autobiography, Angela Davis's autobiography, and Huey P. Newton's *Revolutionary Suicide* all fit neatly into the realm of illocutionary force in that they relayed a personal story as it was connected to the larger struggle of African Americans and were aimed at evoking change in the larger society. Contemporary African American autobiographies have been focused on the lives of celebrities and motivational speakers.[5] People who were formally involved with the civil rights and Black Power movements are also writing autobiographies.[6] However, the crucial element of being connected to a current and contemporary struggle for freedom is missing from these works, and thus they lack the immediacy of political action present in most of the earlier African American autobiographies.

More recently, the vehicle of choice for representing life stories and the ills of society has been rap music. Often criticized for its harsh lyrics and negative images, rap music has been equally praised for representing clearly what is wrong with society so that something can be done to change it. Rap music and Hip-Hop culture's quest to "keep it real" and represent the real has led to the creation of a vast array of lyrics, from the grit of gangsta rap to the playful nostalgia of Will Smith. Thus rap represents multiple aspects of Black life in America. Rap music and Hip-Hop culture function as places from which to tell the truth of one's life. Given the overall lack of opportunity afforded to young African Americans in contemporary society, rap music becomes one of the few spaces in which one can secure a public voice and a place in the public sphere. This space is not totally unproblematic. In fact, it is fraught with conflict and contradiction, especially in terms of representation—specifically, how seriously we can take the rapper claiming to represent the ills of the inner city.

There is also the celebrity factor. Some may view the rappers, because of their celebrity status, as separate from the people they claim to represent—as performing for the people in the same vein as Habermas's nobility and lords (discussed earlier). There is some validity to these concerns; a rapper who is a recognized celebrity travels the country and sometimes the world and is no longer *of* the neighborhood in the same ways as those who live there on a day-to-day basis. There are also complications surrounding those who never even lived the kinds of lifestyles or lived in the neighborhoods they claim to represent. All of these complications make the possibilities for illocutionary force, and by extension bringing wreck, a very vexed project in relation to rap music and Hip-Hop culture.

One way to untangle some of the above-mentioned complications is by focusing on women coming of age in an era of Hip-Hop. Many cultural critiques have been written about what it means to come of age in the Hip-Hop era. Unfortunately, these accounts have often been male-focused and have not sought to theorize women significantly. Kevin Powell and Bakari Kitwana, for example, collapse the Hip-Hop generation with young Black manhood and pay little attention to the unique circumstances of young women.[7]

What does it mean to define oneself within and against these images and constructions? And how can one develop a rhetoric of Black womanhood that brings wreck to these contemporary and historical representations? How can one begin to tell the truth of one's own life? I examine life stories as they occur both in music and in autobiographical texts such as Sister Souljah's *No Disrespect*, Queen Latifah's *Ladies First: Revelations of a Strong Woman*, Veronica Chambers's *Mama's Girl*, and Joan Morgan's *When Chickenheads Come Home to Roost: My Life as a Hip-Hop Feminist*. I examine how these women use the language of the past and present to construct their identities as Black women and create a rhetoric of wreck that claims agency and encourages self-definition not only for themselves but also for contemporary young Black women.

"I Sit on Hills Like Lauryn": The Potential for Black Autobiography in Rap Music

The experience of coming of age as a Black woman in the era of Hip-Hop both builds on the experiences of Black women in the past and also conveys specific experiences unique to that generation.[8] The women of the Hip-Hop generation have unique tools available to them via Hip-Hop culture that allow them to tell their own stories in ways that previous generations of Black women could have only dreamed of. While the use of songs such as slave spirituals and hymns allowed many early African Americans a venue to relate their pain—albeit in a coded manner—it was only after slavery when these songs, once sung in the fields, were sung by choirs such as the Fisk Jubilee Singers and in minstrel shows and therefore taken to a larger audience. Rap music has the capability to reach listeners across the world as soon as an album or single is released, and thus the life stories and tales rap tells are capable of having a more immediate impact. Some women rappers have tapped into the immediacy of this genre in order to share their lives with the world and thus to validate Black women's experiences in the counter–public sphere of Hip-Hop and the society at large. Foxy Brown's "My Life" is one example; Mary J. Blige's "My Life" and Eve's chorus from Beanie Sigel's "Remember Them Days" are others.

There are several examples of artists who use their music to give listeners a glimpse of their lives, or at least to represent some facet of their reality to the public. This glimpse can usually be seen as larger than the artist herself, as something that can stand as a symbol of a larger problem or a larger struggle or is connected in some way to other young Black women like her. Many Hip-Hop artists make use of this dynamic. The listeners connect to the artist's life story because they see themselves represented. Many people, for example, believe that the reason Mary J. Blige became the undisputed queen of Hip-Hop soul is because she poured so much of her heart and soul—her very self—into her first two albums, especially her second album, *Mary,* on which the single "My Life" appears. She represented the average young Black woman coming of age and trying to live and love in an era of Hip-Hop, and listeners were able to identify with her. Likewise, although Lauryn Hill now claims that *The Miseducation of Lauryn Hill* was not about her, many listeners felt that they were glimpsing her autobiography as they listened to the album. When she rapped and sang about her child, her loves, and her losses, it was easy for young women in urban America to identify and connect. From "Ex-Factor" to "To Zion," listeners felt they were getting slices of Lauryn Hill's life.

The Miseducation of Lauryn Hill stands as an example of the way an artist can use Hip Hop to tell her life story and make an impact in the public sphere. The title of the album itself is a political statement. It plays off Carter G. Woodson's work *The Mis-Education of the Negro,* which was written in 1933 but still speaks volumes about the status of Africans in America today.[9] Not only does Woodson offer a powerful critique of the racist state of affairs in the United States in terms of the oppression of Blacks, but he also critiques Blacks' complicity in their own oppression and complicates the notion of education by questioning what counts as meaningful education for Blacks. Lauryn Hill's album, by signifying on Woodson's work, brings forth a history and a legacy of critique. Invoking her own name personalizes the political message. The specificity of *The Miseducation of Lauryn Hill* gives us the sense that we are going to learn about Lauryn Hill's personal miseducation. However, the album as a whole, each track in conversation with the others, paints the picture much more broadly, and we see that Lauryn Hill's miseducation can be compared to our own in significant ways, and her life lessons can teach us some things as well.

Perhaps the clearest example of the ways *The Miseducation of Lauryn Hill* extends one life story to the lives of many other young women coming of age in an era of Hip-Hop is the skits interspersed throughout the album. The skits consist of inner-city schoolchildren and a male teacher talking about life and love, clearing up misconceptions as they go along. There are six skits on the CD, and in them the teacher poses questions such as "How many of you ever been in love?" and "Do you think that TV and music are why people are confused about love?" Listening to the children respond to these questions paints a startling picture of just how much young people do not know about life and love and how some of that ignorance is passed down through the music and the culture.

The Miseducation of Lauryn Hill won the young rapper, singer, and actress an unprecedented five Grammy awards. Lauryn Hill was the first female artist to accomplish such a feat. Critics and reviewers labeled the album deeply personal. Hill herself notes that "it was exactly how I felt the moment I felt it."[10] And she felt validated by the fact that she could "make an album completely from [her] soul and without compromise and be acknowledged for it."[11] Even though Hill would later tell the world that the album was not about her, many fans felt as though they were viewing the real Lauryn Hill as she poured her heart out on track after track. They connected with her trials and tribulations and the sense of honesty that is crucial to any autobiographical moment.

One of the reasons fans felt that they were getting the "real Lauryn Hill"—that she was telling the truth of her life and using music to grant the world her autobiography—is that she presented an aura of being open and honest about both positive and negative aspects of her life, about living, loving, and learning. Part of this aura of honesty is conveyed in the candid nature in which she spoke in interviews about having her heart broken:

> Right now, I'm a lot hurt and I'm a lot disappointed. Half the niggas that I meet, they don't know about relationships. And when they hurt you, they don't know it. Or if they know they don't really give a fuck because they've been so bruised, battered and scarred themselves.[12]

These kinds of interview responses, when read in conversation with the music, allow listeners to make connections and blur the line between art and life. For example, in "Ex-Factor" we get the image of a young woman coming to the age-old realization that "love don't love nobody." The woman is in a relationship where she gives more than she gets, and yet she cannot seem to let go. By acknowledging how she is sometimes complicit in her own heartache and pain, Hill allows the listener to both connect with her and acknowledge his or her own complicity. The listener gets a similar experience from the songs "I Used to Love Him" and "When It Hurts So Bad." Again, it is Hill's willingness to reflect on and share the ways in which she was complicit that draws the listener in, making these more than the typical my-man-did-me-wrong songs. They offer instead a model of critical self-reflection that is crucial to autobiography.

Other songs on the album function as autobiographical texts, such as Hill's ode to her son, "To Zion," and together they expand the possibilities of rap as autobiography. However, it is the song "Every Ghetto, Every City" that makes Hill's story larger than herself and connects her autobiography to those of other young women coming of age in the Hip-Hop generation. The song's title serves two purposes. It both exhibits Hill's many travels and signifies her connection to the young Black women in "every ghetto, every city, and suburban place"—all the young Black women influenced by Hip-Hop culture. The song is also an autobiographical sketch of what it was like for Hill growing up with Hip-Hop in the background. She reminisces about being a young girl getting her hair pressed. She traces growing up through the trends in Hip-Hop fashion, putting Lee patches on the tongues of her shoes and wearing leather. And she notes the Hip-Hop dance trends that informed her youth by mentioning dances like the wop, the jack ya body, and the Bizmark. All of these trends place her in a specific time and place during Hip-Hop's evolution and connect her to other young women who came of age at that moment in Hip-Hop.

The fact that Lauryn Hill was able to convey sketches of her life in her music and received such critical acclaim should not give us the sense that she did not have to bring wreck in order to do so. She did meet resistance, and she spoke candidly about what she had to go through in order to maintain her vision for the album. "I

think when you're a woman, you have to assert yourself even a little more. The record companies sign an act and they have ideas
about how that act should sound."[13] For Hill, that sound was a repetition of the Fugees' remake of Roberta Flack's "Killing Me
Softly." Hill did not want to simply replicate what she had done
with the Fugees. She did not want to repeat the formula. She
wanted to more thoroughly flex her producing muscles. She was
co-producer on the Fugees album *The Score,* but she felt as if she
was not given proper credit because hers was the female name next
to the male name. She reflects, "Men like it when you sing to them.
But step out and try to control things, and there are doubts. This is
a very sexist industry. They will never throw the genius title to a
sister. They'll just call her diva and think it's a compliment. It's like
our flair and vanity are put before our musical and intellectual contributions."[14] The simple fact is that Lauryn Hill had to assert herself
and stay true to her own core beliefs about who she was in order to
share what listeners felt was the true Lauryn Hill.

Not all women rappers are aware of or acknowledge their unique
position as women in the music business or within Hip-Hop culture. There are certainly countless examples—from Queen Latifah's
"Just Another Day," in which she recounts a day in her neighborhood as just plain Dana Owens, to Yo Yo's "Black Pearl," in which
she reflects on and attempts to uplift others growing up young,
Black, and female—of life stories being used in rap by women rappers to convey a sense of what it was like to come of age as women
in an era of Hip-Hop and validate that experience. However, complete autobiographical experiences on wax, such as *The Miseducation
of Lauryn Hill,* are few and far between. Also, reflection on being a
woman in Hip-Hop culture is often missing, not only in the music
but also in the interviews given by popular rappers. When reading
these interviews, one does not often get the sense of serious critical
reflection, whether directed inward toward the self or outward.
Often what we see is the industry image and the industry answers.
This facade and lack of depth limit the space of autobiography—in
the critical self-reflexive sense—in rap music. There are also questions of the artist's input and involvement in terms of production
and image. These kinds of concerns lead us to other examples of

the autobiographical elements of bringing wreck in Hip-Hop culture, the ones found in the prose and more traditionally grounded autobiographies.

Autobiographies and Life Stories: Coming of Age Female in the Hip-Hop Era

The autobiographies of Black women who have come of age in an era of Hip-Hop, like the African American autobiographies before them, provide entry into the public sphere and give the women a chance to tell their stories while making social commentary. They provide us with the materials necessary to foreground the stories of the precious little Black girls that Yo Yo raps about—the Black girls who so often find their stories and the truths of their lives erased.[15] And, like Yo Yo's "Black Pearl," these Hip-Hop autobiographies and life stories operate as tools for uplift and improvement in the lives of other Black women. The autobiographies discussed here each serve dual functions as life stories and message texts. Each of the authors attempts to uplift and heal others through the telling of their stories. For Sister Souljah it is the entire "African race" she wishes to uplift and indeed save through the pages of her text. For Queen Latifah it is other young Black women that she hopes to make strong by the telling of her tale. Veronica Chambers wants to help other mama's girls who yearn for a mother's love and touch to understand the plight of the strong Black woman. Joan Morgan's goal is the empowerment of Black women. In addition to trying to heal others, these women make critiques of society and comment on how society impacts both their own lives and the lives of the others they are trying to save.

These women build on the legacy of Black women's activism and expressive culture, and also chart new ground. In "Third Wave Black Feminism?" Black feminist scholar Kimberly Springer examines the work of Lisa Jones, Joan Morgan, and Veronica Chambers as representative texts of 1990s young Black feminists. Springer finds three predominant themes, all involving relationships: young

Black women's relationships with their personal and political histories, their relationships with themselves, and their relationships with Black men.[16] I agree that these relationships are crucial and provide the groundwork for much of the theory and activism that these new Black feminist works exhibit. Through their theorization of their relationships, these new Black feminist thinkers are able to bring wreck to the misconceptions and stereotypes of Black womanhood that inhibit their lives. Adding the autobiographies of raptivist Sister Souljah and rapper/entrepreneur Queen Latifah to those of Morgan and Chambers reveals the continued activist legacy of Black women and a new understanding of what it means to come of age as Black women in an era of Hip-Hop. Springer notes that these young Black feminist voices grapple with older stereotypes such as the strong Black woman. I maintain that they deal with the old images in new ways and also confront newer images brought on by Hip-Hop culture, specifically rap music. They grapple with these images not only for themselves, but to help other Black women combat them.

For example, Sister Souljah's *No Disrespect* is an autobiography with a mission. She writes, "No matter how backward and negative the mainstream view and image of Black people, I feel compelled to reshape that image and to explore our many positive angles because I love my own people."[17] She adds that "it is with this kind of spirit and that kind of love that I live my life and offer this book, which deals with the African man and woman in America and our ability to relate to and love one another in healthy life-giving relationships. I am especially concerned with the African female in America, the ghetto girl whom nobody ever tells the definition of womanhood, or manhood for that matter."[18]

Sister Souljah shares in the activist project of uplift started by her nineteenth-century foremothers. Like the clubwomen before her, she wants to uplift less fortunate and downtrodden Black girls in an effort to vindicate Black womanhood. Also like the clubwomen, Sister Souljah is in the position of having already been uplifted and thus above the women she seeks to help. Reading Sister Souljah's autobiography from cover to cover, we get a sense of self-righteousness that lets the reader know that Sister Souljah should be not only followed but emulated. This self-righteous tone is one of the pitfalls of any text that is aimed at both uplift and diagnosis of the problems in the Black community. In Sister Souljah's text the most evident biases surface in her text's heterosexism and homophobia. In her privileging of "healthy life-giving relationships," Sister Souljah leaves out several segments of the "ghetto girls" she hopes to reach. They are not all heterosexual women seeking knowledge on how to intimately love a Black man. Some of them intimately love other women. Nevertheless, Sister Souljah's outreach and uplift project, as evidenced in her autobiography, shares a lot with the projects of the Black women who preceded her in that she, like they, seeks to uplift young Black women even as she excludes some Black women.

Similarly, Queen Latifah dedicates her book "[t]o every woman who has ever felt like less than royalty."[19] And she writes, "I am writing this book to let every woman know that she, too—no matter what her status or her place in life—is royalty. This is particularly important for African-American women to know inside out, upside down, and right side up. For so long in this society, we have been given—and we allowed ourselves to take—the role of slave, concubine, mammy, second-class citizen, bitch, ho."[20] The project of uplift is clear in Queen Latifah's autobiography. She is on a mission to bring wreck to stereotyped images of Black women, and she wants to vindicate Black womanhood. Not only does Dana Owens consider herself a queen, but also she wants other Black women to know beyond a shadow of a doubt that they too are queens. Unlike Sister Souljah's *No Disrespect,* one gets the feeling that when Queen Latifah talks about letting all Black women know that they are royalty, she is not excluding large segments. For example, even though she goes to great lengths to proclaim her own heterosexuality when she addresses the rumors of lesbianism that have followed her throughout her career, she does not do so in a way that stigmatizes being a lesbian. Rather, she simply states that people should not look to role models to validate who they are, and that her coming out as a lesbian will not help society view lesbianism any more positively. She does, however, see herself as a role model for young

Black women in terms of finding a place of self-love that validates their self-worth. Both Queen Latifah and Sister Souljah have a goal in writing their autobiographies, a goal that is rooted in the old spiritual tradition of "if I can help somebody." Just as the slave narratives were written to help those still in bondage, these contemporary Hip-Hop autobiographies are out to make changes. By using their own stories as tools of racial uplift, they continue the tradition of Black autobiography in America.

Joan Morgan's and Veronica Chambers's texts have a less pronounced activist/social uplift slant. However, both Morgan and Chambers offer complicated critiques of the status of Black women in America through thought-provoking analyses of race, class, and gender, as well as critical self-reflection that extends their own personal stories far beyond their lives. Morgan's *When Chickenheads Come Home to Roost* is the more forthrightly political of the two in that she is trying to fashion a feminism that is appealing and relevant to her generation of Black women. The topics that Morgan addresses show her desire to make feminism relevant to the Hip-Hop generation. Chapter titles such "Hip-Hop Feminist," "From Fly Girls to Bitches and Hos," "Babymother," and "Chickenhead Envy" present a remixed feminist agenda that not only questions the negative images of women presented by men in Hip-Hop but also calls women of the Hip-Hop generation to task for their own complicity.

Chambers's text is the least overtly political of the four in that she neither has a central uplift message nor is pushing a feminist project. However, *Mama's Girl* offers an understanding of what it means to come of age as a Black woman in postindustrial urban America. Through Chambers's story we get the complex intermingling of race, class, and gender that characterizes the struggles young Black women face. The life stories of Chambers, Morgan, Queen Latifah, and Sister Souljah offer key critiques of society, and through those critiques they offer models of how one might go about effecting change. For example, each writer presents coping strategies and ultimately models of success for other female members of the Hip-Hop generation. The life stories are road maps for how to, and sometimes how not to, navigate life.

Wrecking Images: Issues of Identity Construction and Black Womanhood

Even more than critiquing society and giving advice on how to make changes in society, these autobiographies are very concerned with issues of identity construction as they pertain to Black womanhood. The quote from Queen Latifah given earlier offers a list of the kinds of images and misconceptions that these women confront: "slave, concubine, mammy, second-class citizen, bitch, ho."[21] Some of these labels are legacies from slavery, and some have reached new heights of usage due to contemporary rap music. I might add that the focus on identity construction and Black womanhood is not new to Black autobiography. In fact, the form that the concern surrounding Black womanhood takes in the life stories discussed here builds on the tradition and legacy of Black autobiography in America. Harriet Jacobs was just as concerned with the misconceptions and stereotypes surrounding Black womanhood as Angela Davis or Elaine Brown. What is new or different about the Hip-Hop generation autobiographies is the way they embrace and reject certain identities and the variety in how they do so.

The images I will focus on here are those of the strong Black woman and the domineering Black mother. The strong Black woman in all her glory is an image that has been both embraced and rejected throughout time; it has always been a point of contention. Think, for example, of the outrage that Michele Wallace endured when she called the Black superwoman a myth in her book *Black Macho and the Myth of Superwoman*. Also think of the smile, strut, and shrug of shoulder that goes along with any Black woman acknowledging that she is indeed "a strong Black woman." It is no surprise that young Black women coming of age in the era of Hip-Hop would be grappling with the same image that their foremothers struggled with.

The struggle is just as conflicted within this generation of Black women as it was in Wallace's generation, but women like Queen Latifah and Sister Souljah embrace the label—so much so, in fact, that Queen Latifah subtitles her text *Revelations of a Strong Woman*. And throughout her text Sister Souljah notes that she is a strong

African woman out to save the race and make them strong as well. The references to strength throughout Queen Latifah's and Sister Souljah's autobiographies are definitely linked to the racial uplift projects of their texts. They also call on the tradition and the legacy of the race women and clubwomen who went before them. If one is going to successfully perform uplift and bring the entire race up with her, she had better be strong. The women of previous generations were strong in the mythical sense because they had to be; if they had not been, none of us would be here. Their kind of strength is encouraged in young Black women today to prepare them for everything that society will throw at them—specifically, multiple intersecting oppressions that stem from racism, sexism, and classism. The fact that Black women feel it is necessary to prepare other generations of Black women for these realities accounts for the strong Black woman's lingering presence throughout the generations. Queen Latifah and Sister Souljah, as Hip-Hop embodiments of race women and as young Black women raised to be strong Black women, encourage other young Black women to be strong.

For Sister Souljah, strength is not a luxury; it is a necessity. She sees the situation for Africans in America as a dire one in which Black women must play a crucial role in the survival of the race. The urgency centers on the question "What are the roots of problems in today's relationships between African men and women?"[22] She uses every opportunity she has in the text to give Black women instructions on how to be positive, uplifting influences, particularly in relation to Black men and in accordance with Sister Souljah's heteronormative visions for the Black family. The title of the last chapter in No Disrepect, "Listen Up (Straighten It Out)," can be taken both literally and figuratively, with the "straight" standing for the allowable representations of sexual identity. The Black nation that Sister Souljah envisions has no place for people who are not straight-identified, and thus the common colloquial references to the strong Black woman who does not need a man is countered in her text.[23] For Sister Souljah the strong Black woman not only must have a man but needs one to help her ensure a strong Black community.

From the negative representations of homosexuality that surface in her description of her college love, Nathan—who is portrayed as demon-possessed, sick, and troubled—to the specific prescriptions she gives to Black women to stick to the "life-giving relationships" between Black men and Black women, Sister Souljah's text relies heavily on a heterosexist conceptualization of the Black relationships that in turn repeats some of the most negative elements of heterosexism in the Black community. She urges Black women, "Do not believe that same-sex love will solve your problems. You can be hurt in any human relationship. Leaving your man because you have experienced pain, only to sleep with another woman will not guarantee that you will be treated more kindly. . . . Confront your inner confusion before you enter any relationship."[24] What could be very sound advice is trapped in homophobic undertones and heterosexist messages. This focus on the heterosexual life-giving relationship as the prerequisite for the strong Black woman also narrows the potential of the text. The constant references to how to treat a Black man and the expectations that Black women should have of how Black men should treat them create a cage of heteronormativity that inhibits other kinds of strength and encourages the disavowal of anything that is not straight.

In Queen Latifah's text we are not given the same descriptions and prescriptions for the strong Black woman needing a man to fulfill her duties to the Black community that we are given in *No Disrespect*. However, Queen Latifah does go to great lengths to negate rumors surrounding her own sexuality in the chapter "No, Yes." The fact that this chapter is placed in the "Latifah's Laws" section of the autobiography should not be taken lightly. She writes, "But it's insulting when someone asks, 'Are you gay?' A woman cannot be strong, outspoken, competent at running her own business, handle herself physically, play a very convincing role in a movie, know what she wants—and go for it—without being gay? Come on."[25] She goes on to note that "people fueled those rumors when I wasn't dating anyone. I felt as if I should run out and get a boyfriend, if only to say, 'Look, I have a man, I'm not gay.' Ridiculous."[26]

Both Sister Souljah and Queen Latifah seem to be on a rescue mission that requires them to dispute popular colloquial references that strong Black women do not need men. This makes them the victims of what feminist scholar Suzanne Pharr calls "lesbian baiting"—the use of the word *lesbian* by people who seek to halt women's progressive movement through the use of fear and alienation.[27] Whenever women are working diligently toward the improvement of life for themselves and other women, the word *lesbian* can cause them to stop the good work they are doing and spend the bulk of their time defending their heterosexuality.[28] Queen Latifah's "No, Yes" chapter is one example of this kind of response to lesbian baiting. Imagine if she had used the chapter instead to talk about forming coalitions between people working on gay, lesbian, bisexual, and transgender issues and people working on race and class issues. Or if she had used that chapter to call on Black feminist foremothers such as Audre Lorde, Barbara Smith, and Barbara Christian in order to show that there are indeed some Black women who are Black and strong and lesbian and their work has added to the progression of women and Black people as a race immensely. Or even if she had used the chapter to interrogate why the rumors about her surfaced at the start of her career and what those rumors have to say about how Hip-Hop's heteronormativity and homophobia limit the scope of its political potential.

Instead of problematizing the notion of the strong Black woman, Queen Latifah and Sister Souljah end up conducting a rescue mission for her and represent her as straight and linked to a man. It might be worthwhile to note that as female participants in the masculine discursive space of Hip-Hop, Queen Latifah and Sister Souljah may have found it necessary to be strong Black women in ways that were not as pressing for journalists such as Joan Morgan and Veronica Chambers. They were trying to carve a place for themselves in the testosterone-filled space of Hip-Hop, and they had to show a certain amount of strength in order to be taken seriously as artists. However, this fact does not excuse the heterosexism and homophobia in their texts.

Chambers, Morgan, Queen Latifah, and Sister Souljah each address the multiple and intersecting oppressions of being a Black woman in contemporary U.S. society, and each deals with the history and legacy of images that go along with being a Black woman.

Both Morgan and Chambers grapple with and eventually reject the label "strong Black woman." Each of these women reaches a point in her life when she can no longer be a Black superwoman. And each suffers a near emotional breakdown when coming to that realization. Chambers likens the strong Black woman to a magic act. She writes:

> I remember seeing a magic act when I was little in which the magician would repeat over and over: "The closer you get, the less you can see." And oddly enough, it was true. The people in the front row couldn't see through the deception; they were so close, yet they were looking for the wrong thing while the trick was being pulled right before their eye. Black women are masters of emotional sleight of hand. The closer you get, the less you can see. It was true of my mother. It is also true of me.[29]

Chambers realizes that the strong Black woman is a falsity, a magic act that Black women perform so well even the people closest to them do not realize that an "emotional sleight of hand" is being performed. In the tradition of Michele Wallace, Chambers problematizes the strong Black woman by uncovering the myth. The "making a way out of no way" that we often credit Black women with is complicated somewhat when we begin to see it in light of the magic act. The references to magic do not discredit the wondrous feats that Black women had to complete in order to ensure survival, but instead show the falsity in the notion that strength is some innate trait, that all Black women are born with a strong Black woman nestled deep inside them. The magic act places the strong Black women in the realm of tricks that can be taught and used for their protection and survival.

Morgan takes the realization one step further by symbolically giving her resignation. She questions the quickness with which some Black women take on the "STRONGBLACKWOMAN" marker as they do everything in their power to distance themselves from feminism. She notes that while she is still strong and Black and a woman, she wants to challenge the social conditioning that Black

women experience that tells them they have to be "BLACKSUP-
ERWOMAN." She wants to challenge the notions

> [t]hat by the sole virtues of my race and gender I was sup-
> posed to be the consummate professional, handle any life
> crisis, be the dependable rock for every soul who needed
> me, and yes, the classic—require less from my lovers than
> they did from me because after all, I was STRONG-
> BLACKWOMAN and they were just ENDANGERED-
> BLACKMEN. Retirement was ultimately an act of
> salvation. Being a SBW was killing me slowly. Cutting off
> my air supply.[30]

Her retirement is distinctly different from the rescue mission of Sister Souljah and Queen Latifah. The Black woman as a mythical
self-sacrificing savior to everyone but herself, linked eternally to a
Black man—any Black man—is not worth salvaging for Morgan.
She describes the emotional and mental breakdown she went
through trying to be the stereotypical strong Black woman. She had
accomplished it all. She had the job of her dreams. She was working
hard and trying to save the world when finally she realized that she
could not do it all. Like anyone raised to believe that a Black
woman has to be strong enough to take on and bear the world—
indeed, be the "mules of the world"—the realization that one is
not strong in that mythical sense can be maddening. This is especially true when all around you other Black women seem to be performing that emotional sleight of hand with effortless ease and
when one of those women is your very own Black supermother.

"Dear Mama" or "Mother, Mother": Depending on Your Generational Shift

There are complicated connections between women autobiographers' narratives and the narratives of their mothers.[31] Theorist Jo
Malin notes that since all woman autobiographers are daughters,
they necessarily establish their identities in some way through their

mothers. She contends that "many twentieth-century autobio-graphical texts by women contain an intertext, an embedded narra-tive, which is a biography of the writer/daughter's mother."[32] I believe that these embedded narratives exist in the autobiographies of young Black women coming of age in an era of Hip-Hop.[33] The Black mother in all her glory and controversy is key to the identity construction of women such as Queen Latifah, Sister Souljah, Joan Morgan, and Veronica Chambers. The daughter's story is intimately linked to the mother's life and the mother's story. She teaches the daughter how to be a woman through her actions, which most times are the epitome of strong Black womanhood. The image of the domineering Black mother, à la Daniel Patrick Moynihan, plays an interesting role in the autobiographics.[34] What Moynihan con-cluded in the late sixties was that there were too many female-headed Black families led by domineering Black mothers who castrated their sons. More recently the focus of the Black mother's alleged domination has shifted to the daughters. According to Dr. Jawanza Kunjufu, "some women raise their daughters and love their sons."[35] While I will not enter the debate of whether Black mothers are more domineering in the lives of their sons or their daughters, I will say that the misconceptions surrounding Black women, motherhood, and Black sons have been critiqued at length, and until recently the interaction between Black mothers and daughters has not been as thoroughly critiqued.[36] Thus it is fruitful to explore the images of Black motherhood that surface in these autobiographies and life stories and how those images influence the identities of the writers.

The mothers' strength or lack of strength shapes each writer. Each weaves her mother's story through her own. Where Queen Latifah became strong because her mother was, Sister Souljah be-came strong because her mother was not. While Queen Latifah, Chambers, and Morgan grew up wanting to emulate the strong Black women that they believed their mothers to be, Sister Souljah works to create an image of Black womanhood that she felt poverty and a racist America robbed her of. Sister Souljah's mother falls vic-tim to the trappings of a racist and materialist society and sees her worth only in her body and her looks. She hits rock bottom in Sister Souljah's eyes when she begins to date a white man, an act that signals to Sister Souljah that her mother is no longer the woman whose strength helped them survive the projects. She writes, "It was as though body snatchers had somehow invaded her body and turned her heart cold. Life was too much and too harsh for her." However, she also thanks God for her mother and the fact that

> she had the strength to save us and secure us from the proj-
> ects, the danger, the hunger, and the mental devastation. . . .
> I thanked God for allowing me to know her before the
> world took her. . . . But I had come to believe that the
> woman walking around the house posing as my mother was
> not my mother. She was America's creation and that did not
> belong to me.[37]

I think that it is interesting to note how the combinations of narratives (of mother and daughter) and images (strong Black woman and domineering Black mother) shed light on the inconsistencies inherent in the narratives and the images. For example, in Sister Souljah's mother-daughter narrative we get the dual images of the strong Black woman and the domineering and damaging Black mother coexisting with and contradicting each other, all while being represented through the same person. What Sister Souljah's mother embodies, then, is the contradiction at the heart of the myth of the strong Black woman. Contrary to Sister Souljah's telling of her mother's story, her mother does not change very much from the beautiful young single mother in the projects who decided to date the biggest and baddest young Black hustler in the projects to protect herself and her children to the slightly older, still beautiful single mother who dates a white man who slips her enough cash to take care of house and home. Sister Souljah's reading of her mother's actions is blurred by her Black nationalist tendencies and her dislike for white men and dating outside of the race. The reader is able to see, however, that her mother is still the same woman who will do whatever she has to do to take care of her family. And the reader can also see the glaring holes in the myth of the superwoman that allow us to question how many pieces of the soul get bartered in order to maintain the facade of strength.

This dual representation surfaces again in the autobiography of Veronica Chambers. Watching her mother's strength and ability to remain calm after being hit in the head with a hammer by an abusive husband and take herself to the hospital has a tremendous impact on Chambers. She writes:

> When the hammer connects, my mother doesn't scream. Her head is gouged. . . . My mother sees me watching and tells me to go to my room, she is going to the hospital. She says it in a calm, grown-up, don't worry voice. . . . She presses the towel against the hole in her head. The towel is white, which she isn't thinking about as she bleeds into the snowy terry cloth. . . . My mother grabs her purse off the kitchen table and goes out the front door. She is bleeding so much, but she doesn't cry.[38]

The fact that she more than likely cried once she was out of her daughter's sight is important but not crucial here. What is crucial is understanding the impact that never seeing their strong Black mothers shed one tear has had on young Black women of the Hip-Hop generation.

I, like Veronica Chambers, have never seen my mother cry. She survived and eventually left an abusive marriage. As she raised five daughters into strong Black women she suffered more setbacks and heartache than I can even begin to mention here, but she never once shed a tear in front of us. Because I never saw her cry, once I grew up and became the embodiment of all her hopes and dreams for me, I never thought I could allow others to see me cry. I remained calm and controlled in the face of adversity. I gave off attitude and wore it like armor. And if I wet my pillow at night, well, that was no one's business but mine. Through my mother's giving me the armor I needed to face a world that offered multiple oppressions, I learned how to bottle up the most intimate and vulnerable parts of myself.

Joan Morgan had similar experiences with her own strong Black mother not showing emotions. She reflects on her own status as a strong Black woman:

> Perhaps the image of my mother at my age, with blood clotting in her lungs, trying desperately to immerse herself in an activity as normal as plaiting her hair before she was rushed off to the hospital, is too viscerally implanted in my childhood memory. Perhaps it's the thought of her pushing my tiny hands away as I made attempts to help her. Perhaps, it's because I can't remember my mother ever being afraid unless something threatened her children's well-being.[39]

Stories like Chambers's, Morgan's, and my own are not meant to condemn Black mothers for not showing emotions such as sadness and fear in front of their daughters. I do not think that anyone would question their reasons or intentions. They knew all too well what the world would do to their daughters, and they wanted to ensure our survival. However, these instances of strong Black womanhood being passed down from generation to generation also make us vulnerable to misrecognition and misunderstanding of the myth as a myth as well as the contradictions inside the myth.[40] Still, some women, such as Joan Morgan and Veronica Chambers, are able in time to see the myth of the superwoman for what it is, a falsity.

Just like Sister Souljah's mother, Queen Latifah's mother, and Joan Morgan's mother, Veronica Chambers's mother holds her life together and maintains a strong facade in order to raise her children. Just like Sister Souljah's mother, the strong facade crumbles when she meets and marries a man that she places before her children. Chambers ends up leaving her mother's house and going to live with her father and then her aunt because she cannot get along with her mother's new husband. Unlike Sister Souljah, however, Chambers does not write her mother off at the first sign of weakness, or rather ordinariness. She does not reject her mother at the first sign that she is just a "reglar" Black woman.[41] She still longs for her mother's love and respects all that her mother went through.

I think that her ability to appreciate her regular Black mother and give up on the myth of the super Black mom comes from the vision she receives when she realizes that the superwoman is a magic trick. When she suffered a near nervous breakdown after trying to do it all, her mother came to her and gave her a hug.

> Then she reached over and hugged me and did not let go. This was not how we hugged. Our hugs were quick. . . . This hug was different. . . . It felt so strange. . . . Was I dying[?] . . . Then my mother started to rock me, rock me like I wanted her to when I was seven and terrified of my father. . . . I never thought she'd do it. I never thought she'd see how much I needed it. I started to cry. I figured it was okay to cry now.[42]

It is the mother's touch and the mother's story embedded within this autobiography that free the writer from the images and misconceptions surrounding Black womanhood and allow her to free the other young Black women who will eventually read *Mama's Girl*.

When read separately, the autobiographies and life stories discussed here carry on, in various ways, the tradition of Black autobiography in America. Separately they offer the kind of "flat-footed truths" that Patricia Bell-Scott writes of in "Flat-footed Truths: Telling Black Women's Lives." They tell stories that are "straightforward, unshakable, and unembellished."[43] And they join the lineage of women who always "insisted on speaking truths in the face of disbelief and public criticism."[44] However, when they are read together, as I have hopefully shown, they offer much more. Together, they offer guides to the navigation of the narratives and images that influence us and possible new rhetorics of Black womanhood. When read in conversation with one another, these autobiographies highlight not only what it means to come of age as a Black woman in an era of Hip-Hop but also how to successfully grapple with all the historical and contemporary baggage that comes along with it. Thus, when these Black women "remember them days, living all days in doubt," they do so in search of a way out not only for themselves but also for other Black women coming of age in contemporary America as children of Hip-Hop.

Girls in the Hood and Other Ghetto Dramas: Representing Black Womanhood in Hip-Hop Cinema and Novels

Ghetto-girl: Female ignorant to establishment ways.

Ghetto-queen: 1) Black mothers who live in the inner cities and who struggle to feed their children. 2) Girlfriend who usually lives in the inner city.

—Alonzo Westbrook, *Hip Hoptionary: The Dictionary of Hip-Hop Terminology*

She's the most likely extra in every single one of the *Boyz 'N the Hood*–inspired flicks. She's the one with the head full of braids wearing Hip-Hop gear that marks her as both ghetto chic and female. If it is a warm climate, she might be scantily clad; add more clothing the colder it gets, but not too much. She is always cute in that way only ghetto girls know how to be. She can usually be seen drinking a forty-ounce malt liquor or holding a baby, depending on her relationship to the main character of the film, who is usually young, Black, male, and does not give a fuck. If one of the main characters is a young father who is trying to get it together, the ghetto girl must be holding a baby in each scene she is in. If no baby daddies are central to the plot, then add the lone ghetto girl hanging out with all the guys drinking beer and smoking weed. The ghetto girl is seldom central to the plot of ghetto dramas; ghetto dramas, much like the real life they imitate, usually place men at the center. The ghetto girl has been both demonized and glorified in these ghetto dramas. As the definitions from Alonzo Westbrook's Hip-Hop dictionary show, she can be everything from ignorant to a sister making it the best she can given her surroundings and circumstances. She can be the run-of-the-mill girl from around the way exalted to queen status. Or, as shown in Lil' Bow Wow's anthem "Ghetto Girl," she can be the quintessential every-sister, the shorty who is street-smart, Hip-Hop-savvy, and hip to the game.[1] Like Lil' Bow Wow, many rappers have coined songs to glorify and pay homage to the ghetto girl. Songs such as LL Cool J's "Around the Way Girl," Apache's "Gangsta Bitch," Cash Money Millionaire's "Hood Rat Chick," Another Bad Creation's "Aisha," and Ja Rule's "Down Ass Bitch" all in varying ways give the ghetto girl her props. The ghetto girl has also gone by many names, such as *chickenhead, hoochie, shorty, boo, hoodrat*—the list goes on. Like the ghetto she is named for, she is loved by some and despised by others. She has been equally praised, maligned, and neglected.

I explore the "ghetto girl motif" as it is represented in the ghetto exploitation cinema and fiction of the late twentieth and early twenty-first centuries. I look specifically at the ghetto girl as a motif, as a repeating and recurring element in the cinema and fiction set in urban America and meant to replicate the gritty realities of life in predominantly Black and poor neighborhoods. The ghetto girl, while not always a dominant or central character in these films, is always consistently represented in the caricatured ways described above. The ghetto girl is denied a fullness of womanhood, and societal influences, such as systemic and intersecting oppressions and the implications of these for her life, are not taken into consideration. Therefore, representations of the money-hungry and sexually promiscuous Black woman living in a poor urban area are given as un-problematized truths or humorous stereotyped caricatures.

I explore these representations as they appear in the *Boys 'N the Hood*–inspired cinema of the 1990s and then move to an examination of the supposed upgrade of girls-in-the-hood stories, in which the ghetto girl becomes the main character, looking specifically at John Singleton's film *Poetic Justice* (1993) and Omar Tyree's novel *Flyy Girl* (1993). I maintain that although it appears that the ghetto girl is given top billing in these works, she is still represented as the unproblematized and stereotyped motif. I then move to the work of filmmaker Leslie Harris and novelist, rapper, and activist Sister Souljah and examine how their work depicts the same kinds of ghetto girls with more depth and adds complicated critiques of the historical and material elements of the public sphere that influence and impact the lives of these women. I close by looking at F. Gary Gray's *Set It Off* (1997), a film that depicts variations of the ghetto girl motif, in order to offer observations about the need for Black feminist interventions in the actual lives of young urban African American women.

Girls in the Hood: Bit Parts with Big Implications

In their essay "Sisters in the Hood: Beyond Bloods and Crips," Andrien Katherine Wing and Christine A. Willis examine the complete erasure of women in the public narratives about America's gang-ridden inner cities. The public narratives surrounding gangsterism in the United States has painted the face of the gangster as young, Black, and male. And the gangster culture personified by Los Angeles–based gangs such as the Bloods and the Crips has been popularized via rap, movies, television, and even books.[2] Wing and Willis find that with all the attention being paid to Black men in terms of the gang problem, the roles of Black women in gang life are largely ignored. Wing and Willis demarginalize Black women and their stories by looking at the roles Black women play as gang members and as mothers, sisters, daughters, wives, girlfriends, and comrades of gang members. Wing and Willis believe that these roles place Black women in a position to have tremendous influence and that their influence has the capacity to play a significant role in providing solutions to the gang problem.[3]

The women's roles that Wing and Willis highlight in real gangs are very similar to the roles women often play in the cinematic and literature representations of gang life. These women are represented as peripheral characters; the roles they play are trivialized and their lives are made insignificant. These kinds of representations are especially evident in the cinema of the 1990s influenced by John Singleton's critically acclaimed film *Boyz 'N the Hood* (1991), which set in motion a renewed awareness in Hollywood that Black people like to see films about Black life. In much the same way that Melvin Van Peebles' *Sweet Sweetback's Badass Song* (1971) sparked a wave of blaxploitation films in Hollywood, Singleton's *Boyz 'N the Hood* sparked a wave of ghetto exploitation films. It was followed by films such as *Straight Outta Brooklyn* (1991), *Juice* (1992), *Menace II Society* (1993), *Above the Rim* (1994), *New Jersey Drive* (1997), and a spoof of the genre starring the Wayans brothers, *Don't Be a Menace to South Central While Drinking Your Juice in the Hood* (1996). Each of these films also offers various incarnations of the ghetto girl who in turn becomes a part of the ghetto background that is crucial to these films. Paradoxically, for all the importance that women have in these films, they might just as well be a lowrider, a gang bandana, a tattoo, or some other insignificant prop.

In *Boyz 'N the Hood,* for example, women are both crucial and peripheral. The film is completely male-identified, and women come into play only as they relate to men in the films. The women in *Boyz 'N the Hood* are represented in problematic ways for a variety of reasons. They do not have meaningful roles, but the implications of the roles they play carry a multitude of meanings. The women are mothers, girlfriends, and crack heads (or some combination of the three). They lurk around the margins of the story and are invited in only when they can contribute—either negatively or positively—to the lives of the men.

Michele Wallace critiques the film's negative portrayal of Black motherhood in her essay *"Boyz 'N the Hood* and *Jungle Fever."* She notes the film's demonization of Black single mothers, which encourages a stereotypical view of their lives. And she cautions that the focus on violence against Black men and only Black men mystifies the plight of Black women and girls.[4] But even more crucial for Wallace and myself is the message this film sends to Black women about raising their sons: that Black women cannot raise healthy, strong, and self-sufficient Black men, and that if no father is present, their sons will fail in life and perhaps even end up dead. Wallace aptly credits the film for creating a third kind of Black female character: "I call her the Shahrazad Ali nightmare: Single Black mothers who are white identified and drink espresso (the Buppie version), or who call their sons 'fat fucks' and allow their children to run in the streets while they offer blow jobs in exchange for drugs (the underclass version)."[5] Singleton's *Boyz 'N the Hood* adds to the pathological readings of Black motherhood that circulate in the larger public discourse. From slave mothers who were read as not real women and therefore not really mothers (and whose children, in consequence, could be sold away) to the welfare queens, crack heads, and dominating castrating mothers, the demonization of Black motherhood is nothing new. So while I was, like Michele Wallace, deeply troubled and disheartened as I watched Singleton's remarkable film because of the film's underlying message that Black women cannot raise their sons, I also found the film's representations of ghetto girls problematic.

There are essentially three models of the ghetto girl represented in *Boyz 'N the Hood,* and each is equally marginalized. Each is a girlfriend of one of the main characters: Doughboy (Ice Cube), Ricky (Morris Chestnut), and Tre (Cuba Gooding Jr.). On the surface, the women appear to represent the typical girls in the hood, girls you would more than likely see if you took a trip to your local ghetto. You would see the striving sister with bourgeois aspirations whose family wants better for their child, so they send her to private school. She is represented in the film by Nia Long's character, Tre's girlfriend, Brandi. You might also see a young single mother or baby mama, represented in the film by young football hopeful Ricky's girlfriend, Shanice, played by Alysia Rogers. And last but not least, you might see the braid-wearing, fast-talking, forty-ounce-malt-liquor-guzzling sister represented in the film by Regina King's character, Shalika, Doughboy's girlfriend. Each of these women plays a very minor role in the film. In fact, in some instances they might just as well be palm trees, just another part of the scenery in South Central Los Angeles. To remix Doughboy's now famous and oft-quoted lines from the film, either John Singleton don't know, don't show, or don't care about what happens to girls in the hood.

Each of these women is represented as an appendage. Ricky's girlfriend barely speaks, but she does walk around with that baby in her arms throughout the majority of the film. It is as if she is a prop used by Singleton to show us how much pressure Ricky is under and why he must achieve a 700 on his SAT so he can go to college. She represents, along with her child, the ghetto girl trap, another pitfall awaiting young brothers in the hood. This representation of the ghetto girl is meant to show one of the many negative elements out to get young Black men. This representation is problematic because Singleton grants her no voice. We barely know her name. We do not know her story, her hopes, and her dreams. We do not know if she was a misguided teenager who made a mistake and got pregnant or if she was a calculating, money-hungry woman who wanted to latch on to a future NFL player early. We see her only as an appendage to Ricky.

Tre's girlfriend, Brandi, is problematic for similar reasons. She too is an appendage. She is in the film to show both the thrill of the chase and the sensitive side of the lead character, Tre. Brandi represents the ghetto girl who is in the hood but not of it. A single mother is raising her, but her mother still manages to send her to Catholic school. This fact leads the viewer to believe that her mother is a professional working woman, but we do not learn much about her. Brandi represents the supposed high end of the ghetto girl trio. She is smart. She is pretty. She starts out a virgin. And it is clear that she, like Tre, will make it out of South Central. She does not give in easily to Tre's charm and player antics. She does not have sex with him until—after a run-in with the LAPD—Tre shows his vulnerability. The poignant scene in which Tre and Brandi make love for the first time must be read carefully with the understanding that no matter how wonderful and positive the portrayal of this ghetto girl, she is still a prop in the movie. She is there for one purpose and one purpose only—to renew Tre's manhood in the viewer's eyes after his less-than-flattering encounter with the police. The police roughed him up, and he even cried like a baby.

But because he finally got the panties he was after, he reclaimed his manhood. Again, because we know so little about Brandi, she becomes a flat conquest for Tre.

If Brandi is the high end of the ghetto girl trio, then Regina King's character in the film represents the low end of the trio, with the young, single baby mama somewhere in the middle. Regina King plays the braid-wearing, always-cussing appendage to Dough-boy. I say appendage instead of girlfriend (who in this film would function as an appendage anyway) because it is not clear what her relationship is to Doughboy. She's pretty much always around, and she's usually drinking. Regina King played another version of this particular kind of ghetto girl in John Singleton's *Poetic Justice*. In fact, for a while I was afraid the cute little girl from the television sitcom *227* was going to be typecast as a ghetto hoochie mama. This character is virtually silenced, and we get even less of her story than the other two women. She is a prop who serves no real purpose except to drink all the beer and be told by Doughboy that she better take that shit (the empty bottle) to the store. But she is even more problematic because she is a caricature, one that we would come to see a lot throughout the 1990s in film and on television. From Martin Lawrence's She Nee Nee to Craig's (Ice Cube) fast-talking, braid-wearing girlfriend in the film *Friday* (1995), we can point to various incarnations of this representation.[6] This is the ghetto girl in the first definition of the epigraph. She is the "female ignorant to establishment ways."[7] It is her ignorance that we are made to feel is so amusing.

Films and television depend on this ignorance for jokes and laughs. But these caricatured representations that encourage laughter beg one question: if the plight of Black men represented in films such as *Boyz 'N the Hood* warrants our outrage and encourages our pity, why is it that the plight of these ghetto girls warrants ridicule and laughter? Even if we were to look at the representations from a positive angle and read them as a symbol of the connected plight of Black men and Black women in the urban United States, we would still have to ask that question. While his project is about boys in the hood and not the girls, and—like *Straight Outta Brooklyn, Juice, Strapped,* and *Menace II Society*—is about life for young Black men as they try to escape the pitfalls that the ghetto holds for them, the film is still very problematic.

Boyz 'N the Hood and films like it promote themselves as urban dramas, as the gritty truth about life in U.S. hoods, but it is a one-sided truth. The women in these films have no voice to speak of, and when they are given voice, such as Jada Pinkett Smith's character, Ronnie, in *Menace II Society,* they are not listened to or valued for what they could contribute, for the role as agents for change that they could play, or for the impact and influence that they could have. Casting Jada Pinkett Smith in almost any ghetto girl role almost guarantees that she will be the kind of girl who is in the hood but not of it. She usually fits more in line with definition two of the ghetto queen definition, "the girlfriend who lives in the inner city." But it is clear that the inner city does not live in her. Whether she is walking down the block with clowning brothers in Tupac Shakur's "Keep Your Head Up" video, begging Caine to move to Atlanta and start a new life in *Menace II Society,* the aspiring and striving Lyric in *Jason's Lyric,* or the young bank robber with bourgeois aspirations in *Set It Off,* Jada Pinkett Smith's ghetto girls are always represented as wanting more out of life than the ghetto can offer.

The *Boyz 'N the Hood*–inspired cinema is not concerned with representing the fullness of Black womanhood or the realities of their lives. This in and of itself is not problematic. What *is* problematic is the way in which these women function as props and become caricatured representations. If Hip-Hop culture and rap music made the ghetto a recognizable entity on the U.S. landscape, then the Hip-Hop cinema represented by the *Boyz 'N the Hood*/ghetto exploitation cinema of the 1990s made the ghetto girl a recognizable element of that landscape. The ghetto girl is recognizable because she is usually presented as one of the above-mentioned three types—the young single "baby mama," the "tweener" (with one foot in the ghetto, one foot out of the ghetto, and bourgeois aspirations), and the "hoochie" or "chickenhead" (who is usually represented as a product of her environment, hanging out with or loving bad boys, drinking, and with no desire to change or better herself or her surroundings)—or some combination of these.[8] There is some

variation in the hoochie or chickenhead in that the hoochie is usually represented in a more positive light. The hoochie is usually the
down girl who hangs around the guys because she is cool, almost
one of them. She gets very little respect, but her presence is toler-
ated. The chickenhead is usually the girl who hangs around because
of what she thinks these guys can do for her. She is not just down
with the crew. She hangs around because she wants something,
usually money, protection, sex, or all three.[9]

The fact that variations of these three ghetto girls are represented
in John Singleton's *Boyz 'N the Hood* should not be taken lightly.
This film started the ghetto exploitation era of the 1990s, and the
ghetto girl motif has seeds in the movie, seeds that would sprout
again and again in other films. The baby mama, the tweener, and
the hoochie or chickenhead became necessary appendages to the
male-centered stories later ghetto exploitation writers and directors
were trying to tell. In *Menace II Society*, for example, Caine alone is
helpless, but with the help of a tweener/baby mama like Ronnie,
the viewer can have some hope that the pair just might make it out
of the ghetto. Even though that hope is not realized, without it the
film would be even bleaker than it is. Likewise, the young girl in
the film who claimed she was pregnant and that Caine was the
father is necessary. She represents a mixture of the hoochie, chickenhead, and baby mama, but even more so, because it is her cousin
who defends her womanhood and kills Caine in the end. She, along
with guns and gangs in the hood, represents the danger awaiting
young Black men.

In fact, each of these ghetto girls as they are portrayed in *Boyz
'N the Hood*–inspired cinema represent danger for these young men.
Each of them in some way is represented as a threat to Black manhood. The baby mama traps the young man in the plight of young
fatherhood. The tweener—with her hopes and dreams—controls
her life and by extension his because either she will not have sex for
fear of getting pregnant or she tells him how to live his life so that
they can have a better life, thereby emasculating him. The hoochie
or chickenhead is sexually promiscuous, money-hungry, or both
and will eventually trap the young Black man in the hood if she
does not get him killed first. The question we must begin to ask as

we think about the larger implications of these seemingly bit parts is what it means when Black womanhood is constantly represented as a danger to Black manhood in our popular culture. From the demonized single mother to the ghetto girl trio, the representations of these Black women on the margins of these films turn out to have wider meaning. They in fact grant us a deeper understanding of the negative rap lyrics that men rappers spout about Black women. If the general underlying message throughout the culture is that Black womanhood is a threat to Black manhood, then the negative images take on a different light. That does not mean that they are in any way excusable, but at least we are able to get at some of the underlying reasons for their existence. If Black men see Black women as a threat, it is easy to see why, even when they begin to tell Black women's stories and bring them out of the margins, they get it all wrong.

Ghetto Girl Stories from the Brotha's Perspective: Singleton's *Poetic Justice* and Tyree's *Flyy Girl*

John Singleton's movie *Poetic Justice* and Omar Tyree's novel *Flyy Girl* have several things in common. Both can be classified as girls-in-the-hood stories in which the ghetto girl is taken from the margins and placed at the center of the story. They are both Black women's stories told from the perspective of a Black man, a technique that is not inherently problematic. But given the considerations discussed above, the elements of danger, fear, and distrust significantly influence the telling of the stories. And both rely on variations of the ghetto girl trio, even as they bring these stories to the center.

Singleton's *Poetic Justice* is interesting because he initially envisioned the film as the female version of *Boyz 'N the Hood*. He remarks, "I dealt with the insecurities of Black men. Why not do a movie about a young sister and how all the tribulations of the brothers affect her?"[10] Singleton put a lot of thought into the kind of woman he wanted Justice to be; she had to be a strong Black woman who had suffered great loss and was now distrustful because of that. And the fact that she was a hair stylist was also important to her character and highlights Singleton's thoughts on what a "real" ghetto girl aspires to and can accomplish. Singleton comments, "A regular sister is usually not thinking about college. If she wants to think about making it, she'll go to cosmetology school."[11] He also notes:

> I wanted Justice to be a down-to-earth woman. Think about LL Cool J's "Around the Way Girl"—so many sisters loved that song because it spoke to them, not some bourgie, stuck-up Black American Princess. The song spoke to the regular sister in Compton, Watts, Harlem, South Side Chicago, Atlanta, Mississippi. That's what I want to do with *Poetic Justice*.[12]

The character Justice, played by singer Janet Jackson, represents an interesting blend of the ghetto girl trio. She is not quite a tweener. Although she has aspirations for a better life, these aspirations do not make her want to leave the hood. And the fact that she is a poet and is represented by the moving poetry of Maya Angelou gives her that in-the-hood-but-not-of-it aura. Also, she is not quite a hoochie or chickenhead. Although her dress—braids, big earrings, and Hip-Hop gear—and mannerisms would lead one to identify her as one of these characters, the fact that she works, takes care of herself, and really does not want anything from men removes the supposed negative elements of being sexually promiscuous and money-hungry. That elements of each of these ghetto girl tropes can be found in Justice would lead one to think that Justice is meant to be complicated, to represent the fullness of Black womanhood that we miss out on when filmmakers rely on stock stereotypes and caricatures. However, the promise of depth is not fulfilled in the character for a variety of reasons.

Many critics have noted that Justice was overshadowed by her love interest, Lucky, that Janet Jackson's acting ability—or lack of ability—held no weight against the dynamic and charismatic rapper and actor Tupac Shakur. They may be right. Certainly Tupac brought believability to the character of Lucky, a postman, aspiring Hip-Hop artist, and single father. Tupac was a product of the urban environment that the film sought to portray. Janet Jackson was not. However, setting aside Jackson's positionality, believability as Justice, and her ability to act, I think that Singleton's script, written from a Black man's perspective, did not really place Justice's story at the center, even if she was the title character.

The film itself spends much more time developing Lucky's story line and fleshing out his wants and needs. We never really get to go in depth with Justice in the same ways. As the film opens we see her boyfriend Markell (Q-tip) get shot, but we never see her mourn. We never get the full impact this loss had on her life. Although her distrustful attitude toward Lucky is supposed to make us infer that she is carrying baggage from that loss, we never really see her portraying it in any other ways. We see her taking classes to become a hair stylist and eventually working in a hair salon, but we do not have a clue as to why she made that decision. Part of the problem is that all of the opening shots of the film are meant to show us glimpses of the character and lead us to the current day. They are just brief scenes, almost snapshots, and in all of them, except the opening scene with Markell, she is voiceless, with the exception of the voice-over of Maya Angelou's poetry read in Justice's voice.[13]

On the other hand, we do know why Lucky is working at the post office and why he is striving to have a better life. We get to see Lucky interact with a variety of people, from his coworkers at the post office, to his mom, baby mama, gang-banging and drug-dealing friends, and young daughter. Through Lucky's interactions and the time spent developing his character throughout the film we get a sense of his motivations, hopes, and desires. Even the filmmaker finally had to admit that what he originally set out to do, tell a Black woman's story, may not be what he actually did: "The more I look at this movie, the more I think it's about women, but it's still from a man's perspective. You still got the booty shots, the breast shots of Colette, I'm sorry. The fact is that I'm going to emphasize certain things in certain ways."[14] I would add that in addition to the booty and breast shots, we get a decentering of the woman's story even as it is represented as the center. Justice is pushed back into the margins of the film, and Lucky takes over the center.

Ironically, it is the film's reliance on another ghetto girl trope, the hoochie/chickenhead, that also works to decenter Justice's story. The sidekick character, ghetto girlfriend Iesha (played by Regina King), takes the beer-drinking, voiceless ghetto girl King originated in *Boyz 'N the Hood* to a different level. By allowing this character more space, Singleton is staying true to his attempt to tell the Black woman's story. But just as we see with Justice, he cannot help but tell the story from his perspective. And unfortunately, when it comes to a character such as Iesha and all that she represents to Singleton, the character we get and thereby the story we're told is not a flattering one. In *Poetic Justice,* Iesha falls victim to the same plight as the ghetto girls in the *Boyz 'N the Hood*–inspired cinema because she represents that same mistrust, fear, and danger to Black manhood.

The casting call for Iesha's character sets the scene: "IESHA: An African American 17–22 year old girl. She's Justice's friend and encourages Justice to go on a road trip with herself, her boyfriend Chicago, and Lucky. During the trip, she rules Chicago, putting him down, threatening to leave him, which only puts a strain on everyone's 'goodtime.' At such a young age she has already acquired a drinking problem."[15] The character of Iesha was written with a certain kind of Black woman in mind. She is presented as a Black woman out to rule the Black man—a ghetto girl version of Moynihan's castrating Black matriarch—and therefore a threat to Black manhood. Iesha is quick with her tongue and speaks her mind. Her relationship with Joe Torry's character, Chicago, is complicated by the fact that he is not pleasing her sexually. She likes the fact that he is willing to spend money on her, but he has a tendency to finish his lovemaking before she is ready to climax. And unlike the nice, docile little lady who just grins and bears the limited satisfaction, Iesha gets a ghetto girl attitude.

Singleton reflects on the implications of a character like Iesha: "So many Black men feel that Black women cut them down as bad, if not worse, than society. I'm always denying it but truth be told, I know more than one Iesha—some sisters cut a brother to the quick, in cold blood.''[16] He tries to paint himself as the understanding brother looking for the good in sisters but just telling the truth as he sees it. Sounding eerily like rappers who claim they rap about bitches and hos because that's the kind of women they come across, Singleton too has trouble really envisioning the fullness of Black womanhood.

> I don't want to make Iesha the typical victimized woman. In truth, she's the castrating bitch that downgrades her man at every turn. . . . Basically, Iesha is the same as many other Black American women: a perfect feminine nightmare that might have conjured up Shahrazad Ali. I just have to remember not to make her unsympathetic.[17]

One wonders what *Poetic Justice* would have been like if Singleton had remembered "not to make her unsympathetic," if perhaps his own clearly distrustful attitude toward Black women and the perceived danger they represent to Black manhood had been one of trust and willingness to understand a character such as Iesha in all her complications and contradictions. Even though it appears that Iesha and Justice, and by extension women like them, are having their stories told in *Poetic Justice*, they are still being represented by the ghetto girl motif, as tropes in a larger story that is still all about Black manhood. Particularly with Iesha, we get the unproblematized hoochie or chickenhead who comes off as sexually promiscuous, money-hungry, and a threat to Black manhood because she uses her mouth to emasculate men. She also uses men for what they can give her either materially or sexually. In the unproblematic way she is represented in the film, we do not get a sense of why she is the way she is. What societal influences, for example, make using men such an appealing option for her?

We get a similar version of the ghetto girl in Omar Tyree's *Flyy Girl*. The main character in the novel, Tracy Ellison, is a teenage Black girl growing up in the 1980s in Philadelphia who is obsessed with material things and all the hottest and latest trends. Her desire to have nice things leads her to sleep around quite a bit with a variety of guys so that they will buy her things. Like Singleton's Justice,

Tyree's Tracy at first appears to be a complicated mix of the three ghetto girl types. Like Justice, Tracy is a composite of the tweener and the hoochie or chickenhead. However, unlike Janet Jackson's Justice, Tracy is the center of the story in *Flyy Girl*. At no point is she marginalized and placed on the sidelines of the novel. And like Singleton's *Poetic Justice,* Tyree's *Flyy Girl* is told from a male perspective, which limits the reader's sense of the impact society has on Tracy and why she behaves the way she does.

The novel *Flyy Girl* traces the life of Tracy Ellison from her sixth birthday in 1977 to the end of her first year in college. Tracy was a very spoiled child who had everything her heart desired because she had two working parents, one of whom was a doting father. When her parents split up and her father leaves, the novel brings to the surface the less-talked-about side of the absence of Black fathers in the home. A lot of attention has been paid to what happens to young Black men when they do not grow up with a constant positive male influence. Very seldom do people explore what it means for young Black women to grow up without a father. The novel brings these issues to the surface, but it does not engage them in any significant way. We see the teenage Tracy going from boy to boy, having sex and collecting gifts. However, the novel does not explore the impact on Tracy of losing her father, who lavished her with gifts and was essentially her first love. In fact, in several instances Tyree merely paints Tracy as a cold, manipulative, calculating user who in the end—when she finally meets her match, a drug dealer named Victor who uses her sexually and plays with her very young mind—gets what she deserves, a broken heart.

Tyree has noted in a number of interviews that he likes to have each of his novels deal with important societal issues.[18] In *Flyy Girl* he wanted to explore materialism and the trend of being ostentatious.[19] Given the enormous amount of money Black people in this country spend in an attempt to live above their means, Tyree's desire to tackle the rampant and obsessive materialism in the Black community through the character Tracy in *Flyy Girl* is welcome. We do need to explore the impact that excessive spending has on the Black community, and if we can do it via popular literature or another form of popular culture, great. The problem surfaces in the approach and the distrust/fear of Black womanhood that comes across when the only things on offer are limited stories from a man's perspective.

Tyree writes *Flyy Girl* in the third person. However, even though the narrator has access to what is going on in Tracy's mind, we do not get the fullness of her character—that is, unless Tyree purposely set out to create a shallow, selfish, greedy girl. I do not think that is what he meant to do, because Tracy is endearing on many levels. The fact that—much to Tyree's chagrin—the novel is so very popular with women all across the country says something about the character. Personally, as a former fly girl who grew up without her father, looked for love in all the wrong places, and liked the finer things in life, I identified with Tracy on many levels. This identification, I believe, allowed me and other women who read *Flyy Girl* to read between the lines and understand Tracy in ways that Tyree's words alone did not offer.

It is hard for the reader to muster any sympathy or empathy for Tracy the way Tyree constructs her. And given that he saw his book as making a critique of obsessive materialism, one would expect him to pay a little more attention to the societal influences in the life of this young fly girl. By the end of the novel, her father comes back home, Tracy is away at college, and Victor the drug-dealing heartbreaker who took her virginity at age thirteen is in jail. The fact that Tracy's calming of her wild side coincided with her father's return is not lost on the reader. It suggests that once the Black man returns to the home all will be right with the Black family. Also, the fact that the novel closes with two letters, the first from Victor to Tracy and the second from Tracy to her father, is very telling—the perfect example of the male point of view and the peripheral nature of women's feeling, worth, and well-being in the novel. While most young girls who grew up without a father—and because of that abandonment fell victim to the head games of a player like Victor—might have come to some self-reflective moments at the end and finally appreciated the parent who was there for her, Tyree's Tracy, still shallow and quite frankly stupid, is only able to dedicate herself to waiting for Victor and writing a letter to her father telling him that she forgives him.

It is really not important whether Tracy learns from her mistakes. What is important is that the critique of society that the novel promises is not there for its main character. It is, however, there for Victor. Tyree gets deep into Victor's mind, and we get a clear sense of why he uses and discards women, as well as why he sells drugs. We even get a pseudosocial critique of his situation when he writes Tracy from jail as a converted Muslim:

> The white man has set us up for all this shit we been through. And all I was doing was running around dicking every girl that I could get. . . . And I didn't know who I was, and what my mission was in life. But you know white people have a lot of pitfalls set up to distract us from searching for the truth. They be having us playing them "Super-nigga" roles.[20]

Victor (now named Qadeer) is given space in the novel to reflect on why he did what he did. And while his nationalist critique on society ends up too neatly blaming the "white man" for all his shortcomings and faults, he is showing the beginnings of a consciousness that might begin to look both at outside elements and how he became susceptible to them in more meaningful ways. Tracy, on the other hand, literally just meets some college girls, becomes friends with them, and then realizes that she wants to go to college. She does not have any real moments of critical self-reflection. In fact, the critique of society, when it comes from Tracy, is in defense of her father and Victor. In the final letter to her father, which serves as the epilogue to the novel, Tracy is singing in the society-is-so-hard-on-the-Black-man choir, and writes a poem, "Stop the Critics," to defend her father from attacks about his absenteeism as a dad.

Perhaps this occurs because, as a man, Tyree—like Singleton—is able to think more critically about the whys and why-nots of his male characters, and essentially can conceive of the women only in relation to the men. I maintain that it is not that simple for either Tyree or Singleton. If they had granted the same fullness to their women characters as they did to the men, if they had even tried to give them more depth and dimension or looked at how society influenced them, the works might truly have explored the realities of Black women's lives. A ghetto fly girl like Tracy might still have been sexually promiscuous, money-hungry, and materialistic, but she would have been a whole lot more than that.

Sisters Gonna Work It Out: The Ghetto Girl Refigured

The ghetto girl also takes center stage in Sister Souljah's *The Coldest Winter Ever* (2000) and Leslie Harris's *Just Another Girl on the IRT* (1993). Sister Souljah's novel and Harris's film come to us direct from the ghetto girls' mouths. Sister Souljah's novel is written in the first person, and the main character, Winter, is present and accounted for throughout. We know why she does the things she does because she tells us. The reader may not agree with her actions, but by the end of the novel we know Winter in ways in which it is difficult to know Tyree's Tracy. Likewise, with Harris's film, the main character, Chantel, speaks directly into the camera throughout the film, thereby giving the viewer a clear, firsthand account of her actions and why she does what she does. Chantel's space as the center and driving force of the film is not sacrificed in the same way that Singleton's Justice is sacrificed. While viewers may not agree with Chantel's actions throughout the film, they do get a fuller sense of why she takes each of them. In both Sister Souljah's novel and Leslie Harris's film, we get a clear understanding of the role the larger society plays in not only the choices they make but also the choices they *feel* they can make. Both Sister Souljah and Harris offer a full account of the ghetto girl's life that not only looks at oppression but also takes into consideration issues of complicity. It is this fullness that takes the ghetto girl out of the realm of the stereotypical motif and into the realm of reality and ultimately understanding.

The main character in *The Coldest Winter Ever,* Winter Santiaga, like Tracy in *Flyy Girl*, is a spoiled ghetto princess who grew up with a father who gave her everything she ever wanted. She also figured out quite early the game of tricking—using her body to get money from men. Her actions minus a clear understanding of what really pushes her would allow the reader to place her in the stereo-typed, sexually promiscuous, money-hungry Black ghetto girl category. However, Sister Souljah's clear depiction of Winter's surroundings and her circumstances halt such stock categorizations. Sister Souljah offers a critique of materialism and the ghetto-fabulous mentality promoted in contemporary Hip-Hop culture through a literary exploration of the harsh implications that this materialistic mentality has on Black women such as Winter.

Winter's drug dealer father was targeted for takeover by up-and-coming drug dealers, and her mother was shot in the face. These actions marked the beginning of a slow spiral downward for Winter and the end of life as she had come to know it. Eventually Winter had to fend for herself in the streets, but her surroundings and how she was brought up warped her understanding of survival. Survival for Winter was far more than food and lodging. She had grown up in the projects and seen others surviving that way. For her, it meant having the best of everything and lots of name-brand clothing. Also, her understanding of how to survive and make it in society was warped by what society values. As a product of a capitalist country built on crime and theft, whose "old-money" families got their fortunes by participating in less-than-legal activities, Winter saw value in a life of crime that made it impossible for her to even consider finishing high school. She definitely would not consider working at McDonald's for minimum wage.

Winter sees a life of crime and having a hustle as the only legiti-mate options for herself. The stark reality of her not being able to even consider other choices speaks to the air of hopelessness that some ghetto girls must feel. Even after all the things that happened to her family and the fact that her father will spend the rest of his life in jail, Winter still thinks crime is the way to go and looks for ways to enter the drug game herself.

[M]y father got at least *twenty years of good high living* out of the business. Nobody could argue with that. That's power. To be able to set up your own empire in your neighbor-hood, or even somebody else's neighborhood for that matter. To buy cars, Jeeps, trucks. To sport the flyest shit made by top designers everyday. To be able to buy property, mansions, and still have apartments on the side. To be able to shit on people before they get a chance to shit on you. That's power. Who could argue with that? A regular nigger worked all week for change to get to work plus a beer to forget about how hard he worked. . . . Let's compare it, ten years of good living and twenty years of high living versus sixty years of scraping to get by. Enough said.[21]

I quote this passage at length because it demonstrates the complicated and conflicted issues that *The Coldest Winter Ever* has to offer. Many of the contradictions highlighted in the novel stem from the original contradictions in the "founding" of the United States and the myths central to the country's origins, such as the land of opportunity, the American dream, and bootstraps, to name only a few. Ultimately, Winter just wants her piece of the American pie. Her views about success and power stem not only from growing up the daughter of a drug dealer but also from the things that society as a whole values and sees as markers of success.

To say that contemporary U.S. culture marks success by the amount of things one is able to acquire would be an understatement; contemporary U.S. consumer commodity culture is nothing new. What is new is the way Sister Souljah skillfully weaves the contradictions inherent in the larger U.S. story into the contradictions of Winter's life in order to create a more complex character. Through Winter, Sister Souljah also forces us to acknowledge at least part of the contradictory relationship between the United States and drugs. Winter ponders, "Besides, the drug dealers helped America to be rich. If it wasn't for us, who would buy the fly cars, butter leathers, and the jewelry? We put so much money into circulation. More than them little nickel-and-dime-paying taxpayers. We employed half of the men in the ghetto. Nobody else gave them jobs. So why be a player hater?"[22] This passage also brings to light the very real implications of the joblessness that plagues America's inner cities and a reason why some feel the need to lead a life of crime. Sometimes trying to live the American dream is a one-way ticket to a nightmare.

Sister Souljah complicates the discussion of obsessive materialism even more because she does not let the Hip-Hop generation off the hook by only looking at U.S. complicity. She also uses Winter to make a critique of what Hip-Hop's rampant materialism will bring. Winter describes the scene at a Hip-Hop concert she attends:

> As usual, the show outside the theater was the biggest. Females in spring leathers, patent leathers, plastic, lace, cellophane shorts, skirts, the works. Enough gold on necks, arms, and teeth to fill Fort Knox. Players was rocking fresh Nike, Fila, Armani, Versace, Kani, Mecca, and all the flavors. Hip-hop vibes hugged the airwaves and we filed in looking every person up and down and side to side, checking for authenticity. It was a car show, a hair show, a fashion show, and a hoe show all rolled up into one. Each male and female in the audience was as important as any star on the stage.[23]

Sister Souljah purposely lists the designer names and all the material things that have become so important to the Hip-Hop generation that they check each other for authenticity. This authenticity check serves a dual function. It is a check to see if the gear and the jewelry the person is wearing are real and not knock-off clothing or fake jewelry. And it is also a check on the person to see if he or she really belongs. The authenticity check becomes a self-monitoring that pushes members of the Hip-Hop generation to acquire as many things as they can in order to fully belong. In the words of rapper Ice Cube, you "check yourself before you wreck yourself," with members of the Hip-Hop generation relying on physical appearance and material things for an image, without which they feel less than worthy.

It is the desire to maintain appearances and keep up the facade of being the flyest, best-dressed woman with all the newest and hottest gear that ultimately brings Winter's downfall. She begins to date a drug dealer named Bullet who promises to give her a life better than the one she lost when her father got locked up. And even though

Bullet was down with the young, upstart crew that helped to bring her father down, she still gets involved with him. This lack of judgment is just one example of how the quest for material things leads to Winter's own downfall. She also manages to double-cross her girlfriends and turn them against her. In her quest for things, Winter tries to steal her best friend Natalie's drug dealer boyfriend. Winter also turns her back on her friend Simone. Simone gets caught shoplifting a pink leather suit that Winter wanted to wear to the Hip-Hop show, and Winter does not want to part with the money she's saved from their shoplifting racket to bail Simone out. Thus, Winter's quest for material things leaves her friendless and in a relationship with the wrong man.

In order to bring home the consequences of Winter's actions, Sister Souljah paints Winter's trajectory in vivid detail. She shows us what happens to the young women who get involved with drug dealers and allow the men to make them do foolish things. Bullet convinces Winter to lease an apartment and rent a car in her name. The police find drugs in the car and guns in the apartment; neither belongs to Winter. All in one day, Winter goes from being the beautiful drug dealer's girlfriend to having her faced sliced with a razor by her ex-friend Simone and being carted off to jail. As she sits bleeding in the rented Lexus, the cops come and Bullet takes off. Winter is sentenced to serve a mandatory fifteen-year prison sentence.

Eventually all of Winter's friends and ex-friends end up in the same situation. Winter notes, "Everybody got drug-related charges stemming from their own situations. But we wasn't nothing but the girlfriends to niggas moving weight." Winter does not learn her lesson in the end and does not warn her sister, who is heading down the same path. Her bad attitude has not changed, and all she can say is "Fuck it. She'll learn for herself. That's just the way it is."[24]

Winter Santiaga is not a very likable character. She is conceited, she is obsessed with material things, and she does not learn from her mistakes. She constantly makes bad decisions, and she is sometimes mean and rude. However, what Winter and her friends who end up in jail represent is what makes *The Coldest Winter Ever* a text that brings wreck. Winter Santiaga and her project friends represent the startlingly large and growing Black female prison population. They represent a wake-up call and a glimpse at what Hip-Hop's focus on materialism is doing to young Black girls. They also represent what a lack of suitable choices can do to a life that, but for better circumstances, could have been lived out differently. Winter Santiaga is no stock character. While Winter does fit the description of a ghetto girl, Sister Souljah writes about her surroundings with such detail and gets us so deeply into the mind of the character that we cannot easily dismiss her. Even as readers might be able to guess where Winter is going to ultimately end up, we are forced to question so many aspects of society along the way that the reading shakes up all we thought we knew about Winter and her world.

Viewers of Leslie Harris's *Just Another Girl on the IRT* get a similar unsettling experience when they are let into the world of the main character, Chantel Mitchell. Chantel, like Sister Souljah's Winter, is a Brooklyn girl. Like John Singleton's Justice, Chantel wears long goddess braids and Hip-Hop-style clothing. Like many of the ghetto girls discussed here, she is money-hungry and materialistic. But she is also ambitious, and she wants to have a better life, one that she can use *her own intelligence* to obtain; she wants to be a doctor. She is sassy, smart, and in some instances self-centered. Chantel is a very complicated character who defies easy categorization and caricature. Filmmaker Leslie Harris notes that she made the film because

> I hadn't seen realistic images of myself in film. There've been films made from an African American male perspective about African American males coming of age. The women in those films are just hanging on some guy's arm. I wanted to give people a different perspective of a 17-year-old at the crossroads. I'd see these teenage women on the subway and I'd want to follow them home and show them as they are—with all their energy and all their faults and flaws.[25]

Clearly, Harris realized that she was bringing to the screen a character that viewers have never really seen before. Harris's film accomplishes what John Singleton attempted to do with *Poetic Justice*—tell the story of a girl in the hood with all the richness and complexity that many praised Singleton's *Boyz 'N the Hood* for having.

As theorist Andre Willis writes, *Just Another Girl on the IRT* "employs a rap and hip hop impulse, style, rhythm, and narrative in the most provocative, revealing, enlightening ways ever documented on film. Devoid of gratuitous violence, drugs, homophobia, misogyny, and many stereotypes, *IRT* overcomes most of the flaws of Black male–directed mainstream films with the hip hop theme and adds a very different flavor to the escape from the ghetto story."[26] Leslie Harris's film added the female perspective to the hood genre of cinema, and by doing so she brought wreck to both the way Black women are represented in these films and the way they are represented in the society at large.

Harris uses Chantel to complicate the way we think about the ghetto girl. She does this by creating a character that does not fit neatly into any stereotype. Like the tweener, Chantel is in the hood but not of it. She has bourgeois aspirations and dreams of making it out of the ghetto. Like the chickenhead or hoochie, she is easily impressed by material things and gravitates to men because of what they have or what they can do for her. Like the baby mama, she ends up pregnant at a young age and unmarried. The combination of the ghetto girl trio in one character may seem like a stereotype waiting to happen. However, Harris uses the character Chantel to explode and wreck stereotypes not reify them.

From the very beginning of the film, when we glimpse an unrecognizable figure placing a garbage bag on a pile of trash and Chantel's voice-over informing us that she is going to tell us "how it really is," we are already gearing up to challenge stereotypes. By the end of the film, we realize that the person with the garbage bag was Chantel's boyfriend, Ty, putting their newborn baby on the trash heap. By then we have already gotten to know Chantel, and her words at the beginning of the film come back with force. We cannot easily place Chantel in the stereotyped role of the drug-addicted mother who throws away her baby because it gets in the way of her next fix. We've seen Chantel and know she is not a crack head. She is, however, a very scared seventeen-year-old with dreams bigger than she may be able to realistically obtain, facing an obstacle that has life-altering implications.

Throughout the film Leslie Harris complicates stereotypes and what we think we know about young Black urban girls. We see Chantel go through various shades of personality, from hard-core Brooklyn girl with an attitude to scared insecure teenager and then confident single mother and college student. Because we get to see Chantel in a variety of settings and in a variety of moods, we know that she is not the stereotypical loud-talking girl in the hood with no class and lots of attitude. She does have a lot of attitude, and in some instances a very bad one. However, Chantel's attitude is contextualized in the film in a way that prohibits caricatured representations of Black womanhood. Chantel complicates stereotypes of the ghetto girl with a bad attitude because in each instance where she has a negative reaction, we see the circumstances and frustrations that lead up to the negative reaction.

For example, when Chantel talks back—in the bringing-wreck sense—to her teacher because he is not teaching them about Black history and contemporary Black issues, she is not merely being rude. Although she is very rude, she has a desire to understand what's going on in the ghetto around her, to make sense of the suffering and frustration that she and the other Black people around her feel. While viewers may agree that Chantel did not have to curse the teacher out, we also agree that in the end education should teach us something about ourselves and in some way be relevant to our lives, our wants, and our dreams.

When Chantel is in the principal's office for cursing at her history teacher, we get another glimpse at her ghetto girl attitude and another complication of it. While a simplistic reading of the scene would cause us to think that Chantel is just a rude young Black girl with no respect for authority, Leslie Harris makes it hard for us to rely on simplistic readings. For example, by then we have seen Chantel hold her temper in check and be smart, clever, and witty about the way she tells off a snobby white female customer at the posh uptown grocery shop where she works after school. And we have also seen how badly Chantel wants to get out of her environment. We know how she has planned and strategized, and how much she believes education and becoming a doctor are going to get her out of the hood. We know she wants to graduate early. So when she reacts negatively by yelling, rolling her eyes, sucking her teeth, and giving off major attitude to the principal, who is discouraging her from graduating early and essentially standing in the way of her dreams, we at least understand why she is upset. Having insight into Chantel's desires and the urgency with which she pursues them stops us from reading her as a caricature. We know that she is book-smart and that she can do the work. But we also know that she can go from calmly professional to attitudinal and rude in a matter of seconds if the right buttons are pushed.

Leslie Harris also complicates stereotypes about the sexually promiscuous and always sexually available Black girl in the film. While Chantel does have a desire for material things and a better life, she is not having sex with a multitude of guys in order to obtain them. She is a virgin when she first has sex with Ty. She is also unseasoned and naive about sex; she falls for the oldest "I don't want to wear a condom" line in the book. Because Chantel is not out having sex with anyone and everyone, we cannot read her as a stereotyped chickenhead or hoochie. By the time Chantel has sex with Ty, in her eyes he has become more than just the Jeep he drives. We see that she really cares about him. But we also see the pitfalls that are looming, and we are not surprised when she misses her period.

Chantel's pregnancy is another instance in the film where we are forced to move away from simplistic readings. Because we know all about Chantel's hopes and dreams, we know that she has hit a major roadblock. The way Chantel deals with the pregnancy is thought-provoking, to say the least. She behaves in a way that conveys a complicated mixture of hiding and denial, concealing her pregnancy from everyone close to her except Ty. Ultimately she even manages to hide from her own mind. Her denial is so deep that we often get the sense that she believes that she will wake up one morning and no longer be pregnant, like waking up from a bad dream. She does things while trying to hide her pregnancy that make the viewer question both her motives and her morals. For example, she takes the $500 that Ty borrowed from his uncle for an abortion and goes on a shopping spree with her friend Natete.

Her immature actions at first seem problematic. Indeed, if she were a stereotypical character we would think she was holding out for the real loot, that she is just another sister setting a brother up to take care of her and a child for the rest of her life. But because we know Chantel, we know that getting pregnant was not in her plans; she wanted to make it out of the ghetto, and she was going to use her brain to make it happen. We are forced to see her spending spree for what it is: the attempt of a scared teenager to pretend as if nothing is wrong.

Leslie Harris also uses Chantel's pregnancy to make some interesting comments about class, race, abortion, and a woman's right to choose. While it is easy for some to read the film as anti-abortion—Ty seems to be trying to coerce Chantel into having an abortion—that would be simplistic. Chantel in fact is a poster girl for a woman's right to choose. Throughout the film she repeats, almost mantralike, that it is her body and her decision. Even though she never officially makes a decision and falls into denial, she is steadfast in her belief that she and only she can say what happens to her body. That is why the scene at the free clinic when she meets with the counselor, Paula, for the first time is so intriguing. Chantel wants information about abortion, but because the clinic is government-funded, Paula cannot give Chantel that information. The scene is poignant and brings to bear a lot of conflicted and complicated truths about access and freedom, especially when matters of race and class enter the picture. The choices that Chantel is ultimately able to make depend on where and who she is.

Therefore, in the end, when we realize that Ty is putting their baby on the trash pile because Chantel wants to get rid of it as though nothing ever happened, we at least know why she did it. We may not agree with her actions, but we see the ways in which the larger public sphere worked to influence her actions. We see where she lives in the projects. We see how hard her parents work only to *still* live in the projects. We see the majority of the household responsibilities, such as cleaning and taking care of her little brothers, fall on her young shoulders. We also see that she is exposed—through her job at the posh grocery store uptown—to what must have seemed like another world, one that was only a train ride away on the IRT. She knows firsthand that there are people leading lives where they can spend serious money on specialty groceries, and she wants to live like that. The American dream is a serious draw, and—as we have seen in the case of Sister Souljah's *Winter*—it can make you do some less-than-nice things in order to obtain it. Chantel just wants her version of the American dream. She wants a nice life, and a baby would stand in her way.

Leslie Harris complicates our understanding of the myths that make up the larger public sphere by using Chantel to break them apart. While the ending would appear to play on the bootstrap theory, with Chantel working hard and going to community college while raising her daughter (Ty was unable to go through with placing the child on the trash), we also know that due to the unequal base from which she starts, the bootstrap theory is not what is really being represented; it is being critiqued. Chantel is going to have a rough life, not because she was not bright enough or did not work hard enough, but because the society is set up in such a way that in order for her to make it legitimately—that is, without resorting to a life of crime or tricking her body for nice things and some man to take care of her—she has to go above and beyond the norm. Who she is and where she is, her race, her class, and her gender all influence her path and how she makes it in the larger society.

Hoochies Need Love Too: The Girls in the Hood Are Gonna Set It Off

When I was an undergraduate student at William Paterson College in New Jersey, before I claimed a Black feminist identity, I had a fierce Black nationalist agenda that took with the utmost seriousness the plight of young Black men in America. I also had a major crush on filmmaker Spike Lee because he represented Black genius to me. I thought he was brilliant, and I cut out every magazine photo I could find of him and taped them to my dorm wall. There was something about his early films, specifically *School Daze* (1988) and *Do the Right Thing* (1989), that represented the urgency that I felt, something that spoke to the immediacy of our problems as Africans in America. In addition to my collage of Spike Lee photos, I also had a red, black, and green "Save the Male, Love the Female" poster hanging on my dorm wall. I think about that poster a lot nowadays. It is long gone, and I do not know if I ever really agreed with it or what it represented. But I do remember that when I purchased it, it felt right to my young neonationalist mind. I knew that the Black male needed saving. That was, after all, the message that various media was giving me. The news and magazines all told me about the young Black men filling the jails or ending up dead. I went to the movies and saw films such as *Boyz 'N the Hood, Menace II Society, Straight Outta Brooklyn,* and *Juice,* which portrayed the plight of young Black men in startling realism. After watching *Juice,* I left the theater feeling a tremendous sense of emptiness and sadness. Yes, I thought, young Black men need saving.

It was only after I began to develop a feminist consciousness that I began to see the contradictions in that poster. I began to ponder what the message "Save the Male, Love the Female" meant for the girls in the hood. Is love all they really need? Or do they need a community that loves them enough to want to save them as well? Why the dichotomy—save/love, Black male/Black female? Are men's and women's needs really that different? I've tried to show here that when we really take a look at the representations of ghetto girls we get to know how young Black urban women navigate and negotiate a place in the larger public sphere that continuously denies them a place or a voice. The ghetto girl trio and the stereotypical tropes of Black womanhood that the *Boyz 'N the Hood* genre of cinema relies on convey flat representations of Black womanhood, but critical interrogation allows us to see that both Black men and women need saving *and* love. Indeed, as the title to this section announces, hoochies need love too, the real love that centers their stories and validates their lives.[27] When the girls in the hood become the center of the story, we get to see how society is implicated in the choices—and the lack of choices—young Black women living in urban areas feel they have. No film shows this more clearly than F. Gary Gray's *Set It Off* (1997).

Set It Off stars Queen Latifah, Jada Pinkett Smith, Kimberly Elise, and Vivica Fox as four friends who grew up together in the hood, fall on hard times, and end up robbing banks. Vivica Fox plays Frankie, a bank teller who happened to know the bank robber who held up the bank where she worked and lost her job because of it. Queen Latifah plays Cleo, a lesbian who works nights cleaning office buildings and spends her days working on her lowrider car. Jada Pinkett Smith plays Stoney, a young woman whose parents were killed in an automobile accident, so she gave up her life to take care of her younger brother. And Kimberly Elise plays Teshawn, a young single mother who is trying hard to maintain a life for herself and her child. Both Stoney and Teshawn also work cleaning office buildings at night. The characters in this film all represent complicated variations and mixtures of the ghetto girl trio. And the film, although it is directed by a man, does not decenter the stories of these women or offer caricatured representations of Black womanhood.

In order to fully understand the complicated space that the film occupies, it is important to contextualize the film and think about the moment in which the film was released—just after the *Boyz 'N the Hood*–inspired ghetto exploitation era and during the moment when gangsta rap had peaked in popularity. The film was also released after the megasuccess of *Waiting to Exhale* (1995), a film based on Terry McMillan's best-selling novel, which glorified Black buppiedom and showed America the Black professional woman in all her glory and glamour. *Waiting to Exhale* is about four professional, upwardly mobile, middle-aged Black women who are successful, can buy anything they want, live in nice homes, and drive nice cars. But they cannot find decent Black men to love. *Waiting to Exhale* was the template for much of the sistah/girlfriend fiction that would come after it, which would always have as main characters three or four Black professional women who are good friends. This formula even made it to television with the hit sitcom *Living Single*. *Set It Off* provided a Hip-Hop/ghetto girl remix of the *Waiting to Exhale* template by making the girlfriends urban, working-poor young women who barely had time to think about men and one lesbian who was not thinking about any man. *Set It Off* thus was neatly positioned to take advantage of two markets, the *Boyz 'N the Hood* gangsta flick market and the market of Black women readers and movie viewers that made *Waiting to Exhale* both a best-selling novel and a blockbuster movie.

A chain of events outside the girls' control leads them to a life of crime. When Frankie loses her job at the bank and ends up cleaning office buildings with her friends, she is more than a little bitter. She had worked hard for the bank, and they did not have any faith or trust in her. Stoney needed money to send her brother to UCLA, so she had sex with a man who had been trying to sleep with her for years. She later finds out that her brother was never even admitted to UCLA, and then he is killed by the police while they were looking for the bank robbers who got Frankie fired, a classic case of mistaken identity. Teshawn cannot afford to pay a baby-sitter and pay taxes to Uncle Sam at the same time. When she cannot find a sitter and has to take her son with her to work, he ends up drinking cleaning fluid. Child protective services considers bringing the child to work as a form of neglect and takes her son away from her. She has to prove that she has money and can afford a baby-sitter in order to get her child back. Cleo, on the other hand, is tired of guys showing her up in their nice cars, and tired of being broke. For four Black women trying to make ends meet on an office cleaner's budget, money is a scarce commodity. Their circumstances and the choices they feel they can make are greatly impacted by their surroundings and who they are. Frankie's rationale for robbing a bank—"we just taking away from the system that's fucking us all anyway"—is telling when we take into consideration the systemic oppression and roadblocks that stand in the way of these women achieving their dreams.

For example, when we take a closer look at Teshawn, we see that in many ways she is in a no-win situation. She really cannot navigate a space for herself where she can come out ahead and free of blame. If she does not work, she is considered a lazy welfare mom living off the state. If she does work and does not have a baby-sitter or cannot afford one, she is stuck with no real options. If she leaves the child at home alone, she is a bad mother. If she takes the child to work with her, she is a bad mother. What else could she have done?

What about Frankie? Did she really have a choice in the opening bank robbery situation? She knew what would happen if she followed procedure. She did not want to be blamed, even though that was what eventually happened. So, she tried to stop the robbery from happening because she knew the robbers. Frankie, like Teshawn, Stoney, and Cleo, had very little choice; they all had very few options.

Another telling line in the film occurs when Stoney asks her love interest, played by Blair Underwood, if he feels free. When the Harvard-educated Black buppie banker replies that he does, Stoney says, "Well, I don't feel free. I feel very much caged." This line captures the ways in which intersecting oppressions work in the lives of these women. Marilyn Frye's description of oppression as a birdcage comes to mind. Frye suggests the image of the birdcage because if we look at it wire by wire we cannot really understand why the bird does not just fly around the wire and flee the cage. It is only when we step back and look at the entire cage that we see how all the wires work together to keep the bird trapped. Frye writes, "[T]he experience of oppressed people is that the living of one's life is confined and shaped by forces and barriers which are not accidental or occasional and hence avoidable, but are systematically related to each other in such a way as to catch one between and among them and restrict or penalize motion in any direction. It is the experience of being caged in: all avenues, in every direction, are blocked or booby trapped."[28] *Set It Off* offers interesting and varied examples of how intersecting oppressions influence the lives of African American women and the choices they feel they can make. While they are not forced into a life of crime, it is safe to say that they did not have doors flung open for them in other areas. Their choices are so limited, in fact, that they cannot really think far into the future in terms of their own lives. Cleo puts it best when she says, "I ain't thinking about five years from now. I'm just trying to get through the day."

The film *Set It Off*, like other girls-in-the-hood stories, specifically *The Coldest Winter Ever* and *Just Another Girl on the IRT,* rips a hole in the American-dream and bootstrap mythologies. The notion that if people work hard enough they can make it is disproven, particularly by the character of Stoney. The ploy is very subtle, and if it is not engaged critically, it would appear that the ending of *Set It Off* reaffirms instead of disproves the myth that hard work and bourgeois aspirations will free one from the ghetto.

For example, Stoney is the classic tweener. She has high hopes for her younger brother and sees his education as their way out of the hood, but the police kill him. After she meets a nice buppie banker, she dares to have dreams for her own life. The banker, played by Blair Underwood in classical condescending fairy-tale style, opens her eyes to the finer things in life and foods from other cultures and countries. Stoney begins to open up and shed her hard ghetto girl shell. But, lest we think it was only the desire of a buppie banker that gave Stoney her bourgeois aspirations, we should note that she was always an anomaly in the hood. Even her friend Cleo remarks on it: "Stoney, you can go to suburbia and start a new life. But we ain't nothing but hoodrats. And I can live with that but you can't. The hood is where I belong." Viewers sense early on that Stoney is going to fare better because she wants more out of life. In fact, casting Jada Pinkett Smith in the role almost guarantees tweener status for the character. She played the tweener Lyric who wanted to move away to a better life in the film *Jason's Lyric* (1994). And she played the tweener Ronnie who wanted to escape the harsh gang realities of Los Angeles for a nicer life in Atlanta in the film *Menace II Society*. The fact that Jada herself captured the hearts of such diametrically opposed rappers in the spectrum of Hip-Hop as Tupac Shakur and Will Smith cements her in-between status. Jada Pinkett Smith cast as Stoney almost guarantees that she will be a character torn between the hood and wanting more out of life than the hood can offer.

All of these elements—the casting of Pinkett Smith, the character's bourgeois desires, and the fact that in the end she is the only one of the four to live—could lead us to a reading of the film that supports the American dream/bootstrap mythology; that is, she wanted more and she worked hard, so she lived. But she did not work any harder than the other girls did. They all cleaned office buildings for little pay and even less respect. They all plotted and robbed banks because they felt trapped and wanted to clear a way out of the hood for themselves. When we engage critically with the film we see that she made it out only because she got lucky. In the end, it did not mean anything that she was the one with the strongest bourgeois aspirations and that she wanted out of the hood and was determined to have a better life. If Stoney and Frankie had chosen to run in different directions when they were fleeing the cops, then Stoney would have run directly into the police, and Frankie would have been the lucky one who happened upon the crowd of people lining up for a bus ride to Mexico. And it was also pure luck that at the moment when Stoney is spotted by the cop who got Frankie fired and Stoney's brother killed, the cop experiences a pang of guilt. If he had not just watched Frankie get shot to death, who knows if he would have let the bus continue with Stoney on it. When we really look critically at the film, we have to acknowledge that hard work does not necessarily equate with success and being able to leave the hood.

There are plenty of real girls in the hood with lives and stories similar to the ones represented in the films and novels discussed here. They are young women whose circumstances and surroundings limit the choices they are able to make, whose lives have been placed in the background of a Black public sphere so obsessed with saving young Black men that it ignores the plight of young Black women. But, as Wing and Willis caution, we need to think critically about improving the status of young Black women in the hood. They write that "young women must be given educational and employment opportunities to lower the risk that they will become involved with criminal gang activity. Mothers must be given adequate resources so that they will be better able to raise their children in a caring and supportive environment, eliminating or at least lessening the need for gang involvement. Linking childcare, healthcare, education, job training, and positive emotional support will make a difference."[29] While Wing and Willis are concerned with how young Black women might better be steered away from gang activities, their suggestions also ring true for what needs to be done to stop young Black women from falling victim to other detrimental aspects of their environments, such as tricking their bodies for material things and getting involved with drug dealers, to name only two. Wing and Willis both realize that it will take real and attainable choices and access to resources to save the girls in the hood.

The dedication in *The Coldest Winter Ever* ponders the disappearance of love in the Black community. The phrase "there is no such thing as love anymore" is repeated several times throughout the poem. The two middle stanzas are very telling in their representation of the "love" that is left. For Sister Souljah, the absence of love in the Black community means the absence of loyalty, truth, honor, respect, humility, appreciation, family, and God. The fact that this poem is the dedication at the beginning of the novel foreshadows what she thinks will come to a community that lacks love: "the coldest winter ever." While we know that love is not all we need to begin to think about effecting change in the Black community, we know that without it we are doomed. As the prolific writer and activist Alice Walker tells us, "Anything we love can be saved."[30] When we apply this mind-set to the girls in the hood, both fictional and real, we can begin to see the truth of that logic.

Hip-Hop Soul Mate?
Hip-Hop Soul Divas and Rap Music:
Critiquing the Love That Hate Produced

As Fanon says, "Today, I believe in the possibility of love, that is why I endeavor to trace its imperfections, its perversions." Dialogue makes love possible. I want to think critically about intellectual partnership, about the ways black women and men resist by creating a world where we can talk with one another, where we can work together.

—bell hooks, "Feminism as a Persistent Critique of History:
What's Love Got to Do With It?"

In her article "Love as the Practice of Freedom," bell hooks discusses the need for an "ethic of love" in the fight against oppression.[1] For hooks love has liberating potential and could free us from oppression and exploitation. She also believes that until we revere love's place in struggles for liberation we will continue to be stuck in an "ethic of domination."[2] I believe that Hip-Hop culture and rap music provide a starting place for us to begin talking about and implementing an "ethic of love," love meant to liberate. The dialogue that bell hooks believes makes love possible is the kind of dialogue that I am searching for, a dialogue that will extend the possibilities of bringing wreck to a project capable of combating racism, sexism, and homophobia. Black feminist criticism, if it goes beyond admonishing rap for its sexist and misogynist lyrics, can aid in starting the dialogue. As third-wave Hip-Hop feminists such as Joan Morgan and Eisa Davis remind us, there is a public dialogue between male and female rappers and between Black men and women. Therefore, rap music and Hip-Hop culture can be used as a springboard for various kinds of conversations and actions. Feminism needs to change its focus in order to take full advantage of the possibilities in rap music. Instead of admonishing rappers, it is time to do something that will evoke change. Here I probe the public dialogue about love found in rap songs; furthermore, I challenge Black feminism to interrogate rap as a site for political change.

How is love expressed in the Hip-Hop community? And what kind of love is this? My aim here is to look at love and Hip-Hop as a place to further the dialogue between Black men and women and create a space for more progressive conversations about gender and sexuality. My aim is also to look at the ways this dialogue can be used to bring wreck and help us reconsider some long-standing notions about gender and sexuality.[3]

"I Need Love": My Need for Love and Hip-Hop

I remember the first time I heard LL Cool J's soulful rap ballad "I Need Love" (1987). While it was the first rap love song I had ever heard, it will not be the last. Rap and rap artists' never-ending quest to "keep it real" is not limited to the struggles on American streets. Some rappers show a dedication to exploring aspects of love, the struggles of building and maintaining intimate relationships between Black men and women, and maintaining a public dialogue about love, life, and relationships. The beginnings of this public dialogue can be seen in the love raps of the 1960s made famous by Isaac Hayes, Barry White, and Millie Jackson. As William Eric Perkins notes, the love raps were essentially monologues, recorded over a simple melody, that spoke to matters of the heart. Millie Jackson, thought of today as the mother of women rappers, got her start in this genre by recording love raps from a female perspective.[4]

Her raps were often X-rated and she held her own in duets with Isaac Hayes.[5] Talking about love and romance over melodious beats is nothing particularly new in the world of Black music. Black men and women have before and after that moment in the 1960s publicly hammered out their differences through song. In the blues tradition of Black music, Angela Davis finds that the mother of the blues, Gertrude "Ma" Rainey, participated in the call-and-response tradition in that many of her songs about love and sex were meant to be responses to the songs of male country blues singers.[6]

In rap this dialogue can be viewed in the answer/"dis" raps of the 1980s, which gave rise to the women rap stars Roxanne Shante and Salt-N-Pepa.[7] These women paved the way for other women rappers by recording very successful songs that were responses to the hit records of men who were their contemporaries. Roxanne Shante gave the woman pursued in UTFO's "Roxanne, Roxanne" a voice, and ultimately let it be known that women would no longer suffer insults and degradation in silence. Salt N Pepa's "Showstopper" was a direct refutation to Doug E. Fresh and Slick Rick's "The Show," a song in which women are portrayed as objects of conquest. While the response or talking-back element of bringing wreck does appear to be reactionary and therefore limiting, at that particular moment in Hip-Hop, when female voices were few and far between, those response or answer raps performed by Roxanne Shante and Salt-N-Pepa added a missing part of the conversation. By adding this part, they paved the way for the women who would later initiate their own conversations. Songs such as TLC's "Scrubs," Destiny's Child's "Bills, Bills, Bills," Alicia Keys's "A Woman's Worth," and Lauryn Hill's "Doo Wop: That Thing" represent contemporary initiations of the conversation about men, women, and relationships. The public dialogue between men and women can also be seen in contemporary elements of Hip-Hop culture and rap songs.[8] The dialogue surfaces when observing the construction of male and female gender identities and sexualities as well as expressions of love. And although love in the traditional romantic sense is not the first thing to come to mind when one thinks of Hip-Hop culture and rap music, it is important to note that the Hip-Hop generation does talk about and express love. While it may be a different manner of expression than the love that is found in the romantic melodies of the 1960s and 1970s with their sweet harmonies and equally sweet lyrics—more in line, perhaps, with the rugged and raw sex-filled lyrics such as those performed by contemporary crooners such as Ginuwine, Blackstreet, and B2K—it is still a form of love.

The need for Black men and women to take these private issues into the public sphere is not a new phenomenon. The legacy of racism in the United States made it impossible for Blacks to obtain the luxury of a clearly defined public/private split. The public discussions about love, sex, and identity found in the lyrics of Hip-Hop soul divas and rap artists bring wreck and flip the script on Habermas's notions of the public/private split and identity formation.[9] The necessities that Habermas says are taken care of in the private sphere are the very necessities Black people have been fighting for in the public sphere. These necessities also become a site of public struggle for Black men and women. The issue of identity formation, which is not a concern of Habermas, also becomes a matter for public debate for Blacks participating in the public sphere. Blacks in America have constantly struggled against stereotypes and tried to define themselves against labels put forth by American racism. In fact, the quest for self-definition, self-actualization, and self-determination has been a guiding theme in classical and modern Black nationalism. These themes all lead back to Black Americans' determination to define themselves in the absence of a clearly located homeland. For all of these reasons, then, the struggle for identity becomes a matter of public debate.[10] By using rap lyrics about love, sex, and identity to have an effect on public debate and at the same time shape the subjectivity of listeners and performers, the Hip-Hop generation sheds new light on the possibilities of the public sphere.

Tricia Rose notes four dominant themes in the works of Black women rappers: "heterosexual courtship, the importance of the female voice, and mastery in women's rap and black female public displays of physical and sexual freedom."[11] While men rap artists cannot claim rapping about heterosexual courtship as a dominant theme, the release of "I Need Love" (1987) and other rap love songs crooned by Black men suggest that when the rapper is a man, the discourse about relationships, courtship, and love is also predominantly, if not exclusively, heterosexual. Hip-Hop, just like the larger society, is guilty of heterosexism along with homophobia. With the exception of rapper Queen Pen, whose duet with Me'Shell NdegéOcello, "Girlfriend," deals with a woman pursuing another woman, rappers have yet to expand the discourse beyond male-female courtship.

Queen Pen's "Girlfriend," unlike the lyrics in the ballads of the Hip-Hop soul divas, which offer strictly heterosexual tales of love and relationships, tells the story of a very confident woman who will woo a woman right off the arm of a man. "Girlfriend," while it was never released as a single, became popular in various clubs in New York and Florida. Making the song was very much a political act that has personal implications. Realizing that women rappers have constantly had their sexual orientation called into question because of various reasons too ridiculous to name, Queen Pen decided to record "Girlfriend" on her debut album in order to squelch rumors about her sexuality before they even got started.[12] However, she has yet to officially come out. She simply says, "I'm black. I'm a female rapper. I couldn't even go out of my way to pick up another form of discrimination. People are waiting for this hip-hop Ellen to come out of the closet. I'd rather be a mystery for a minute."[13] Thus her political act loses some of its momentum. While she is clearly the first rapper to rap about a homosexual experience, she waffles on completing her stance.

The lyrics of "Girlfriend" are very similar to the boastful lyrics found in the raps of men. She raps about having a lot of bitches that all want her and how her sex is good enough to pull someone out of the closet. She brags that she has women leaving their men and giving her their phone numbers.[14] While Queen Pen's lyrics are boastful, derogatory toward women, and objectifying in some of the same kinds of ways found in the lyrics of men, they break free of the heterosexist hold currently on Hip-Hop culture and rap music by recognizing that same-sex courtship exists in society as well. As Queen Pen asks in a *New York Times* interview, "Why shouldn't urban lesbians go to a club and hear their own thing?"[15]

Perhaps one day more rappers will take a stance similar to Queen Pen's and expand the definition of love to include same-sex relationships.

Even if rap has not reached a stage where it is ready to critique its heterosexism, it is particularly fertile ground for observations and conversations about male-female relationships and the fight against sexism. Rap music can be viewed as a dialogue—between rappers and a racist society, between male rappers and female rappers, and between rappers and the consumer—and the dialogue on love and relationships between the sexes is a productive location for inquiry.[16]

As a woman born in 1970—I was nine years old when the first rap record hit the airwaves (the Sugar Hill Gang's "Rapper's Delight")—I pretty much grew up on rap music. Reading Tricia Rose's discussion of the evolution of Hip-Hop culture through the changes in clothing commodified by rappers and Hip-Hop audiences reminds me of my own evolution from a teenage b-girl in Lee jeans, Adidas sneakers with fat laces, LeTigre shirts, gold chunk jewelry, and gold tooth to a college freshman in leather jacket, baggy jeans, sweat hood, and fake Louis Vuitton. My relationship with Hip-Hop changed when I stopped consuming the female identities put forth by men rappers. Once willing to be LL Cool J's "Around the Way Girl" (1989), I took issue with the very notion of Apache's "Gangsta Bitch" (1992). Today, while I still consume the music, I have begun to question the lyrics and constructed identities.

Like many of the academics and Black popular critics writing about rap, I have a love for Hip-Hop culture and rap music. This love at one time stopped me from writing about rap, but now it prompts me to critique and explore rap in more meaningful ways. I am no longer the teenage girl who spent Friday nights listening to Mr. Magic's "Rap Attack" and writing rhymes, Saturdays reading her mama's Harlequin or Silhouette romance novels, and Sundays writing rhymes and short stories. Now I am *all grown up,* and although I still listen to rap music and read a romance novel every time I get a chance, Black feminist and womanist theories and politics inform my listening and reading. When I think about the definition of a womanist—"committed to the survival of a whole people, male and female"—I cannot help but wonder how that kind of commitment can be achieved, or even if it can be achieved in rap.[17] Frantz Fanon's and bell hooks's hope for the possibility of love, quoted in the epigraph to this chapter, urges me to look for it in Hip-Hop. June Jordan's poignant question "Where is the love?" haunts me. In her article of the same title Jordan discusses the need for a "self-love" and "self-respect" that would create and foster the ability to love and respect others. She writes, "I am talking about love, about a steady-state of deep caring and respect for every other human being, a love that can only derive from a secure and positive self-love."[18]

As I think about Hip-Hop and the images of "niggas" and "bitches" that inhibit this kind of "self-love" and "self-respect," I am faced with questions concerning the forming of a subject that cannot only survive but must become a political subject—someone who can evoke change in the larger public and disrupt oppressive constructs. All of these issues inform my critique of Hip-Hop. I am concerned particularly with rap and the love that hate produced— the love that is fostered by a racist and sexist society. This is the kind of love that grows in spite of oppression but holds unique character- istics because of it. In many ways it is a continuation of the way Black men and women were forced to express love during slavery and segregation.

It is common knowledge that during slavery Black people were not allowed to love one another freely. Family members could be taken away at any moment. African American historian Lerone Ben- nett notes in his book *The Shaping of Black America:*

> Slave marriages had no standing in law; the slave father could not protect his wife and children and the planter could separate slave families at his convenience. This had at least three devastating results. First of all, the imposed pat- tern of mating limited the effectiveness of the slave family and had a sharp impact on slave morale. Second, it isolated the black woman and exposed her to the scorn of her peers and the violence of white women. Third, it sowed the seeds of sexual discord in the black community.[19]

Lerone Bennett's work is thought-provoking because it recognizes the influence that the enslaved past has had on the way Black men and women relate to one another in the present. It is fascinating to me that they continued to build family units even as they were torn apart, and they went looking for lost family members as soon as they were free to do so. Black people found ways to love each other and be together during the era of slavery despite separations and sales of partners. During the days of segregation and Jim Crow, Black people, especially Black parents, had to practice tough love in order to ensure that loved ones would live to see another day and not become the victims of Klan violence.

While the Hip-Hop generation has the legacy of African American history to build on and strands of these kinds of love still persist, the Hip-Hop generation also has its own demons. As Kevin Powell writes in *Keepin' It Real: Post-MTV Reflections on Race, Sex, and Politics,* the Hip-Hop generation, plagued by AIDS, drugs, guns, gangs, unemployment, and a lack of educational opportunities, faces more obstacles in their quest to love than other generations.[20] Powell offers the acknowledgment that life for young Black Americans is different, and the very nature of relationships within Hip-Hop culture is necessarily going to represent both the historical struggle and the unique aspects of the Hip-Hop generation. What continues to fascinate me is that in spite of all the historical baggage and contemporary struggles, these young Black people are still trying to find ways to love, just as their ancestors did.

A new direction for Black feminism would aid in the critique and exploration of the dialogue across the sexes. Black feminists such as dream hampton, Tara Roberts, Joan Morgan, and Eisa Davis have begun to explore the relationship between love and Hip-Hop. Joan Morgan maintains in *When Chickenheads Come Home to Roost: My Life as a Hip-Hop Feminist,* "Any feminism that fails to acknowledge that black folks in 90's America are living and trying to love in a war zone is useless to our struggle against sexism. Though it's often portrayed as part of the problem, rap music is essential to that struggle because it takes us straight to the front lines of the battlefield."[21] Rap music and Hip-Hop culture more generally, along with Black feminism as an activist project, can be a part of the solution. It is not just about counting the "bitches" and "hos" in each rap song. It is about exploring the nature of Black male and female relationships. These new Black feminists acknowledge that sexism exists in rap music. But they also recognize that sexism exists in America. Tricia Rose and other Black critics of popular culture argue that rap music and Black popular culture are not produced in a cultural and political vacuum. The systems of oppression that plague the larger public sphere plague Black public spheres as well.

Michele Wallace and bell hooks examine the larger society's role in Hip-Hop's sexism and encourage Black women to speak out against sexism in rap. The new Black feminists, however, are looking for ways to speak out while starting a dialogue right on the "front lines of the battlefield." In "Some Implications of Womanist Theory" Sherley Anne Williams notes that womanist inquiry assumes a proficiency in talking about men and that this assumption is necessary because stereotyped and negative images of Black women offer only part of the story. In order to get the full story, we have to be able to acknowledge and interrogate what Black men are saying about themselves.[22] While Williams is looking at the potential of womanism for examining the work of Black men writers, she offers a useful lens for understanding Black men rappers as well. Some of the questions that will form my analysis of Black men rappers are: What are they saying about themselves? What kind of lover is described in the Hip-Hop love song? What is the potential for meaningful and productive dialogue found in the lyrics? What are the implications of a real and continued dialogue in this new direction? What impact do the songs of these men rappers have on the songs of Black women rappers? How have women rappers begun to internalize the images put forth by the men? How do all of these songs impact other young Black women? What is its political and rhetorical relevance? What happens when we really begin to critique and explore the love that hate produced?

Hip-Hop Meets R&B: An Overview of Hip-Hop Soul Divas

My use of the Hip-Hop soul diva's lyrics is threefold. First, the blending of Hip-Hop and R&B has added a new dimension to rap, which is already noted for the way it makes connections with and takes from other forms of Black music via sampling.[23] Thus the Hip-Hop soul diva is helping rap evolve to yet another level of crossover appeal. Second, the Hip-Hop soul diva has changed the nature of the rap love song. We can now hear a soulful singing voice on many rap love songs. During the time of LL Cool J's "I Need Love," this use of R&B singing was not as prevalent as it is today. Third, the love songs on the albums of Hip-Hop soul divas open up the floor for questions about love, thus providing a starting point for dialogue between the sexes.

Hip-Hop soul has opened the largely masculine discursive space of Hip-Hop culture to include more women. In fact, there are now more recorded women Hip-Hop soul artists than there are re-corded women rap artists. It has always been a struggle for women to disrupt the masculine space of Hip-Hop, but the success of Hip-Hop soul offers more possibilities for women's voices and issues to be heard. Rap magazine writer Dimitry Leger notes that the "singing sisters" of Hip-Hop soul use the gained space to sing about their lives as members of the Hip-Hop generation. These women come from all regions of the country in which Hip-Hop has a presence, and their music reflects that regional influence with shades of hard-core reality.[24]

The release of Michel'le's 1989 self-titled album marks the beginning of a new era: that of the Hip-Hop soul diva who skillfully blends R&B soul melodies with gritty urban beats. While many credit Mary J. Blige and Puff Daddy with the creation of Hip-Hop soul—Mary J. Blige's *What's the 411?* was the first complete album with R&B lyrics over Hip-Hop beats throughout the entire album—her predecessor, Michel'le, shares some of the credit. Her career makes evident key elements of what constitutes a Hip-Hop soul diva. And her career and work helped lay the foundation for Mary J. Blige's success. The criteria includes the backing of a male rapper entourage, a rap record label, and the influence of men producers largely known for their work in the field of rap. In Michel'le's case, the entourage includes her then labelmates Niggas With Attitudes (N.W.A.); they appear in her videos and set up the Hip-Hop soul diva as queen bee surrounded by a hive of men rappers. The record label for Michel'le's first album was the late Eazy E's Ruthless Records. The male influence is Dr. Dre—the producer of her album—and he can be heard rapping and talking throughout the various numbers. Indeed, the fact that her album was financed by Eazy E, a known womanizer with seven children by six different women, who is now deceased due to complications from AIDS, and produced by the woman-beater Dr. Dre, who attacked rap video hostess Dee Barnes and was rumored to be the cause of Michel'le performing at concerts with black eyes, calls forth many questions about the way a woman rises to the top of a male-dominated field such as rap. Michel'le's on again, off-again career is also a testament to how hard it can be.

The acclaimed queen of Hip-Hop soul, Mary J. Blige, started out with a slew of male rappers and singers as part of her entourage but has since gotten rid of the men who surrounded her early in her career. Perhaps this is why her career has outlasted Michel'le's. Many of Blige's early songs and remixes feature men rappers, not women rappers. Her first label, Uptown Records, started as a largely rap label but found more success with Hip-Hop soul acts such as Jodeci and herself. In fact, Blige, like Jodeci, got her start singing backup for Uptown rap artist Father MC. The producer of her first two double platinum albums, *What's the 411?* and *My Life,* Sean "Puffy" Combs, got his start at Uptown and now has his own rap label, Bad Boy Records. Puffy, like Dr. Dre on Michel'le's album, can be heard talking throughout Blige's entire album, and he and his Bad Boy rappers are in many of the videos from the *My Life* album. Former Bad Boy rappers such as Craig Mack and the late Biggie Smalls rapped on many of Mary J. Blige's early remixes.

Similar to Michel'le, Blige's career reveals how a dominant male influence can sometimes overshadow the accomplishments of women in the world of Hip-Hop. Numerous magazine articles about Blige mention Combs's role in shaping, molding, and creating her, as if she were a lump of clay and not an extraordinarily talented woman. There is also evidence of mental if not physical abuse. In several interviews Blige talks about getting rid of all the negative people and negative influences around her because the men she was working with made her feel bad about herself.[25] "I had a lot of people around me who were trying to hurt me—who were able to hurt me because I couldn't see that I meant something. Now my family is more involved in my career. There's nothing but love surrounding me. I don't allow anything else."[26] She also says, "[W]hen you love people, you don't wanna let them go because you love them. It's hard to let them go—family members, boyfriends, girlfriends—but you just gotta because if you keep them around, they'll drain you and try to hold you back. You gotta cut them off, because it's important. I'm important to me now."[27] Mary J. Blige started out as the classic ghetto girl with an attitude. She has evolved into a spiritual person who values herself and her life more than the things she almost let destroy her, namely, men and drugs. She speaks so openly and honestly about the things she believes that she has become a voice for young women in the Hip-Hop generation.

Mary J. Blige has undeniable talent, as Joan Morgan notes in her interview with her, "Hail Mary." Blige offers a different kind of blues that caters to a Hip-Hop generation devastated by crack, AIDS, and Black-on-Black violence. Her voice offers the reality of a ghetto that is simultaneously beautiful and ugly. And Blige can be credited with bringing the entire Hip-Hop generation back to R& B.[28] Even renowned Hip-Hop activist Sister Souljah recognizes Blige's talent and what she brings to the Hip-Hop community. Sister Souljah credits Blige for the issues she brings to public attention about the state of Black communities in her lyrics, and notes that Blige brings to light the real implications of our future if we continue to lose sight of love and family. Although Sister Souljah notes that Mary J. Blige is not a revolutionary in the tradition of Harriet Tubman or Angela Davis, she has managed to accomplish in her music what other divas have not: she stayed true to herself. She sang in her own rough voice and opened up her own bruised heart to the world. "[S]he pronounced her words in unashamed Black English and she danced her un-choreographed unladylike steps with class."[29]

Mary J. Blige represents the average Black woman from the projects who shared her message with the world through song, managed to get her voice heard, and in doing so brought wreck to the glamorous notions and stereotypes of the recording industry. She also helped make it possible for other young Black women to share their voices. Blige has basically paved the way for other Hip-Hop soul divas such as Sisters with Voices (SWV), Xscape, Total, Adina Howard, Monifah, and Faith Evans. And she offers many women born and raised on Hip-Hop a representation of Black womanhood they can relate to. Former Uptown president Andre Harrell sums her up best when he says, "[H]er interpretation of soul has given women in the inner-city pride. She took the girl from around the way and made her something cool to be."[30]

Mary J. Blige's music becomes the outlet of expression for many of the wants and needs of young Black women. Dyson aptly notes the strength of Blige's voice and music in relation to Hip-Hop culture when he compares her to Aretha Franklin. While Blige represents the gritty explicitness of Hip-Hop culture, he finds that Blige and Franklin are saying similar things in different ways. "Blige's hip-hop soul feminism seeks 'real love.' But it remakes edifying love confessions into gut-wrenching pleas of faithfulness. It makes self-love the basis of loving others. And it bitterly, defiantly refuses to accept sexual infidelity."[31] In interview after interview Blige offers advice on relationships and love to her fans. She stresses the importance of self-love and of staying away from abusive relationships. "I believe in love. I believe good relationships do exist, but you've got to have a love affair with yourself first and really know yourself from the inside out before you can have a good relationship with a man or anyone else."[32] It is as if through her music and her interviews, especially the later ones, Blige is trying to heal a generation and open them up for the possibilities of love.

There is really no other artist to use as a guide when coming up with questions about love that are relevant for the Hip-Hop generation. No other soul artist has had such an enormous impact on the Hip-Hop generation. Her Hip-Hop understanding of the yearning for love can clearly be seen in her first two albums. In her songs "Real Love" and "Be Happy" we get a glimpse of what the Hip-Hop soul diva is looking for in a mate. In "Real Love" Blige sings about wanting a lover who will satisfy her every need and give her inspiration and real love.[33] In "Be Happy" she questions how she can love anyone else without loving herself enough to leave when things are not going right in the relationship. She sings about finding a love that belongs only to her and being happy.[34] At first glance, Blige's requests seem simple: love and happiness. But anyone familiar with the lyrics of Al Green knows to wait a minute. The questions may appear simple, but can the Hip-Hop lover love? Can he make her happy? The notion of "real love" is not that uncomplicated. What is real love to a Hip-Hop soul diva? What can we find in the lyrics of rap love songs that testify to the fulfillment of every need? Are the love needs expressed by Hip-Hop soul divas different from those of other women in mainstream America?

In the introduction to her book *Wild Women Don't Wear No Blues,* Marita Golden notes that Black girls of every class and complexion grow up believing that there are no Prince Charmings in their neighborhoods. Golden questions the possibility of love existing without fairy tales, because in our society the two, fairy tales and love, are so intimately connected.[35] I think it is important to note that society has indeed made fairy tales and love inseparable. And because living in and taking part in mainstream society influences Hip-Hop divas and indeed all Black women, various versions of the fairy tale do exist. The success of novels such as Terry McMillan's *Waiting to Exhale* attests to some Black women's need to find Mr. Right. Assuming that Black women do not believe in and internalize mainstream images of love and romance promotes essentialist notions of Blackness that claim romantic love does not affect or is not important to Black people.[36] An example of a young Black woman's view of the fairy tale comes from Lesley D. Thomas:

> I know gangsta bitches that believe in princes and shining armor. Like them, I interpret "hard-core" as an earned status qualifying Black men to rescue Black women from all this pain and bullshit. The desire to be freed is not a result of being weary and worn. And no, fantasizing as a Black woman is not unrealistic. . . . Hoes, tramps, bitches, whatever, we want our men, at home, being fathers and lovers— not making excuses and angry babies.[37]

Clearly some Black women, to quote Julia Roberts in *Pretty Woman,* "want the fairy tale." It might be a slightly different fairy tale, but it is a fairy tale all the same, with heterosexual relationships, "real" love and happiness, being saved from a life of strife, a man at home being a father and a lover, and living happily ever after. This same need is echoed in the writing of dream hampton, who decided to spell her name in lowercase letters like her feminist role model bell hooks. Like Thomas, hampton envisions a future with a Black man who would marry her and give her beautiful brown babies.[38] The political implications are important to note. Given the lack of clarity on gender roles, these dreams of heterosexual romance hint at a firmly established patriarchy—indeed, what comes to mind are the dreams of the normal bourgeois family described by Habermas, where all the necessities of life are met. However, these descriptions of strong Black male female relationships also offer possibilities for a united struggle against oppression; a divided house cannot stand, but Black men and women united offers other alternatives. Perhaps a way to use this vision as a base without reinventing the patriarchy would be to do so with what Michele Wallace calls "black feminism with a nationalist face." Black women and men would need to look at their relationship as working together against oppression and not as men being the head of the family.

With the Hip-Hop soul diva's (and, by extension, Hip-Hop culture's) unique relationship to love in mind, I turn now to the songs of the rapping lovers. What kind of rapping lover do we find in the lyrics of rap love songs? What does the man say about himself? What, finally, is the potential for a meaningful productive dialogue, let alone a relationship with the man we find? What happens when we really begin to critique and explore the love that hate produced?

Love and Happiness? Critiquing the Love That Hate Produced

Third-wave feminist cultural critic Joan Morgan gives a probing reason for her continuing to listen to and grapple with rap music.

She maintains that she exposes herself to the sexism of rappers like Snoop Doggy Dogg and the Notorious B.I.G. as a move toward understanding who her brothers really are as people. She listens as a Black woman and a feminist so that she can be clear about what she is dealing with.[39]

I believe that rap love songs can tell us things about what Black men and women of the Hip-Hop generation have to deal with as they seek to build relationships with each other. Two of the songs on the late Biggie Smalls's debut album, *Ready to Die,* can be classified as rap love songs, although they are very different models of love songs.[40] "Me and My Bitch" is an ode to a deceased girlfriend that begins with Sean "Puffy" Combs and an unidentified woman having a discussion. Puffy asks the woman if she would kill for him. The woman hesitates and then responds in the affirmative. He then questions what took her so long to answer, to which she replies she does not know. Puffy then asks, "What the fuck wrong with you bitch?"[41] In the background, Biggie says, "The act of making love, ha ha . . ." Instead of a sung chorus on this cut, there is Puffy and the woman's discussion. At the end of each of Biggie's stanzas we are taken back to the talking couple. It is through the dialogue between lovers that we get our first glimpse of the rapping lover and what kind of lover he wants. "Would you kill for me?" he asks in the first chorus. "Would you ever fuck around on me?" he asks in the second chorus. It would appear that the rapping lover wants a faithful woman who would kill for him.

We get a clearer picture in the lyrics of Biggie Smalls. Is the fairy-tale lover desired by the Hip-Hop soul divas and Black women present here? Biggie lets us know that moonlit strolls are not his thing. And while he admits that he will treat women right if they behave the way he wants them to, he also acknowledges that he will beat them if they do not.[42] And what does Biggie have to say about the possibility for marriage and beautiful brown babies? Biggie asserts that his notion of a wife does not include rings and traditional marriage, but rather involves "main squeeze" status and a set of keys to his home.[43] So what makes this a love song? Besides Biggie paying homage to his "main squeeze" and "best friend" and in spite of the constant repetition of "Just me and my bitch, me and my bitch" throughout the song, the song gives an insightful look at a relationship between a young thug and hustler and his woman, trying to survive in postindustrial New York City—a city with few opportunities for Black people.

However, what really makes the song problematic is that while giving respect to the woman who lost her life because she was murdered in order to get to him, Biggie's "love" for her is defined solely by all the things she did for him and how she made him feel as a man. Undoubtedly it is her love that's the "real" love in this rap love song, a love she dies for. He loves her because she loves him. She helps him in his drug business by bagging up marijuana for him, while he admits he was unfaithful. And he did not have to worry about her telling the authorities about him, because she loved him broke or rich. Even though Biggie raps, "And then we lie together, cry together I swear to God I hope we fucking die together," he is the one who lives to rap about it, because she is killed by men seeking revenge against him.[44]

We get an even clearer picture of the kind of rapping lover Biggie is in his song "One More Chance," which features his then-estranged wife, Hip-Hop soul diva Faith Evans, singing the background chorus. This song is different from "Me and My Bitch" because of its use of Hip-Hop soul. However, just as in "Me and My Bitch," the woman is doing all the loving. The song starts with Faith singing a remixed version of the 1980s group DeBarge's "Stay with Me." The chorus is sung in the same melody. This use of the R&B classic is an example of what Russell Potter calls "sonic signifying"—rap's sampling of other Black music forms—and thus sets up a dialogue across generations in Black music. The use of an old-school love song provides familiarity for the listener; it is "repetition with a difference; the same and yet not the same."[45] Sonic signifying helps give the rap love song validity as a love song.

During the chorus Biggie can be heard repeating that he has the good love.[46] But what exactly is his good love? What picture of the rapping lover are we viewing in "One More Chance"? Biggie's lyrics offer some insight. He raps about the many women he has sex with. He raps about how he will essentially have sex with any kind of woman.[47] And he marvels over his own ability to attract and have sex with all these women because he describes himself as Black and ugly and not a heartthrob.[48] He brags about his player skills and his ability to steal another man's girl, because he is both member and president of the players' club.

While his lyrics may be viewed as simply boasting rap, it is important to look at and critique the things he chooses to boast about, his sexual prowess and promiscuity. This is not a stay-at-home, faithful kind of guy. However, what makes this a rap love song is that Biggie uses this boasting as a method to secure female companionship. He is wooing the ladies with promises of all he can do for them. He raps about how wonderful sex with him is and how deep he can go in order for women to have the kind of orgasm that their men cannot give them. He offers cruises, pearls, gator boots, crush linen, Cartier wrist wear with diamonds, luxury cars, diamond necklaces, and cell phones.[49] If fulfilling a woman's every need were based only on material things, Biggie would have been Mr. Wonderful. But somehow I think the love Mary J. Blige sings about is a little deeper than that. Judging Biggie by what he has said about himself in the two songs discussed (he's a womanizing, woman-beating thug who wants a "real bitch" who can take everything he puts out, who would kill and die for him), what does this say or mean to the woman who would love him?

Method Man's Grammy-award-winning "I'll Be There for You/You're All I Need," featuring Mary J. Blige, is perhaps a more hopeful example of love in Hip-Hop. And it offers perhaps a somewhat better picture of the rapping lover. However, Method Man displays more similarities with Biggie than differences. Even though it has been acclaimed as a classic rap love song and has won several music awards—not to mention high praise and accolades from Black women, who cried out, "Finally, a rapper rapping about loving and being with one woman"—"I'll Be There For You/You're All I Need" still has room for critique.

Like Biggie's "One More Chance," "I'll Be There for You/You're All I Need" makes use of sonic signifying by its use of Marvin Gaye and Tammi Terrell's Motown classic. This use of a classic love song places them in a larger tradition of Black love songs and validates "I'll Be There for You/You're All I Need" as a love song.

It also creates a space for dialogue across generations. This dialogue is jokingly hinted at in the Coca-Cola commercial where an older Black man turns on the Gaye and Terrell version and sits down to enjoy his Coke only to be interrupted by the booming bass of his teenage son upstairs, who is also enjoying a Coke but bopping to the Method Man and Mary J. Blige version of the song. The possibility for dialogue is stifled, however, when the angry father bangs on the ceiling with a broom as if to say, "Turn down that noise." The Coca-Cola commercial sets the scene for possible conversations between younger and older generations, and sonic signifying is the rapper's first move toward such a dialogue.

I will focus on the Puff Daddy razor mix here because it has a hypnotizing rap beat and a longer second stanza by Method Man. I believe that while this is truly a sweet and gripping urban love song, it does not quite fill the model of what the Hip-Hop soul divas and many Black women are looking for. As with Biggie's "Me and My Bitch," we get the sense that the love expressed in "I'll Be There for You" is more a description of her love, and he loves her because she loves him. For example, Method Man raps about her making him feel like somebody even before he became a star, and notes that he loves her because she did so. He makes it known that because she was with him through the bad times, she has shown herself to be real and true. He also warns her not to give her sex away and to keep her vagina tight for him.[50] The love that's "real" to the rapping lover in this song is the same kind of put-up-with-everything love expressed in "Me and My Bitch." And interestingly enough, a sample from Biggie's "Me and My Bitch" is used as a second chorus in the song. In addition to Mary J. Blige singing the Motown classic, we have Biggie's lyrics: "lie together, cry together, I swear to God I hope we fucking die together." As an answer to that we have Mary J. Blige's soulful lyrics, "I'll sacrifice for you, dedicate my life to you." We get the sense that, like Biggie's bitch, she is the one who gives the ultimate love, sacrificing her life for him.

Again, if we keep in mind the questions about love and the fairy-tale-like qualifications that were discussed earlier, Method Man shares a lot of answers with Biggie. In response to the husband question, he too makes it clear that rings and traditional wedding vows are not for him.[51] But in his favor, at least he professes to always be there for his woman and not go out tricking like Biggie. But just like Biggie in response to the romance question, Method Man lets us know that hugs, kisses, Valentine cards, and birthday wishes are romantic crap that he and his woman are far above.[52] I find it interesting that Method Man's rap ends with a request for her to show her love.

While the two express similar views on marriage and romance, they differ in matters of fidelity. Method Man feels that he does not have to shop around because he already has the best. And although they both express unromantic pet names for their women—Biggie's "bitch" and Method Man's "shorty," "boo," and "you my nigga"—Method Man's pet names show much more love. It is a high form of respect—"giving props"—to say "you my nigga" or "that's my nigga" in most Hip-Hop communities. And Method Man, unlike Biggie, expresses some elements of his love in the song—his mad love that he intends to share only with her.[53] One gets the feeling that this love goes deeper than the physical. As if to show this mad love, the video for "I'll Be There for You" shows Method Man getting evil looks from his girlfriend's mother, being hassled on the streets of New York, running from the cops, and a host of other things just to bring her a box of tampons. In the male mind that might just be the highest form of love. The possibility for a love that somewhat resembles what the Hip-Hop soul diva is looking for seems attainable with the man we find in Method Man's song. Maybe that's why "Real Love" songstress Mary J. Blige is singing the chorus.

"I'ma Stay Dat Bitch": Lil' Kim and Foxy Brown

The conversation in rap is complicated even more when we take the work of women rappers Foxy Brown (Inga Marchand) and Lil' Kim (Kimberly Jones) into consideration. Their songs work as a direct response to the lyrics of the men. They take on many of the characteristics that men rappers put forth. Lil' Kim becomes the bitch Biggie raps about. In fact, as the title of her song suggests, she is the "Queen Bitch." And the lyrics remind listeners that she will indeed "stay dat bitch." She has no plans of changing. It is clear that like Biggie's lost love, who would kill to save her lover's life, Lil' Kim would readily kill for her man. Some feel that the reclamation of the word *bitch*, like the reclamation of the word *nigger* or *nigga*, is an empowering act. Indeed, listening to the lyrics of Lil' Kim as she forcefully raps "I'ma stay dat bitch" exudes a certain sense of power. She comes off as a woman in control—assertive and sexually assured. She is tough, not someone to mess with. She re-creates herself as the bad Black momma from 1970s blaxploitation flicks. Not only is she sexy but she is tough; she will kill you if she has to.

In other songs Lil' Kim exhibits the same tough but sexy image. She raps about her sexual exploits. And like many of the men rappers, she uses boasting as a method. She raps explicitly about her sexual exploits and the things she is willing to do in order to be sexually satisfied. However, Lil' Kim is not about sex for the sake of sex alone. She reminds listeners that she likes to be compensated by her lover with money, jewelry, designer clothing, furs, and expensive cars. In her song "We Don't Need It" Lil' Kim raps about her desire for good sex, her irritation with men who cum too fast, and her ability to masturbate and please herself if the man is not giving her what she needs.[54] Lil' Kim's songs offer a woman who knows what she wants sexually—to experience pleasure and to cum—even if she has to satisfy herself.

The public image that Lil' Kim grants the listeners is of a strong, self-assured woman who knows what she wants and knows how to get it. That image also seemingly falls in line with the image of a woman that the rappers discussed earlier want. What is interesting in the case of Lil' Kim is that she has constructed dual and conflicting public images: the sexy, self-assured rapper that surfaces in her music and the vulnerable girl with low self-esteem that surfaces in her magazine interviews. Her parents spilt up when she was young, and her mother left her with an abusive father. She left home as a teenager and used men to support her. She has mentioned in interviews that she grew up thinking that she was not pretty. While she now believes she is beautiful because she has a beautiful heart, she still slips into self-consciousness about her looks: "[B]ut, like Halle Berry, Salli Richardson, Stacy Dash, Jada Pinkett Smith? I used to wish I looked like them motherfuckers!"[55]

The fact that each of these actresses is fair-skinned and has what is called in Black colloquial expression "good hair" should not be dismissed when thinking about Lil' Kim's desire to look like them. In fact, some might think that she has taken her desire to look like light-skinned, straight-haired Black women to another extreme, with her blond wigs and blue contacts. She also notes that "when I was young, I didn't feel like I got enough attention."[56] Because she left home when she was fifteen years old, Lil' Kim learned the art of tricking at a young age in order to keep a roof over her head. She talks about living with a man for eight months the first time she left home. "I had a Panamanian boyfriend. I thought he was just so cute. He had a lot of money because he was illegally involved. He was taking care of me and I was living with him."[57] Any critique of Lil' Kim, her sexualized image, and her explicit lyrics must take both of her public images into consideration. The things that come out in her interviews about her abusive father, relying on men for food and shelter, and not feeling pretty complicate our understanding of the things she says on wax and require that we look at her in a more critically engaged way.

Similarly, Foxy Brown expresses tough and sexy lyrics. Like Lil' Kim and Biggie's bitch, Foxy helps her man with his drug business. Like Lil' Kim and Biggie's bitch, she would kill and die for her niggas. In "Holy Matrimony" she raps about being married to her male crew, the Firm, and being willing to lie and die for them.[58] Foxy Brown and Lil' Kim fit very well into the image of Biggie's dearly departed bitch. But they appear to be bitches with agency. Foxy Brown, like Lil' Kim, is very expressive about her sexuality and very boastful about her sexual exploits. In "Get You Home" Foxy Brown lets men know exactly where to kiss her and how to get her excited sexually.[59] She boasts that she has no problem getting her "swerve on." Both of these women combine sex and materialism in their lyrics. Sex and money constitute the good life. Indeed the woman they construct would be more than happy with the man Biggie constructs in "One More Chance."

Like Lil' Kim, the public images that Foxy Brown puts out are dual and conflicting. In addition to the self-assured sexy rapper, in interviews we get the vulnerable Black girl with low self-esteem, a darker sister who did not feel pretty growing up. However, that is where the similarities between Foxy Brown and Lil' Kim end. Foxy Brown lived a fairly pampered life compared to Lil' Kim's homelessness, abusive father, and having to use men to keep a roof over her head. While her parents also split when she was young, she grew up having her wants and needs taken care of by her family. She did not have to trick to earn a living. There was no physical abuse in her family. She remembers, "[I]n our family, we said 'I love you' every night."[60]

Even though she felt nothing but love in her mother's home, she still yearned for her father. His absence influenced her relationships with men: "I thought it was normal for a guy to mistreat me. My father wasn't there to show me the right way."[61] She also grew up not feeling pretty because of her complexion: "My number one insecurity is being a dark female. If you take any beautiful dark-skinned sister nowadays, guys are like, 'Oh she's beautiful.' But back in the day, it was not the cool thing. That was just something I had to get over, because for a while I couldn't stand myself."[62] The estranged relationships with their fathers, ill-fated relationships with other Black men, and uncertainty of self-worth are things that Lil' Kim and Foxy Brown have in common. Their stories fit a lot of young women coming of age in an era of Hip-Hop, though to some extent these are age-old problems for Black girls. We could no doubt find some connections and similarities between their stories and the stories of the girls in the hood discussed earlier. And, like the girls in the hood, Lil' Kim's and Foxy Brown's stories beckon Black feminism to find more meaningful ways to intervene in the lives of young Black women.

Ultimately, behind the sex and glamour of their songs and public personas we see the public dialogue about love and relationships in Hip-Hop coming full circle. Just as the men rappers can be read in response to the Hip-Hop soul diva, Lil' Kim and Foxy Brown can be read in response to the men rappers. And while there were some questions about the men rappers presenting what the Hip-Hop soul diva wants, the same cannot be said of these women rappers. The representations of Black womanhood put forth by men rappers are internalized and surface in ways some view as problematic. The questions about Lil' Kim and Foxy Brown being too sexy, too raunchy, too pornographic, and so on have been addressed in every Black popular magazine currently in print. Along with these questions go the charges that Lil' Kim and Foxy Brown are puppets, victims of their male crews—the late Biggie Smalls, Junior Mafia, and Puff Daddy in Lil' Kim's case and Jay-Z, Nas, AZ, and Cormega in Foxy Brown's case. Some feel that because Biggie wrote some of Lil' Kim's lyrics and Jay-Z and Nas penned some of Foxy Brown's hits, these women are not legitimate rappers; their use of the word *bitch* in their lyrics is not an empowering act because a man wrote the lyrics, and they are not exploiting their own sexuality but rather are being exploited.

Angela Davis discusses this issue of agency and the woman performer in her work on the blues woman. In her discussion of Gertrude "Ma" Rainey and the song "Sweet Rough Man" Davis maintains that although the song was written by a man, Rainey's enthusiastic rendition rescued the issue of men's violence against women from the private sphere and gave the issue prominence as a public discourse.[63] For Davis the issue is not who wrote the song but how the women blues artists used them to bring women's issues into the public sphere. Even the blues woman's sexually frank lyrics are read as women taking control and having a stance that spoke to their freedom as sexual beings. Another example of the way a woman performer exhibits her own sense of agency when performing songs that were written by men can be seen in Aretha Franklin's "Respect." Otis Redding may have written the lyrics, but no one is going to question Franklin's strong presence or her agency when she sings the lyrics. She performs the lyrics so forcefully that the song has become an anthem for women's liberation.

Therefore, rather than labor the question of who is exploiting whom, I would like to look at all of the lyrics discussed as a fertile ground for dialogue and communication aimed at evoking change—at how the conflicting public images of Foxy Brown and Lil' Kim can be used to bring wreck and help destroy existing notions and stereotypes about Black womanhood and also help improve the lives of young Black women. Joan Morgan notes in her article "The Bad Girls of Hip-Hop" that when Hip-Hop is truly significant and meaningful it gives us images of Blackness that we refuse to see and dares us to get mad enough to do something about them.[64] What the conflicting images of Lil' Kim and Foxy Brown represent is clear if we choose to see it. They have based their womanhood and sexuality on the images that men rappers rapped about, just as I tried to be LL Cool J's "Around the Way Girl" many years ago. With no real constructive conversations going on about sex, Black female identity, and the shaping of public gendered subjects outside of the academy, their lyrics and images are inevitable. "[T]he success of these baby girls speaks volumes about the myth shrouding feminism, sex, and black female identity," writes Morgan.[65] The success of Lil' Kim and Foxy Brown is a direct result of a Black community consumed with saving the male and not about the problem facing young Black women. As Morgan points out, very few people are aware of or alarmed by the fact that Black girls growing up in America's inner cities, surrounded by violence and materialism, will suffer their own pathologies. She notes that Black women die disproportionately of AIDS, cancer, and drugs, that the female prison population is exploding, and that teenage pregnancy rates have skyrocketed for Black women. And she asks a very important question: "Is it really surprising that some female MCs (like their male counterparts) would decide to get paid by glamorizing that reality?"[66]

We are constantly bombarded with discourse about the situation of young Black men in America. And while that is a legitimate and worthwhile cause for concern, few are noticing that young Black women are living and trying to grow in the same oppressive environments as these young Black men. If the Black man is endangered, what about the Black woman? No one stops to ask. This neglect is the plight of the Black woman. It has been around since the days of the Black Power movement and definitely gained momentum with Daniel Patrick Moynihan's 1965 report on the Black family.[67] The stereotype of the strong Black woman, because we refuse to dismantle it, prevents us from seeing the very real danger that the lives of young Black women are in.

Lil' Kim's and Foxy Brown's lyrics help bring light to things once ignored. They can also help Black women face and maybe even get rid of some of the myths and stereotypes about Black women's sexuality and Black female identity that have existed in one form or another since the days of slavery and which continue to influence the way Black women live their lives and express themselves. The fear of being labeled sexually promiscuous or always sexually available plagues many Black women. It is a legacy passed down from generation to generation. Foxy Brown's and Lil' Kim's acknowledgment that they are sexual beings who enjoy sex, and lots of it, is hard to face when one is taught to be ashamed of such desire.

What these rappers offer is the opportunity to embrace the sexuality of the self. Their boldness does exhibit a kind of freedom. Ironically, it is this same freedom that exposes the myths surrounding feminism. Morgan suggests that "their success drives home some difficult truths. The freedom earned from feminist struggle is often a double-edged sword. Now that women are no longer restricted to the boundaries of gender expectations, there will be those who choose to empower themselves by making some less than womanist choices—and they are free to do so."[68] While I take issue with Morgan on the exact extent to which women have broken the boundaries, I do acknowledge the fact that women have far more choices today than they did thirty years ago.

I contend that the sexually explicit lyrics of these women rappers offer Black women a chance to face old demons and not let the stereotypes of slavery inform or control their lives. After years of Black women being read as supersexual—or asexual, in the case of the mammy stereotype—the lyrics of these women rappers offer Black women a chance to be proud of—and indeed flaunt—their sexuality. And, after the images of the Black bitch that have stilted assertiveness in Black women, it's almost nice to have a line such as "I'ma stay dat bitch." It does create a certain amount of agency.

In an era when men rappers are presenting problematic images of Black womanhood—ones that encourage the kind of "ride or die"/"kill a nigga for my nigga" mentality and an obsessive focus on sex, drugs, and materialism—we cannot simply cast aside artists such as Lil' Kim and Foxy Brown because they are not as positive as we would like them to be. The lifestyles that they rap about are a reality for some women, who were never told any different. The images young Black women get from contemporary Hip-Hop culture and rap music tell them that they should be willing to do anything for their men. The "ride or die" chick who will do anything and everything for her man is placed on a Hip-Hop pedestal as the ideal woman. From Ice Cube and Yo-Yo's "Bonnie and Clyde Theme" and "Bonnie & Clyde II" to Jay-Z and Beyoncé's "'03 Bonnie & Clyde," rap shows a warped obsession with remixing and remaking the tale of the white criminal couple who went out in a blaze of bullets. At first glance this appears to be just another obsession with gangster culture, but it is much more than that. The obsession with Bonnie and Clyde tells us a lot about the state of Black male-female relationships in America. Nowhere is this more telling than in Ja Rule's "Down Ass Bitch" and "Down 4 U."

The video of Ja Rule's "Down Ass Bitch" is very problematic. It is yet another video all about how women should stand by their men and be down for whatever. His rough voice croons, "Every thug needs a lady. Would you ride for me? Would you die for me?"[69] In the video Ja Rule and female rapper Charlie Baltimore remix the Bonnie and Clyde theme with Hip-Hop flavor. They rob the mansion of an unidentified rich person, taking a safe full of diamonds. However, before they can make off with the bag full of diamonds the alarm sounds and they try to escape. Charlie Baltimore is caught. The cops really want Ja Rule, but she, being a "good bitch" and a "down ass chick," does not snitch. She does the time. We see her in her prison-issue orange jumpsuit. She goes from being scared to running the other women prisoners. She becomes a survivor in jail. We see her pushing around the very women who pushed her around when she first entered the prison. When she is released, presumably years later, Ja Rule picks her up. All is well. The message that this video sends to young women, specifically to young Black women, is very troubling because it essentially tells young women that it is okay to commit crimes for their men. It tells them that even if they spend time in jail, it is okay because it will pay off in the end when their man picks them up from jail in a luxury car and flies them off to a remote island to lavish them with tropical drinks and beautiful clothes. The video tells young women that the only way to obtain material possessions is to let some man use them to commit crime and then depend on him for their reward.

The fastest-growing prison population in this country is Black women. They are going to jail for things like smuggling drugs, largely because of their relationships with men who are involved with criminal activities. The recently pardoned Kemba Smith simply fell in love with the wrong man and was too afraid to leave. She recounts, "At age 24, without so much as a parking ticket on my record, I was sentenced to more than 24 years in prison—without parole. Technically, I was convicted of conspiracy to distribute crack cocaine, but I contend that I went to jail for dating a drug dealer."[70] She was finally pardoned as a last-minute act by President Clinton, but she still feels that justice was not served. "You'd think I'd have been doing cartwheels when I was released. Truthfully, my feelings were in conflict. It was tough to leave behind the incredible women I met in prison—especially since many of them were victims of the same laws that put me away."[71]

Of another woman, who like Kemba Smith (and the others still in jail) did time for drug-related crimes, dream hampton writes that she "used to be so fly, the first girl in Detroit with her own Benz. Candy-apple red and convertible, with customized plates that spelled CASH. She bought red boots to match. . . . She liked to make the trip back then. She could drive all the way without stopping (he never did like to drive long distances), but he'd keep her awake with promises about the next forty years."[72] This woman, like Charlie Baltimore in Ja Rule's video, did not snitch on her man. "She's proud of the fact that she never snitched. Doesn't seem suspicious that he served 18 months, went home, and has forgotten to put money on her books for the past ten years."[73] She brags that "little girls like [Lil'] Kim are rhyming about her life."[74] However, the Black female prison population is rising because of stories like these—because of the messages young women are getting from the videos.

Ja Rule's message to women about being a "down ass chick" would not be so bad if it was the only one. But the message is everywhere, and it's not just coming from men. Women rappers such as Lil' Kim and Foxy Brown also rap about the illegal things they would do for their men. And even though Alicia Keys's video for the hit single "Fallin'" somewhat flips the script on this message by having the woman out of jail and visiting the male inmate, the message of the song is eerily similar to those discussed above. She sings, "I keep on fallin' in and out of love with you. I'll never love no one the way I love you."[75] In the video we see a field of women in prison-issue orange jumpsuits—mostly Black and Latina—singing the lyrics. Instead of falling in and out of love with these men, the young Black women need to love themselves. They need to love themselves enough to recognize that no love is worth going to jail for.

The remix of "Down Ass Bitch," The Inc.'s "Down 4 U," is just as problematic as the first version. It features the entire The Inc. roster, Ja Rule, Ashanti, Charlie Baltimore, and Vita. The video is the typical beach-and-yacht party scene that most rap videos trying to showcase a rich and glamorous lifestyle take advantage of. The video has lots of bikinis and objectified women. The video also ironically features a cameo appearance by the contemporary R&B incarnation of Bonnie and Clyde, Whitney Houston and Bobby Brown. There are no robberies and prisons, just lots of fun and frolicking in the sun and lots of people living the glamorous life on the beach. The carefree nature of the video is what makes it even more problematic than the video for "Down Ass Chick." Combined with the lyrics, the video sends a false message to young Black women about love, life, and money.

The down-ass chick is both an image and a reality that Black feminism needs to deal with. It has a lot of Black women serving time and countless others taking incredible risks with their lives. It is the inevitable conclusion of a community that does not value Black womanhood. Joan Morgan offers the perceptive observation that Foxy Brown's and Lil' Kim's success reflects Black feminism's lack in teaching younger Black women about sex, feminism, and power. For both Morgan and myself, Black feminism needs to be accountable to young Black women, saving their lives and widening their worldview and the choices they feel they can make.[76]

In order to accomplish this—in order to reach the young Black women—feminism needs to come down from its ivory tower. Young Black women, like it or not, are getting their life lessons from rap music. And because voices like Queen Latifah, Salt-N-Pepa, and Queen Pen are few and far between, it's up to Black feminism to pick up the slack. In short, there are many ways that Black feminism can begin to work with Hip-Hop. The first step is recognizing the tremendous possibilities Hip-Hop culture and rap music have to offer.

You Can't See Me/You Betta Recognize: Using Rap to Bridge Gaps in the Classroom

Rap and Hip-Hop culture offer many political possibilities for bringing people of various backgrounds together and for effecting change. The youth that created the culture in the midst of urban decline and postindustrial urban neglect found a way to create something out of nothing; they created a form of music and developed a culture that today expands far beyond that original audience in the South Bronx. As Tricia Rose notes, middle-class and upper-middle-class white consumers make up a significant percentage of the buying audience for rap music.[1] And Chuck D notes that rap music is worldwide; youth all over the world are learning the English language—specifically the Black vernacular—so that they can follow the lyrics of their favorite rappers.[2] Rap is the music of today's youth all over the world; it is their rock and roll. But more than rock and roll, rap has the potential to effect change and bring wreck in meaningful ways. Because of rap's diverse population of listeners, it has the possibility to cross boundaries of race, sex, gender, sexuality, nationality, and class.

Indeed, because rap crosses so many dividing lines, it is the sound track of today's youth. And I believe that rap, as a successful crossover genre, has an enormous potential for effective teaching, bridging gaps and maneuvering contact zones. Because such a large majority of rap's consumers are white middle-class youth and many African American, Latino, and Chicano youth claim ownership of the music and the culture, meaningful conversations about race, class, the effects of capitalism, commodification, and co-optation can occur. As Angela Ards notes in "Rhyme and Resist: Organizing the Hip Hop Generation," rap's ability to move the crowd has the possibility to do more than make them dance; it could very well be used to spark political activism.[3]

I maintain that rap has untapped potential that can be unleashed in the classroom, and so here I expand on the possibilities for using rap in the fight against sexism by combining the theories discussed earlier with actual classroom practice. I examine the use of rap music and third-wave/Black feminist theories in a race- and gender-diverse critical reading and intensive writing course entitled "Introduction to Women's Studies" that I taught at a small midwestern university in Ohio. Since the class of thirty-five was almost evenly split in regard to gender and also had six Black students, four of whom were men, I believe the class offers an ideal space to observe the ways in which rap influences diverse groups of people as they grapple with difficult issues such as race, class, and gender and their intersections; as students' ideas about difference surface in their writing about rap; and as they reach beyond those ideas, disrupt previously held ideas about race, class, gender, and sexuality, and begin to bridge gaps.

Part of the students' ability to bridge gaps comes from their active participation in the classroom as a "protopublic." In "From Writers, Audiences, and Communities to Publics: Writing Classrooms as Protopublic Spaces," Rosa Eberly contends that viewing the classroom as a protopublic space encourages students to realize themselves as participants in multiple, different, and overlapping publics, and this realization can help them examine and ultimately experiment with the situated nature of rhetoric which requires specific needs for effective writing.[4] She feels that thinking of the classroom tasks we perform as public processes allows students to begin to recognize themselves as participants in the public space. In Eberly's protopublic space, classroom activities such as thinking, talking, and writing about different publics allows students to practice public discourse and form different overlapping publics.[5] While Eberly does not think that classrooms can be true public spheres because of institutional constraints, she does believe that students and teachers can create and enter real-world discourse in the classroom.[6] Viewing the classroom as a protopublic space and allowing students to address difference through various language acts allows them to see both the social aspects and the process aspects of reading and writing. And "classrooms understood as protopublic spaces allow teachers and students to engage in education as the praxis of public life, widely defined."[7] The classroom then becomes a space in which students engage in building a public sphere and a place for them to practice working with difference.

Rap in the classroom gives students an example of a cultural space where public dialogue and debate are occurring from the inside and the outside. In addition to the public outcry and moral panic rap provokes in some listeners, rap also looks inward and takes issues with itself. Because of rap, issues such as misogyny, sexism, and violence have become matters of public concern and debate. It is one medium for putting these kinds of issues on the table. As Mark Costello and David Foster Wallace note, rap is both self-conscious and radical and as such is well equipped to break apart the racial, political, sexual, and economic prejudices that listeners bring when they hear rap.[8] Rap then becomes a tool to help students think about diversity of voices in a variety of ways: in terms of rap's diverse audience, issues of debate and controversy, the diversity of the class itself, and the variety of ideas each student has on the subject. Students can use rap to evaluate and possibly bring wreck to their own ideas about difference and possibly change their ideas and society as well.

In my women's studies class, I wanted students to explore the Black feminist critiques and begin to make their own observations. The readings I offered had common themes dealing with rap, gender, and sexuality. The students were asked to stake out their own opinions with those items in mind. Given the nature of the course and my desire to teach for change, my students were told to also be mindful of the ways they could make a difference in the situations we discussed. I wanted students to use rap and the critiques of rap music to develop an awareness of the world outside of their immediate surroundings.

Pedagogical Issues

Clearly, Black women in academia have been thinking and writing about pedagogy since they first entered American classrooms during the days of Reconstruction. For Barbara Omolade, Black feminist pedagogy is not only about Black women teaching Black women about other Black women. It also offers learning strategies informed by and ultimately linked to Black women's historical struggles with race, class, and gender biases as well as their experiences with marginalization and isolation. Black feminist pedagogy "offers the student, instructor, and institution a methodology for promoting equality and multiple visions and perspectives that parallel black women's attempts to be and become recognized as human beings and citizens rather than as objects and victims."[9] Omolade's ideas about Black feminist pedagogy show an understanding that Black feminist pedagogy—indeed, Black feminist struggle—can be used as a tool to construct a better world. She realizes that students— white, Black, male, and female—can learn something from the ways Black women have struggled to have their voices heard and to be recognized as citizens.

Her sentiments about Black women and how their status in society can be used to instruct and empower students put a slightly different slant on feminists such as the Combahee River Collective and Anna Julia Cooper. The Combahee River Collective asserted that "[i]f black women were free, it would mean that everyone else would have to be free since our freedom would necessitate the destruction of all systems of oppression."[10] Years before their statement, however, Anna Julia Cooper wrote, "Only the black woman can say when and where I enter in the quiet undisputed dignity of my womanhood, without violence and without suing or special patronage, then and there the whole Negro race enters with me."[11]

In each of these instances it is clear that true freedom for all could reside in the freedom of Black women from the interlocking forms of oppression that inhibit them. It would logically follow, then, that Black feminist pedagogy has liberatory potential.

Omolade is an activist teacher and understands the power that college teachers have in the classroom. She identifies three core issues that should inform how we all think about and approach Black feminist pedagogy: "the clarification of the source and use of power within the classroom, the development of a methodology for teaching writing skills, and the need for instructors to struggle with their students for a better university."[12] She believes in being up-front with her students about power dynamics. She tries to maintain a balance that gives students a significant amount of agency. She holds that writing and literacy are important skills we give our students. And she believes we need to push students and ourselves to effect change. The classroom setting and the goals that I tried to accomplish in my "Introduction to Women's Studies" classroom can best be described by the three contexts that guide Omolade. I practiced the feminist model of a decentered classroom and tried to have power move as much as possible.

Rappers use the term "power moves" to describe the actions taken to better one's position in life. The committee that developed the Power Moves Hip-Hop Conference at UCLA maintains "that power does not stand still; in fact, power moves on a regular basis. And in a society such as ours, art often challenges various systems of power and influences public opinion."[13] As the instructor, I of course held the majority of the power in the classroom; it would be naive of me to suggest otherwise. However, students with the ultimate goal of bettering their positions in life were in a sense making power moves.[14] I wanted my students to experience what Adrienne Rich calls "claiming an education," to take responsibility for their learning.[15] In that regard, a large part of the power indeed rested with them. I also used group presentations and student-led class discussions as another method of sharing class power and allowing students the opportunity to aid in structuring the classroom proto-public.

Another element that informed the classroom discussion and the way the students related to the information was my physical presence as a Black woman instructor. Because I was blessed with knowledge of Cheryl Johnson's and Shirley Wilson Logan's work on their experiences as Black women teachers in predominantly white classrooms, I was able to maintain an awareness of students' reactions to the class materials and my physical presence. Thus I tried to prevent any instance where my presence as a Black woman could stifle conversation or growth. This, of course, was not always fully accomplished, and could not be. But, given the things my students felt comfortable saying in class—things that I know I did not always want to hear—I would say the students felt comfortable and did not hold their tongues because of my presence. In fact, during a class discussion in which we talked about minority groups reclaiming the negative words that oppressors used to define them, I heard the word *nigger* come out of quite a few white mouths— several times. While I do not pretend to know if that is good or bad, I do know that they felt free enough to use the word in my presence.

Both Logan and Johnson write quite eloquently about what it is like for Black women to teach Black texts to a classroom full of white faces. Johnson's questions—"How, then, can students refigure the black woman in their consciousness? And how are they to read the African-American texts in the presence of this African-American female body?"—informed the way I taught Black texts in class.[16] I realized, as Logan does, that "tensions surrounding black women who teach in predominantly white institutions might be converted into catalysts for change."[17] She also notes that "difference can be a force for change. Yet it would be naive to think that the simple presence of a Black female teacher guarantees change."[18] Both Logan and Johnson note that the space they navigate as Black women in the academy is a tricky one, and what they are able to accomplish with their students is contingent upon their navigation of that space.

The views of the students in "Introduction to Women's Studies" on rap music and Hip-Hop culture were largely shaped by the things they had read, heard, or seen on MTV. For some, the only recollection they could gather about the music and the culture was the media and other attacks on gangsta rap. Some also had the media images of slain rappers Tupac Shakur and Biggie Smalls in their minds. Though young white teenagers make up the majority of rap's consumers, I had students in the class who did not listen to rap and who voiced their opinions on the music's negativity. These students also attached their own ideas about Blackness and Black culture to the music. There were also white students who listened to the music, but it was their only link to Black cultural practices; thus they were getting all their ideas about Black people from the contemporary rap CDs in their collection. Their own experiences did not provide them with a context for the music or even the things that the Black feminists wrote about the music.

Viewing the classroom as a public space in which to grapple with, discuss, and write about these wide and varied experiences and connections to rap music and Hip-Hop culture can open the floor for other possibilities. The combination of the classroom as public space, Black feminist pedagogy, and rap music grants students the opportunity to see and recognize things they might not in other classroom situations. "You can't see me" is a Hip-Hop boast that touts how wonderful and superb the person doing the boasting is. Its translation is "I am so fantastic that others do not come close," that is, close enough to see. "You betta recognize" is a Hip-Hop warning that cautions the hearer to have respect for the person giving the warning. When combined, the two convey that rap in the classroom is a rich tool that we would do well to value and make use of.

Discussing rap music and Hip-Hop culture in the class allowed students to explore sexism in popular culture as well as the race and class issues that sexism is connected to. Rap provoked a discussion that went beyond the dismissive "This is sexist, therefore this is bad" response. It complicated the discussion and disrupted dismissive attitudes. And rap, more than any rock song, MTV alternative video, cartoon, or real-sex talk show, offered the perfect way into discussions on intriguing intersections of race, class, and gender that I felt would spark the passionate and lively debates I desired. It was also a form of music I believed all my students had strong feelings about.

Rap has the power to make people love or hate it, even sometimes without knowing the first thing about it. One white male student wrote, "I love rap music. My CD collection is made up of mostly rap and R&B." A white female student wrote, "I fervently condemn all forms of misogyny, rap music is not an exception. I cannot understand how any woman would support such an obtrusive form of sexism." Responses such as these are exactly why it is a wonderful classroom tool. The controversy provides a significant amount of fuel for intellectually rigorous discussion.

By the time we reached the part of the syllabus dealing with rap music, my students had already been exposed to some rap music in class. During a group presentation by five of the six African-American students in the class on the objectification of women in the media, the students listened to some rap lyrics by rapper Too Short. This rapper is known for his sexually explicit lyrics and the raw and raunchy way he discusses the female body, not to mention the way he brags and boasts about certain parts of his own anatomy. Some of the students were shocked at the content of the Too Short songs, while others owned copies of Too Short's CDs and liked his music. One student wrote, after reading the course articles on rap,

> In one of our presentations, the group played rap music and I must say this was probably the first time I ever heard lyrics like that. At first play, I was quite offended. . . . The images this music portrayed of women as hoes, bitches, etc. were more than I could handle. However, after reading these articles my opinion has slightly changed.

I did not have the goal of changing students' opinion about rap. However, I did aim to provide students with a space to open their minds to other possibilities that differ from the ones they held and to disrupt each other's realities through reading, writing, and critiquing. This student's response shows how the class readings prompted the students to think and re-think the things that happened in class and their own likes and beliefs.

You Can't See Me: Seeing Black Women as Agents of Their Own Sexuality

During our class discussion, I played various songs from women rappers such as Salt-N-Pepa, Queen Latifah, Lil' Kim, and Foxy Brown. I wanted the discussion to include female constructions of identity in addition to the objectification and exploitation we discussed in the male lyrics. Considering female constructions of identity and sexuality provides an alternative tool for critiquing and discussing the sexism in rap music. It takes us out of the "sexism–Black male–bad" space and into a space where women rappers have some agency and voice.[19] As cultural critic Tricia Rose points out, "Black women rappers affirm black female popular pleasure and public presence by privileging black female subjectivity and black female experiences in the public sphere."[20] Rose also emphasizes that the Black female rappers offer varied and sometimes contradictory stances in terms of Black womanhood, feminism, and Black women's sexuality. And she problematizes the woman rapper's entrance into the public sphere—especially when it is linked to the woman rapper objectifying her own sexuality. My students found the focus on female rap lyrics useful and wrote about them in their response papers. One Black female student wrote:

> There have been countless arguments on the debate of whether or not the degradation of women can be blamed on rap music, and how American history has plagued us with stereotypes and internal conflict that has played out as a continuum that has poisoned our minds. However, men can no longer be viewed as the only offenders. Recently we have seen female rappers such as Lil' Kim and Foxy Brown step onto the scene and play such roles. They have changed the direction of what some may describe as the women's movement in music that was created by such artists as Queen Latifah, who talked about gaining respect from men. Instead they flaunt their sexuality in a raunchy and somewhat obscene manner. Are these new female rappers re-

claiming their sexuality or taking the feminist movement back 20 years?

This student's response offers an example of the Black feminist outrage against Foxy Brown and Lil' Kim. She was, however, able to begin to question whether the two women rappers were doing something positive in reclaiming their sexuality. The readings and class discussion provided her with a space to open her mind and bring wreck to initial knee-jerk reactions that dismiss without dialogue and critical inquiry. This student's writing also offered an example of the way Black women have been conditioned to think about their sexuality. She noted the historical past of U.S. racism and sexism as it applies to and still haunts Black women. And the fact that she's such a young woman showing this kind of uneasiness with sexual expression gives credence to the unrelenting hold of slavery's past—at no point in United States history have Black women known a true place of freedom from these issues.

These sorts of discussions and questions allowed students to experience the kind of joy in learning that bell hooks discusses in *Teaching to Transgress*. And it also gave them an experience of ecstasy when they exchanged information and learned from one another, making the classroom itself a space for critical thinking.[21] I practiced engaged pedagogy because I believe, as hooks does, that critical thinking can potentially lead to change, and if we are able to think critically about our lives and ourselves we will be able to progress in meaningful ways toward change.[22] As hooks notes, even if the classroom has some limitations, it is still a space of possibility in which we can work toward freedom. We can demand open minds from each other, allowing us to face the realities in front of us and imagine ways to transgress boundaries together.[23] So no matter what my students started out thinking about rap music, I hoped that by engaging with the articles, music, and one another we could move beyond those thoughts. In fact, I hoped that we would wreck the boundaries that inhibited critical thinking.

Through the music of women rappers, articles, and class discussions, the students were able to see how intersections of race, class, and gender inform our readings of popular culture. After listening to the songs by the women rappers, they were able to discuss issues of self-commodification and female rappers embracing their sexuality. We also discussed women embracing terms once thought of as negative, such as Lil' Kim's and Foxy Brown's reclamation of the word *bitch*. We asked if Salt-N-Pepa's highly sexualized images and rap personas were that much different from those of Foxy Brown and Lil' Kim.[24] We also compared the co-rapped lyrics from Queen Latifah's and Monie Love's critically acclaimed women's anthem "Ladies First" (1989) with some of Foxy Brown's lyrics. Foxy Brown bragged about her "ill na na"—a slang term for vagina. And Monie Love bragged about making love and giving birth. Both placed a woman's power in her vagina. This inevitably led us to discussions of the madonna/whore dichotomy and discussions of positive/negative images. We explored why, in general, the concept of motherhood and giving birth is separated from the concept of sexual freedom and agency for women. We began to wreck commonly held ideas about the proper role for women. The class also discussed issues of authenticity and power, in reference to women rappers whose lyrics were written by men. And they grappled with the question of whether the words "I'ma stay dat bitch" hold power when they come from a woman's mouth but were written by a man. Were Lil' Kim's lyrics "clean bitch, murder scene bitch, disease free bitch" any less powerful and provocative coming out of her mouth because male rapper Biggie Smalls helped write the lyrics?[25] We went around in circles trying to answer that question and never came to a consensus. Some students felt Lil' Kim held the power because she spoke the lyrics and brought the image to life. Other students felt she was a puppet being used by the now-deceased male rapper.

After reading bell hooks's article "Gangsta Culture—Sexism and Misogyny: Who Will Take the Rap?" the students grappled with several questions: Are young Black male rappers being used to sow the field of misogyny for the white patriarchs? Are they the expendable workers who keep the patriarchy alive and kicking? We also questioned why other (white) forms of popular culture are not as demonized as rap music. Why was there, as hooks astutely asks, no feminist outcry over the sexism in the movie *The Piano*? What happens when we ignore the ways in which women are complicit in carrying out the same damaging, sexist, stereotyped images as the patriarchy? What happens when we fail to critique it? These were all tough questions to grapple with, and they exposed us to the intricate intersections of race, class, and gender. Needless to say, the conversations were not always warm and pleasant. The conversations can best be described as the contact zones Mary Louise Pratt writes about. The class sessions were "social spaces where cultures meet, clash, and grapple with each other, often in context of highly asymmetrical relations of power, such as colonialism, slavery, or their aftermaths as they are lived out in many parts of the world today."[26] With such a diverse mixture of students, the conversations were at the very least passionate and opinionated.

The women's studies class centered on gender issues, but race, class, and sexuality inevitably and necessarily came up. This combination made for heated discussions. Since many of the Black students in the class felt a sense of ownership and connection to the music, we had to find "ways to move into and out of rhetorics of authenticity."[27] It was important that none of the white students who did not like rap be silenced and that the Black students—and even some of the white students—who grew up listening to rap have a chance to express why they felt the way they did about the music. There were several times when the discussion of rap and articles about rap contributed to the clashing of cultures. In fact, it was the perfect setting in which to use conflict as a pedagogical tool.

Given the fact that rap music prides itself on "the battle," is used to sell every kind of merchandise imaginable (making it capitalism's money-earning poster child), and is attacked by politicians on the right and left (making it the United States' punching bag), conflict in relation to rap music and Hip-Hop culture is inevitable.[28] But as Susan Jarratt tells us, "Recognizing the inevitability of conflict is not grounds for despair but the starting point for creating a consciousness in students and teachers through which the inequalities generating those conflicts can be acknowledged and transformed."[29] The students' divergent views on the topic were expected and welcomed. A space for argument was made with the hope that we could use rap to help us think differently about the fight against sexism. Or, to use Jarratt's words, "In the heat of argument—feminism and rhetoric become allies in contention with the forces of oppression troubling us all."[30] Viewing rap as a rhetorical practice, and using Black feminism to aid that viewing, can help bring about new ways to think about the fight against sexism and the patriarchy that troubles us all and lead us to the possibilities of bringing wreck to oppression.

Seeing Differences Among Women: Generational and Racial

The students also grappled with third-wave feminist views that called into question age and the role it plays in how we read popular cultures. Since rap music has been touted as the music of this generation, some students felt torn by their love for the music and the music's sexism and violence. By reading articles by third-wave feminists that dealt with the same kinds of issues, they were able to contend with their feelings. For example, Eisa Davis's article "Sexism and the Art of Feminist Hip-Hop Maintenance" provoked heated discussion. Davis brings to bear the complicated and conflicted relationship she has with rap music as a young Black feminist, but she also refuses to censor and dismiss the culture, language, and sense of community she considers her own. For Davis, Hip-Hop "after all, is the whipping boy for a misogyny that is fundamental to western culture."[31] And she questions why she should deny Hip-Hop in exchange for grounding in the classics represented by Aristotle. She instead chooses to listen and begin a dialogue with the rappers in order to get at the root of their sexism and how that sexism shapes their view of the world.[32]

The students debated for almost an entire class period on the effectiveness of Davis's stance. Some felt she was an elitist and did not take into consideration other, less educated women's inability to rationalize their exploitation. Others felt she was too dumb to realize how the negative lyrics have a serious impact on her and all women. And some felt her stance offered the solution they had been waiting for, a way to both enjoy and critique the music they loved. All of the students were able to note how Davis's stance was both different from and similar to bell hooks's stance. The students noted how both saw Hip-Hop as a pawn in a larger game being played by the white supremacist patriarchy. For hooks, the rappers are sowing the fields like Blacks before them planted cotton. For Davis, rappers become the whipping boys and suffer mental lashes as opposed to the physical lashes the slaves suffered. By finding similarities in these second- and third-wave Black feminists, students were thus able to partially bridge the gap between these two periods in feminism.[33] The discussion also allowed us to see that boundaries between age groups are not as neatly drawn as we would like to believe, and that people of the students' age might have more in common with previous generations than they would like to admit. All of the class discussions tried to move beyond the articles and the music and on to larger societal issues.

The students had varied responses to Davis's piece; she was viewed as the ultimate feminist by some and not a real feminist by others. We did not accomplish a definitive reading of her text. Some students changed their views on the piece and others did not. What is most important, in my opinion, is that the class discussions and the student responses showed critical thinking and engagement. They were able to disrupt their own ingrained thinking patterns and maintain a space for possibility and thought. They exhibited the open minds necessary for education. When reading their response papers, I could hear and see them grappling with the text. One student titled her response paper on Davis "A Voice for One and Silence for All." The student wrote, "In her attempt to remain faithful to her culture and language she has sacrificed her feminist principles by rationalizing hip-hop's misogynist lyrics." This student used rap to continue views she expressed earlier on race and feminism. She had a hard time grasping the notion that women of color have a different relationship to feminism that is largely influenced by race. It was interesting to see her continue to grapple with the notion that the women's movement does not currently encompass the needs of all women. She had a hard time dealing with the fact that even in the women's movement there is sometimes a need for more safe spaces within the safe space of all women and that sometimes women of color have to enter into safe spaces and alliances with men of color. In her view, Davis was not true to feminism because she was trying to understand and better relate to Black men. The student continued:

> Davis's fear of ostracism from her community has already occurred because she is separating herself from her African-American sisters. As an educated feminist, Davis writes from a somewhat privileged position. . . . As an educated woman, Davis is able to dissociate herself from the misogynistic lyrics of some hip-hop music because she understands that they are not defining *her as an individual woman*. However, those women who identify themselves as "hoes/bitches" cannot separate themselves as individuals from the stereotypes portrayed by male rappers.

In noting Davis's privileged position, the student fell into her own privileged conclusions. She granted Davis a space of privilege but denied other women an intellectual space. She did not take into account the fact that these women may have reasons just as intellectually sound as her own or Davis's. However, this student and the others who critiqued Davis's stance were engaged and beginning to think of themselves as participants in discussions not only with their classmates but also with the teacher and with the critic. The students were beginning to recognize the uses of writing and reading in relationship to thinking and their participation in the public space. The students' writings were also a space for pushing further and bridging gaps.

You Betta Recognize
Recognizing Connections: Race, Sexism, and Culture

The students were able to make connections between rap and other forms of popular music, which inevitably allowed them to question issues of race. They also began to question race, sexism, and culture and offer their own solutions about why rap is attacked and other forms of music are not as demonized. One student, who was one of the only two male students who would label himself as feminist at the beginning of the semester, came to the conclusion that race is one determining factor. He wrote:

> This isn't exclusive to rap though. Most love songs deal in an ideal world, talking about mostly ideal situations. If you look at country, it seems that most country folk, according to the songs, have their dog killed, their momma killed, and that leaves them with drinking and feeling sorry for themselves. You might even have the occasional woman shooting her cheating husband or men just walking out on their family. My point is that the only reason rappers seem to take the heat is because they are African-American. It's like the men in power are saying "those people" shouldn't be sending bad messages to "our children." You don't hear the press hammering on Garth Brooks for singing about committing suicide over a lost love, or singing about a woman shooting her husband for cheating. What about those messages to children? I guess those don't have an impact because Garth is white and everybody knows that those songs are supposed to make you think how stupid a solution that is, right?

This student saw the double standard, and he began to offer reasons it occurs. He was not condoning or excusing the negative lyrics in rap but rather complicating the discussion. While this is an argument that many rappers themselves use, the fact that this student, who confessed he did not really listen to rap, came to a similar argument is telling. One can surmise that the student was able to reprocess the argument that bell hooks makes in her article about rap music and the movie *The Piano*, and use country music as another example of sexism in popular culture that is not critiqued as much as rap.

A female student also wrote about rap in comparison to country music. She wrote:

> I'm not a country fan, but the few songs I have heard have never once had a woman of good sense act of her own free will, as central to the song. I always hear about little lost girls who need guidance from the man who is singing with his twangy guitar. Why are there not studies taken on the effect of young girls who primarily listen to country? Is hip-hop and rap that much more offensive?

This student did not listen to country any more than she listened to rap. She was able, however, to see how various elements of pop culture could be degrading to women. In her paper she even questioned authors such as Shakespeare, Byron, and Kipling; she did not limit herself to popular culture. Once she started questioning she was unstoppable.

Another student wrote:

> I did like bell hooks' article, "Sexism and Misogyny: Who Takes the Rap?" noting that rap is not the only music that disrespects women. "A Hip-Hop Nation Divided" discussed the dilemma of a black woman that wanted to listen to music of her culture but was offended by the lyrics. Now I can relate to that because there are lyrics in some of the songs I like that don't speak kindly of women. The fact that these songs I like are not hip-hop songs would support bell hooks' article.

This white male student did not listen to rap music. In fact, he noted, "I like many genres, just about anything except rap, R&B, and country." However, he was able to see how rap gets a bad "rap" based on an evaluation of the lyrics in music he does listen to. These students were able to use rap to bridge gaps between various forms of popular culture. They were also able to make connections between elements of popular culture that they were interested in and rap. In spite of the various forms of popular culture they took part in, the students—using the class texts and discussions—were able to think critically about a form of music that they did not like or had not listened to in the past. The class discussions were not aimed at making them like rap. They were aimed at showing them how rap could be a tool in political change. I wanted them to begin to bridge gaps between politics, popular culture, and other societal elements.

Recognizing Connections: Economics, Sexism, and Race

Some of the Black students in my class found that they wanted economic issues to be highlighted a little more in the articles and in the class discussion on rap music. One Black woman found it hard to relate to the feminist articles because they did not focus enough on the rappers' needs to pay their bills and provide for themselves and their families. This student had a hard time moving past the economic issues for young Blacks in America. In a time of rampant consumerism and materialism, the need to "get paid" is a constant theme of Hip-Hop. In this student's eyes a feminism that does not take into account the need these rappers have to make the money they need to live was not relevant. A Black male student also made note of the economic issues:

> Rap music has also been an avenue for some people to better themselves. If making rhymes is what they have to do to better their financial status, I cannot blame them. No one talks about rock-n-roll and it is bad also. And some of it is worse than rap.

These economic issues were also addressed in class and allowed us a space to expand the dialogue started by the articles while giving the students the opportunity to further explore the economic inequities that came up in other class discussions. Why is it that most Black millionaires are performers or sports figures? Is that the only space they are allowed to excel in? Rap offered students an example of intersections and how discussions of gender are linked to discussions of race and class. We were also able to move the discussion further and talk about the women who perform in rap videos scantily clad by making connections between the lack of economic possibilities for women in general and the women of color in the rap videos specifically. We were able to further question why there are so many opportunities for women to make money objectifying themselves.

These economical issues surfaced in other ways as well. Another student questioned the economic aspects involved and pushed it further than our class discussion of the limited economic possibilities for young Blacks in our society. She realized that rap was making a lot of people a whole lot of money. However, she did not give up hope. She wrote:

> So what I don't understand is black men, and white men are abusing all women through these songs, so why isn't it stopped? One group of people is abusing another group of people and yet, everyone stands by and watches it happen. I guess an answer to my own question would be the fact that the capitalist society we live in, run by males who are making money off of it, continue to allow it to happen. I see this as a depressing fact in our society, but continue to hope that women can change the world or at least the way we live in it.

This student continued to grapple with the issues discussed in class. And, although she did not come up with definitive answers, I believe her critical thinking and constant questioning in writing were positive steps in that direction. In all of these instances rap was the springboard for broader discussions and connections.

Another student offered a delicate reading informed by the intersections of race and gender. He was able to see that negative lyrics also defame the men who rap them:

> Misogynist rap lyrics both defame women and the black man by presenting a negative image of the rapper and his rap. For example, when a rapper such as Snoop portrays women negatively, he not only perpetuates societal stereotypes of women, but also cultivates a negative stereotype

about black men. This duality, which the patriarchy utilizes to perpetuate itself, is, in my opinion, one of the core obstacles to any real change in this country.

This student preceded the above statement with the observation that "every time an advancement is made in the area of improving women's rights, race equality, etc. . . . the patriarchy adapts in order to preserve itself." While he was not as hopeful about change as the previous student was, he did see some value in Eisa Davis's stance because it allowed a "human angle in the examination of feminist issues." This student was the other male student who identified himself as a feminist on the first day of class. His reading of rap was interesting because he was beginning to look at male constructions of gender and interrogate them.

One female student did not like rap music and thought it was negative; however, she was able to move beyond her dismissive stance and see the value in discussion and critique. She was able to see and recognize the ways in which rap could be used as a tool. She found usefulness in what we tried to accomplish in class. She wrote:

> Artists such as Tupac, who present a conflicted view of women, give the feminist movement honest tools with which to work. By this I mean that sexist lyrics may serve as subject matter to critically think about—a learning opportunity. My reading of these articles is a good example. I have always quickly regarded the lyrics as offensive, demeaning, and stupid. However, I now have a better understanding of the cause of such offensive words. I learned an important history lesson as offered by the writers of the texts. It is only through critical, historical analysis that one can move on to improve a problem. I do not think it is wise to dwell on or ignore a negative situation. Instead, it must be assessed and improved upon.

I would like to discuss this student's paper at length, because her reading of the classroom texts epitomizes what I was trying to ac-

complish in class. This student went through each of the class readings on Hip-Hop and was able to make some connection to the
course goals. Of Eisa Davis she wrote, "I believe that she is stress-
ing, above all else, the importance of critical thinking." Of hooks's
and Davis's take on young black men being used by the patriarchy,
she wrote, "I found this equally interesting and disturbing and yet,
the situation, I believe, is not hopeless." She closed her essay with
this:

> As someone said in class, research shows that there is a con-
> nection between rap music and an increased violence
> against women. I think it is naive to disregard the effects of
> any medium, whether it be music, television, or film. All of
> these have a tremendous impact. Since it is highly unlikely
> that the media is going to change anytime soon, it is essen-
> tial to equip our children with the necessary skills to criti-
> cally think about the media and the constructed images of
> women it portrays. Perhaps they will be the ones to change
> the portrayals as adults.

This student recognized the difficulties in fighting against sexism
but saw the value in learning from oppression and using it to fight
oppression. I think that each of the students took steps we can all
learn from. As academics, it would behoove us to take heed. Rap
provokes the kinds of discussions and student writing teachers for
change desire. It gathers passionate responses from the students and
creates a space to practice the critical thinking we say we want
from our students. As my students' writings show, it also allows students a space to think critically about and critique themselves and
the popular cultures they consume. Rap is a place where popular
culture can meet the academy and make some changes in society.
As Costello and Wallace write, "Rap is the self-conscious–self-
consciousness loop academic feminists and deconstructionists drool
over."[34] In his book *Spectacular Vernaculars: Hip-Hop and the Politics
of Postmodernism*, Russell Potter echoes Costello and Wallace with a
caution against thinking that academic theories or rap music alone
or combined can change society. But he believes that a full-fledged

alliance and interchange between the two vernacular expressions, theory and rap, can expand our understanding of the contemporary moment and the turns it might take in order to make real progress toward change.[35] People are continually trying to tap the political potential of rap, and I believe that people will continue to do so until there is a breakthrough. Rap is too rich a tool to pass up. And with so many academics like myself bringing rap music into our classes and research, those changes could happen sooner than anyone might imagine. It would be a shame to miss out on such a provocative teaching tool because you just cannot see it. You betta recognize!

Conclusion
Imagining Images:
Black Womanhood in the Twenty-first Century

I've really got to use my imagination. To think of good reasons to keep on keepin' on. I've got to make the best of a bad situation . . .

—Gladys Knight and the Pips, "I've Got to Use My Imagination"

The imagination has long occupied conflicting spaces in our nation's consciousness. On one hand, it is valued and respected; on the other, it is seen as idle play and shunned. It is thought of as something better left for those who have enough free time to be creative. Those who do possess this kind of time are usually held in high regard, as they are our esteemed creative people and give us great works for our consumption and pleasure. The idea that the imagination can become a tool for social change is always lingering in the background, but seldom do we give it serious attention. Yet in a speech given during the World Trade Organization talks in Seattle, former president Bill Clinton said that it would take a certain amount of imagination to change the existing order of things. As an example of why imagination is needed, the former president offered a paraphrase from Machiavelli, which I will paraphrase yet again. Basically, imagination is needed because of the age-old truth that people who do not have power are afraid of what they might gain and the people who do have power are afraid of what they might lose. And while I'm not in the habit of quoting or even listening much to the former president, I have to admit I found myself agreeing with him. It will take a whole lot of imagination to begin to make things right and end oppression in the United States and in the world.

As Arjun Appadurai informs us in "Disjuncture and Difference in the Global Cultural Economy," the imagination can be a social practice that leads us to something critical and new. "The imagination is now central to all forms of agency, is itself a social fact, and is the key component of the new global order."[1] Much like Clinton at the World Trade Organization talks, Appadurai realizes and stresses the importance of imagination in an increasingly global economy. When we think about the creative force that is Hip-Hop culture and how it now has a global impact, with large audiences in France, in Japan, and across the continent of Africa, it is not so much of a leap to think about the implications for imagination, globalization, and change within and utilizing Hip-Hop culture. And as I close, I realize the importance for imagination if we are going to imagine ways to work together and imagine ways to change the way things are. As feminist Gloria Steinem advises, we have to be able to envision change before we can act on it, lest we become mired in the self-doubt imposed on us by the status quo and blame ourselves instead of the status quo for the current state of affairs.[2]

My arguments here have largely been about imagining change, about bringing wreck and disrupting the status quo. And as I think about the conflicting spaces that imagination holds in relation to social change—particularly social change and Black people—the dual spaces that Black people occupy in the U.S. imaginary come to mind. Spaces of respect and admiration are juxtaposed with spaces of demonization and blame. And sometimes these spaces of praise and criticism overlap. How else can we account for the co-optation of Hip-Hop cultural forms even as Hip-Hop, specifically rap music, is demonized and evokes moral panic all across the nation?

One of the reasons Black people occupy this dual space involves the ways they are imagined by others and the multiple images and representations that have plagued Black people from at least as far back as the days of slavery. In the case of Black woman specifically, one can easily recall images of the welfare queen, the matriarch, the mammy, the seductress, the strong Black woman, and the always sexually available Black woman. These are the images that Black women have fought against for years. And in working against these definitions, sometimes we deny who we really are or forget what we have accomplished. For example, it takes a lot of energy to be the strong Black woman. Strength in the face of adversity is the legacy left by many Black foremothers. But because of their strength, people such as Daniel Patrick Moynihan labeled them "matriarchs" and blamed them for the ruin of the Black family and the castration of the Black male.[3] This is only one example of the kind of double-edged sword the images have become.

Given the ideological turn the country is taking and the images representing Blacks in this country, we need to imagine new ways to disrupt prevailing images and claim a voice in the public sphere. Imagination as a social practice, as a tool for change, becomes essential. A large part of this work has dealt with the images and representations of Black women in the U.S. imaginary and the ways in which real women negotiated these realities in order to create spaces for themselves in the larger public sphere and the counter-public sphere of Hip-Hop culture. The struggle over representation is one that has been fought by Black women for a long time, and I have no doubt that it will continue for a long time to come. Our participation in the public sphere is connected to this struggle over representation and identity. How we are seen continues to be an issue. Thus, spectacle continues to be a part of resistance. Yet spectacle in the way we have been using it has some problems. While it is at first controlled by the person or group creating the spectacle, certain images can become distorted and be used against the group, especially ones that deviate far from the status quo.

However, the more I think about spectacle, image, representation, power, and the ways they have been and still are connected for most Black people, especially most Black women, I recognize that in order to realize true freedom in the United States we will have to do more than control the images. After all the years of trying, maybe it's time to realize that we *cannot* control the way we are seen. The time and energy we spend doing that can be better spent on things we *can* control. For example, the current NAACP fight to put more Blacks and minorities on network television, while noble, is also a waste of energy, especially when we look back through the years and see the same group having the same fight time after time. While it would probably help young Black people to see positive images on television in a variety of capacities, we have been down that road before. Why not come up with a plan or project that gets young Black people away from the television and into political classrooms and community projects? What about some more youth-oriented, progressive, Hip-Hop-influenced think tanks like the Urban Think Tank that publishes *Doula*, the first Hip-Hop journal? The far right is grooming young leadership as we speak. Who will be *our* next young leaders? These kinds of proactive interventions provide youth with positive images and in turn ensure that they will be positive images for others. All the Black television shows in the world are not going to prompt the kind of revolutionary change we need; "the revolution will not be televised."[4] And revolutionary change is what we are in dire need of. It can be accomplished, I believe, in the public spaces and discourses I have highlighted here, if we start to use our imaginations. If we begin to look for wreck and make better use of those spaces, we can begin to enact change. Imagine if Queen Latifah's release of "U.N.I.T.Y." was followed by a wide-reaching dialogue orchestrated by Black feminist thinkers in Black communities with Black youth!

If we continually ignore the political potential of rap music and Hip-Hop culture more generally, not to mention that of our own classrooms and students, things will not change. And perhaps instead of blaming Hip-Hop culture for the negative images that some rap artists present, our time might better be spent imagining and then implementing projects for change geared toward the youth involved in Hip-Hop culture, change that draws on the culture in meaningful ways. This kind of change would entail not dismissing the culture as negative and therefore not worthy of consideration, but rather engaging with the culture and in turn with our youth. Blaming rappers is useless, because they are not political leaders. They are entertainers. We need leaders, young and old, to provide useful alternatives. And we need to be there in order to help the youth interpret the messages they are getting from the music.

At the end of 2001, I contemplated giving up my subscription to that bastion of professional Black womanhood, *Essence*. The magazine had ceased to be relevant to me and just did not address what I saw as the most pressing issues for Black women today. They had articles on fashion, being fit, and being upwardly mobile, and they printed the requisite number of "save our sons" articles. But they did not seem to have a clue or a care as to what was happening in the lives of young Black girls. The Black professional women's magazine did not engage with Hip-Hop culture in ways that I felt were particularly fruitful or meaningful to the lives of young Black women. Sure, there was the occasional poignant article by Hip-Hop feminists such as Joan Morgan, dream hampton, and Tara Roberts, and even some special issues devoted to Hip-Hop. But something was missing.

I had decided to let my subscription lapse when, in what would have been my very last issue of *Essence*, some visionary, some imaginative person on the editorial board, decided that 2002 would be the year in which *Essence* would take on what they heralded as the "war on girls." I was stunned. I fished out my renewal notice, wrote out my check, and continued my subscription. *Essence* was finally speaking the words that I longed to hear from Black feminists, Black professional women, and indeed the Black community: "We recognize that the war against our girls is just as insidious, potentially deadly and capable of compromising the lives of innocent victims as the one that currently obsesses our government [the war on terror]. We also know that its casualties are far more likely to go unchampioned."[5]

Beginning in January 2002, *Essence* has published six articles addressing the war on girls. In the June 2002 issue, Joan Morgan examined the impact that rap music videos have on young Black girls. Morgan suggests swift action in this war: "It's time to set some standards. Instead of resigning ourselves to being at the mercy of the media, we have to recognize our power to have an impact on it."[6] She encourages people to write their cable companies and have the video shows that exhibit adult content shown at later times, after kids have gone to bed. Morgan's suggestions are innovative and useful because she does not blame the parents, point the finger at the artists, or even wish to ban the videos. She simply suggests a course of action that moves us away from the obsession with images to a space where we can actually think about change.

The August 2002 issue took the war on girls global by looking at the child rapes currently happening in South Africa. In September 2002 the subject turned to child prostitution in the United States and the exploitation of young girls. The article offered real stories about how tricking to get things and rampant materialism can leave young girls vulnerable and mark them as easy prey. It also offered a provocative critique of the materialism that contemporary rap music provokes. The contradiction, however, is that Puff Daddy and Eve are on the cover of the issue dressed in expensive clothes and are quoted inside the magazine on their love of fashion and expensive things. The October 2002 issue places Queen Latifah in a roundtable discussion with real young women, talking about how they cope in a society that does not value them. They talk about body image, female-to-female friendships, male-female relationships, sex, STDs, and rape, to name only a few things. The roundtable represents the kind of interaction I would like to see Black feminism take with Hip-Hop culture and young Black girls.[7]

The November 2002 issue grappled with the startling growth of battering in teenage male-female relationships. Those of us who listen to rap music and participate in Hip-Hop culture are not surprised by this recent trend. When Black womanhood is not valued or validated, and there is a climate that posits Black womanhood as something to be feared, as one of the elements out to destroy Black manhood, then it is not surprising that there is abuse. The task for

Black feminism is imagining ways to do something to combat this fear. Black feminism *has* to work within Hip-Hop culture or else we will be the losers in this war on young Black girls.

As I close a quote from Thomas Holt that explores the possibility of a contemporary Black public sphere being "a space for critique and transformation" comes to mind. He maintains that if the Black public sphere is not a space of transformation, then "this is only idle talk."[8] I think the public spaces discussed here highlight several that are ripe for critique and transformation of the existing order. And I know that with a little imagination we can make full use of them. We need to change the way we think about these issues from *rational* to *imaginative*. As Audre Lorde reminds us, "The master's tools will never dismantle the master's house." Thus being rational about this will not eliminate the many problems that confront us. And besides, who ever heard of a rational solution to a completely irrational, insane, and inhumane problem? The words of the late poet June Jordan in the film *A Place of Rage* come to mind: "And just what in the hell is everyone being so reasonable about?" Oppression, hatred, and the horrid images that have come to represent Black womanhood in this country are not rational or reasonable; they are completely irrational. And the only way to move beyond them is to bring wreck and imagine a better way.

NOTES

INTRODUCTION

1. Leschea, "Hip Hop," *Rhythm & Beats*, Warner Brothers. Inc., 1996.

2. I use capital letters throughout to signify Hip-Hop as a worldwide youth cultural movement that deserves scholarly critical attention. I also capitalize *Black* throughout this work because it signifies a people with a shared history and culture both in the United States and throughout the African diaspora.

3. *Beat Street*, dir. Stan Lathan, 1984; *Breakin'*, dir. Joel Silberg, 1984; *Breakin' 2: Electric Boogaloo*, dir. Sam Firstenberg, 1985.

4. For thought-provoking critiques on the capitalist exploitation of Black music, see N. Kelly, ed., *R&B, Rhythm and Business: The Political Economy of Black Music* (New York: Akaschic Books, 2002), and N. Kelly, "Rhythm Nation: The Political Economy of Black Music," *Black Renaissance Noire* 2:2 (1999). *Check It While I Wreck It* does not delve deeply into issues of capitalism and Hip-Hop production, but it does open the door for further conversations, especially as they pertain to issues of materialism, commodification, exploitation, and Black womanhood.

5. *Wild Style*, dir. Charlie Ahearn, 1982.

6. See, for example, W. E. Perkins, "The Rap Attack: An Introduction," *Droppin' Science: Critical Essays on Rap Music and Hip Hop Culture* (Philadelphia: Temple University Press, 1996); J. Yasin, "Rap in the African-American Music Tradition: Cultural Assertion and Continuity," in A. K. Spears, ed., *Race and Ideology: Language, Symbolism, and Popular Culture* (Detroit: Wayne State University Press, 1999).

7. See, for example, M. Gladney, "The Black Arts Movement and Hip Hop," *African American Review* 29 (1995): 291–301; E. Henderson, "Black Nationalism and Rap Music," *Journal of Black Studies* 26:3 (1996); G. Pough, "Seeds and Legacies: Tapping the Potential in Hip-Hop," *Doula: The Journal of Rap Music and Hip Hop Culture* 1:2 (2001).

8. See, for example, M. Morgan, "'Nuthin' But a G-thang': Grammar and Language Ideology in Hip Hop Identity," in S. Lanehart, ed., *Sociocultural and Historical Contexts of African American English* (Philadelphia: John Benjamins, 2001); G. Smitherman, "The Chain Remain the Same: Communicative Practices in the Hip Hop Nation," *Journal of Black Studies* 28:1 (1997); G. Smitherman, "Word from the Hood: The Lexicon of African American Vernacular English," in S. Mufuwene et al., eds., *African American English: Structure, History and Use* (New York: Routledge, 1998); G. Smitherman, "Introduction," *Black Talk: Words and Phrases from the Hood to the Amen Corner* (New York: Houghton Mifflin, 1994); B. Wood, "Understanding Rap as Rhetorical Folk-Poetry," *Mosaic* 32:4 (1999).

9. K. Maurice Jones, *Say It Loud: The Story of Rap Music* (Brookfield, Conn.: Millbrook, 1994), p. 17.

10. See, for example, S. H. Fernando Jr., *The New Beats: Exploring the Music, Culture, and Attitudes of Hip Hop* (New York: Anchor Books, 1994); N. George, *Hip Hop America* (New York: Viking, 1998); Jones, *Say It Loud;* C. Keyes, *Rap Music and Street Consciousness* (Urbana: University of Illinois Press, 2002); A. Light, ed., *The Vibe History of Hip Hop* (New York: Three Rivers, 1999); D. Toop, *Rap Attack #3: African Rap to Global Hip Hop,* 3d edition (London: Serpent's Tail, 2000).

11. For critical analyses and interpretations of this particular moment in Hip-Hop history and the lack of opportunities for young Blacks and Latinos, see M. Forman, *The 'Hood Comes First: Race, Space, and Place in Rap Music and Hip-Hop* (Middletown, Conn.: Wesleyan University Press, 2002); R. D. G. Kelly, *Yo' Mama's Disfunktional! Fighting the Culture Wars in Urban America* (Boston: Beacon, 1997); T. Rose, *Black Noise: Rap Music and Black Culture in Contemporary America* (Middletown, Conn.: Wesleyan University Press, 1994).

12. George, *Hip Hop America,* p. 184.

13. Ibid.

14. "Hip-Hop heads" describes a group of people totally immersed in the culture of Hip-Hop.

15. *Rhyme & Reason,* dir. Peter Spirer (1997); *The Show,* dir. Brian Robbins (1995). Each of these films has small—usually five- to eight-minute—segments that I like to call "and now a moment for the women" or "what about the women" segments.

16. Freestyle rap is rapping on the spot with no written rhymes, right off the top of one's head.

17. There are no doubt arguments regarding the viability of the answer rap as a space of power for women rappers. And I would agree that the answer rap is a limited space. However, its limited nature does not discount it as a space of possibility.

CHAPTER 1

1. Jürgen Habermas, "Concluding Remarks," in Craig Calhoun, ed., *Habermas and the Public Sphere* (Cambridge: Massachusetts Institute of Technology Press, 1996), p. 463.

2. Black Public Sphere Collective, "Preface," in *The Black Public Sphere: A Public Culture Book* (Chicago: University of Chicago Press, 1995), pp. 2–3.

3. Ibid., p. 3.

4. Habermas, "Concluding Remarks," p. 466.

5. Jürgen Habermas, *The Structural Transformation of the Public Sphere: An Inquiry into a Category of Bourgeois Society,* trans. Thomas Burger (Cambridge: Massachusetts Institute of Technology Press, 1991), p. 27.

6. For more readings that refigure the public sphere and acknowledge the presence of women and people of color in the public sphere, see the Black Public Sphere Collective, *The Black Public Sphere* (Chicago: University of Chicago Press, 1995); H. Baker, *Critical Memory: Public Sphere, African American Writing, and Black Fathers and Sons in America* (Athens: University of Georgia Press, 2001); J. Landes, *Women and the Public Sphere in the Age of the French Revolution* (Ithaca: Cornell University Press, 1988); M. Lara, *Moral Textures: Feminist Narratives in the Public Sphere* (Berkeley: University of California Press, 1998); J. Meehan, ed., *Feminists Read Habermas: Gendering the Subject of Discourse* (New York: Routledge, 1995).

7. Bruce Robbins, ed., *The Phantom Public Sphere* (Minneapolis: University of Minnesota Press, 1993), p. xvii.

8. Nancy Fraser, *Justice Interruptus: Critical Reflections on the "Postsocialist" Condition* (New York: Routledge, 1997), p. 118.

9. For fascinating critiques of homophobia in Hip-Hop culture and rap music, see F. Chideya, "Homophobia: Hip Hop's Black Eye," in K. Powell, ed., *Step into a World: A Global Anthology of the New Black Literature* (New York: John Wiley, 2000); Touré, "Hip Hop's Closet: A Fanzine Article Touches a Nerve," in D. Constantine Simms, ed., *The Greatest Taboo: Homosexuality in Black Communities* (Los Angeles: Alyson Books, 2000).

10. The Black Panther Party is by no means the first or the only Black group to make use of spectacle and representation in this way. In fact, a large part of the argument here is that Blacks have historically had to make use of and skillfully navigate spectacle and representation in order to claim a space in the public sphere. In that regard, similarities can also be seen and connections can also be made between other Black nationalist groups and their use of spectacle and representation, namely, Marcus Garvey's Universal Negro Improvement Association, Elijah Muhammad's Nation of Islam, and Maulana Karenga's United Slaves. Most of the founding members of Hip-Hop as a youth movement would have been aware of the images of the 1960s and early 1970s that the Black Power movement and by extension the Black Panther Party represented. More study is needed in this area in order to fully shed light on the multiple ways that Blacks in the United States have treaded the lines between spectacle, representation, and public voice.

11. Habermas, *The Structural Transformation of the Public Sphere*, p. 8.

12. Kobena Mercer, *Welcome to the Jungle: New Positions in Black Cultural Studies* (New York: Routledge, 1994).

13. Ibid., p. 23.

14. Paula Giddings, *When and Where I Enter: The Impact of Black Women on Race and Sex in America* (New York: Bantam, 1984).

15. Angela Davis, *Women, Culture, Politics* (New York: Vintage, 1990).

16. Darlene Clark Hine, "Rape and the Inner Lives of Black Women in the Middle West: Preliminary Thoughts on the Culture of Dissemblance," in Roger Lancaster and Micaela di Leonardo, eds., *The Gender and Sexuality Reader* (New York: Routledge, 1997), pp. 434–39.

17. Hazel Carby, "Policing the Black Woman's Body in an Urban Context," in *Cultures in Babylon: Black Britain and African America* (New York: Verso, 1999), pp. 22–39.

18. Ibid., p. 24.

19. W. E. B. Du Bois, "The Talented Tenth," in *The Negro Problem* (New York: James Pott, 1903).

20. For an interesting and enlightening discussion of how the civil rights movement gave way to and created the era of Hip-Hop, see T. Boyd, *The New H.N.I.C.: The Death of Civil Rights and the Reign of Hip Hop* (New York: New York University Press, 2002).

21. Scholars are increasingly interrogating the impact that exceptionalism, respectability, and notions of a talented tenth have had and continue to have on Black communities. For thought-provoking critiques of issues of exceptionalism and representation, see Hazel Carby, *Race Men* (Cambridge: Harvard University Press, 1998); Joy James, *Transcending the Talented Tenth: Black Leaders and American Intellectuals* (New York: Routledge, 1997); and D. L. Lewis, "Two Responses to American Exceptionalism: W. E. B. Du Bois and Martin Luther King, Jr.," *Black Renaissance Noire* 4:3 (2002). For provocative critiques of the impact that the quest for respectability and likeability have had on Blacks, see Baker, *Critical Memory*, especially the first two chapters, and E. F. White, *Dark Continent of Our Bodies: Black Feminism and the Politics of Respectability* (Philadelphia: Temple University Press, 2001).

22. Elaine Brown, *A Taste of Power: A Black Woman's Story* (New York: Pantheon, 1992), p. 136.

23. For a critique of the Black Panther Party's use of the lumpen proletariat, see Hugh Pearson, *The Shadow of the Panther: Huey Newton and the Price of Black Power in America* (New York: Addison-Wesley, 1994), and C. Booker, "Lumpenization: A Critical Error of the Black Panther Party," in C. Jones, ed., *The Black Panther Party Reconsidered* (Baltimore: Black Classics, 1998).

24. An earlier example of a group that controlled the gaze and navigated spectacle in ways that sparked fear in the U.S. government—indeed, the world, given the diasporic scope of the movement—and some bourgeois "respectable" Black folk is Marcus Garvey and the Garveyite movement.

25. Bakari Kitwana, *The Hip Hop Generation: Young Blacks and the Crisis in African-American Culture* (New York: Basic Civitas Books, 2002), p. 202.

26. "Represent" or "representin'" is Hip-Hop terminology for being the best one can be in order to show the best of where one comes from. On some levels, it can be likened to the nineteenth-century notion of racial uplift in that one represents not just for oneself but for the entire race. On other levels it means that once the rapper or the member of the Hip-Hop community achieves a space from which to speak, she or he must speak up for everyone left behind—she or he must "represent."

27. *Michael Eric Dyson: Material Witness: Race, Identity, and the Politics of Gangsta Rap.* prod. and dir. Sut Jhalley, The Media Education Foundation, 1995, videocassette.

28. During the later years of the Black Panther Party, they were openly criticized for the ways they used or misused donations given to the group's various defense funds and public service projects. Some felt that they were helping themselves to the funds given to them to help the people. Criticism occurred from both outside and inside the party. Huey P. Newton purchased a penthouse apartment while rank-and-file members lived in substandard houses and apartments. Some of the more prominent members received an enormous amount of media spotlight and sometimes reveled in it.

29. Patricia Hill Collins, *Fighting Words: Black Women and the Search for Justice* (Minneapolis: University of Minnesota Press, 1998), p. 15.

30. Habermas, *The Structural Transformation of the Public Sphere.*

31. Collins, *Fighting Words.*

32. For a critique of the way contemporary state surveillance measures inhibit the lives of Blacks in the United States, see Collins, *Fighting Words,* White, *Dark Continent of Our Bodies.*

33. Ibid.

34. Ibid.

35. Ibid.

36. Oskar Negt and Alexander Kluge, *Public Sphere and Experience: Toward an Analysis of Bourgeois and Proletarian Public Spheres* (Minneapolis: University of Minnesota Press, 1993), p. xii.

37. Mark Anthony Neal, *What the Music Said: Black Popular Music and Black Public Culture* (New York: Routledge, 1999), pp. 1–2.

38. Black Public Sphere Collective, "Preface," p. 1.

39. Fraser, *Justice Interruptus,* p. 14.

40. Michael Hanchard, "Black Cinderella? Race and the Public Sphere in Brazil," in the Black Public Sphere Collective, eds., *The Black Public Sphere: A Public Culture Book* (Chicago: University of Chicago Press, 1995), p. 172.

41. Michael Dawson, "A Black Counterpublic? Economic Earthquakes, Racial Agendas, and Black Politics," in the Black Public Sphere Collective, eds., *The Black Public Sphere; A Public Culture Book* (Chicago: University of Chicago Press, 1995), p. 200.

42. Ibid., pp. 219–21.

43. Neal, *What the Music Said,* p. 15.

44. Baker, *Critical Memory,* p. 17.

45. Ibid., pp. 50–51.

46. Elsa Barkley Brown, "Negotiating and Transforming the Public Sphere: African American Political Life in the Transition from Slavery to Freedom," in the Black Public Sphere Collective, eds., *The Black Public Sphere: A Public Culture Book* (Chicago: University of Chicago Press, 1995), p. 123.

47. Ibid., p. 126.

48. Ibid., p. 150.

CHAPTER 2

1. For discussions on Black women's early literacy and public speaking, see M. Ferguson, ed., *Nine Black Women: An Anthology of Nineteenth-Century Writers from the United States, Canada, Bermuda, and the Caribbean* (New York: Routledge, 1998); S. Logan, *"We Are Coming": The Persuasive Discourse of Nineteenth-Century Black Women* (Carbondale: Southern Illinois University Press, 1999); S. Logan, ed., *With Pen and with Voice: A Critical Anthology of Nineteenth-Century African-American Women* (Carbondale: Southern Illinois University Press, 1995); C. Peterson, *Doers of the Word: African-American Women Speakers and Writers in the North 1830–1880* (New York: Oxford University Press, 1995); J. Royster, ed., *Southern Horrors and Other Writings: The Anti-Lynching Campaign of Ida B. Wells, 1892–1900* (Boston: Bedford, 1997); J. Royster, *Traces of a Stream: Literacy and Social Change Among African American Women* (Pittsburgh: University of Pittsburgh Press, 2000).

2. For some interesting and provocative reconsiderations of Black feminism, see P. Collins, *Fighting Words: Black Women and the Search for Justice* (Minneapolis: University of Minnesota Press, 1998); J. James, *Shadow Boxing: Representations of Black Feminist Politics* (New York: Palgrave, 1999); E. White, *Dark Continent of Our Bodies; Black Feminism and the Politics of Respectability* (Philadelphia: Temple University Press, 2001).

3. Elaine Richardson, " 'To Protect and Serve': African American Female Literacies," *Journal of the Conference on College Composition and Communication* 53:4 (2002): 680.

4. Ibid.

5. Maria Pia Lara, *Moral Textures: Feminist Narratives in the Public Sphere* (Berkeley: University of California Press, 1998).

6. Ibid., p. 166.

7. For fascinating work that interrogates and rethinks the usefulness of the wave model for Black women's studies, see K. Springer, "Third Wave Black Feminism?" *Signs: Journal of Women in Culture and Society* 27:4 (2002), and B. Guy Sheftall, "Response from a 'Second Waver' to Kimberly Springer's 'Third Wave Black Feminism,' " *Signs: Journal of Women in Culture and Society* 27:4 (2002).

8. Royster, *Traces of a Stream,* p. 103.

9. For a detailed discussion of Black women's literacy practices, see Logan, *"We Are Coming"*; Peterson, *Doers of the Word;* Royster, *Traces of a Stream.*

10. Joanne Braxton, "Harriet Jacobs' *Incidents in the Life of a Slave Girl:* The Re-Definition of the Slave Narrative Genre," *Massachusetts Review* 27 (1986): 385.

11. Ibid., p. 380.

12. Sandra Mayo, "Sassy Assertiveness and 'Somebodyness': The Poetry of Black Women During the 1960s and 1970s," *MAWA Review* 5 (1990): 7.

13. Maya Angelou, "And Still I Rise," in *Maya Angelou Poems* (New York: Bantam Books, 1981).

14. For more detailed readings of *Incidents in the Life of a Slave Girl* as a subversive text, see F. Nudelman, "Harriet Jacobs and the Sentimental Politics of Female Suffering," *English Literary History* 59 (1992); V. Smith, "'Loopholes of Retreat': Architecture and Ideology in Harriet Jacobs' *Incidents in the Life of a Slave Girl*," in H. Gates, ed., *Reading Black, Reading Feminist: A Critical Anthology* (New York: Meridan, 1990), pp. 212–26; L. Tanner, "Self-Conscious Representation in the Slave Narrative," *Black American Literature Forum* 21 (1987); A. Taves, "Spiritual Purity and Sexual Shame: Religious Themes in the Writings of Harriet Jacobs," *Church History* 56 (1986): 59–72; M. Vermillion, "Reembodying the Self: Representations of Rape in *Incidents in the Life of a Slave Girl* and *I Know Why the Caged Bird Sings*," *Biography* 15:3 (1992).

15. Harriet Jacobs, *Incidents in the Life of a Slave Girl: Written by Herself* (Cambridge: Harvard University Press, 1987), p. 63.

16. For a more detailed reading of the gaps and silences in *Incidents in the Life of a Slave Girl*, see J. Moody, "Ripping Away the Veil of Slavery: Literacy, Communal Love, and Self Esteem in Three Slave Women's Narratives," *Black American Literature Forum* 24 (1990); Nudelman, "Harriet Jacobs and the Sentimental Politics of Female Suffering"; Tanner, "Self-Conscious Representation in the Slave Narrative"; Vermillion, "Reembodying the Self"; Taves, "Spiritual Purity and Sexual Shame."

17. Darlene Clark Hine, "Rape and the Inner Lives of Black Women in the Middle West: Preliminary Thoughts on the Culture of Dissemblance," in Roger Lancaster and Micaela di Leonardo, eds., *The Gender and Sexuality Reader* (New York: Routledge, 1997), pp. 434–39.

18. Jacobs, *Incidents*, p. 161.

19. Ibid., p. 54.

20. Ibid., p. 55.

21. Ibid., p. 1.

22. Ibid., p. 2.

23. Darlene Clark Hine and Kathleen Thompson, *A Shining Thread of Hope: The History of Black Women in America* (New York: Broadway, 1998), pp. 180–81.

24. Ibid., p. 181.

25. Ibid., p. 183.

26. Logan, *With Pen and Voice*.

27. Anna Julia Cooper, *A Voice from the South* (Oxford: Oxford University Press, 1988), p. 42.

28. Ibid., pp. 24–25.

29. Ibid., p. 31.

30. Royster, *Southern Horrors and Other Writings*.

31. Ibid., p. 52.

32. Ibid., p. 54.

33. Ibid., p. 70.

34. Ibid., p. 74.

35. Even when we look more thoroughly at feminist struggle in the United States in general we see continuations after suffrage with the work of Margaret Sanger and the struggle for birth control. These continuations show us that feminist struggle—despite headlines and propaganda to the contrary—never dies.

36. For more detailed accounts of the blues women and issues of sexuality, see H. Carby, *Cultures in Babylon: Black Britain and African America* (New York: Verso, 1999), particularly the four essays in the section titled "Women, Migration and the Formation of a Blues Culture"; A.

Davis, *Blues Legacies and Black Feminism: Gertrude "Ma" Rainey, Bessie Smith, and Billie Holliday* (New York: Vintage, 1998); T. Kernodle, "'My Handy Man Ain't Handy No More': The Classic Blues and the Black Woman's Transition from Private to Public Music-Making," in Linda Williams, ed., *African American Women Musicians and Black Feminism* (Champaign: University of Illinois Press, 2004).

37. Kernodle, "'My Handy Man Ain't Handy No More.'"

38. Hine and Thompson, *A Shining Thread of Hope.*

39. In the film *Barbershop,* comedian Cedric the Entertainer's character, Eddie, makes several comments about the leaders of the civil rights movement. He makes a derogatory reference about the Reverend Dr. Martin Luther King Jr.'s womanizing. He blatantly and quite vulgarly dismisses and disregards the Reverend Jesse Jackson. And he says, "Rosa Parks ain't do nothing but sit her ass down." At first hearing, this statement flies in the face of the present-day revisionist history that is trying to grant Rosa Parks her rightful place in the civil rights struggle. She did more than sit down. She was already actively involved in the struggle, and she knew the implications of her actions. However, further thought and interrogation of Eddie's words and the way he brings in other nameless, faceless people who sat down and sat in at lunch counters forces us to realize the very classed nature of the civil rights movement and even some of our revisions of history. For example, how often do we hear about Claudette Colvin, a young, single Black woman, who refused to give up her bus seat before Rosa Parks? The young woman's past was not as "suitable" as Mrs. Parks's was—and her pregnancy out of wedlock prevented the NAACP from building a case around her.

40. Rosa Parks, "'Tired of Giving In': The Launching of the Montgomery Bus Boycott," in Bettye Collier-Thomas and V. P. Franklin, eds., *Sisters in the Struggle: African American Women in the Civil Rights–Black Power Movement* (New York: New York University Press, 2001), p. 61.

41. Ibid.

42. Dorothy Height, "'We Wanted the Voice of a Woman to Be Heard': Black Women and the 1963 March on Washington," in Bettye Collier-Thomas and V. P. Franklin, eds., *Sisters in the Struggle: African American Women in the Civil Rights–Black Power Movement.*

43. Ibid., p. 86.

44. Ibid., p. 87.

45. Ibid., p. 90.

46. Stokely Carmichael (Kwame Ture) is often credited with making the statement that the only position for women in the movement is prone. References to "pussy power" can be found in Elaine Brown, *A Taste of Power: A Black Woman's Story* (New York: Pantheon, 1992), and Bobby Seale, *Seize the Time: The Story of the Black Panther Party and Huey P. Newton* (Baltimore: Black Classic, 1991). Both former Black Panther Party members make reference to "pussy power" as women's power to help the revolution by not having sex with men who were not revolutionary.

47. "Double-consciousness" is a term coined by W. E. B. Du Bois that speaks to the dual and conflicted experience of being an African in America. He writes, "One ever feels his twoness—an American, a Negro; two souls, two thoughts, two unreconciled strivings; two warring ideals in one dark body" (W. E. B. Du Bois, *The Souls of Black Folk* [New York: Penguin, 1989]).

48. Rebecca Carrol, *I Know What the Red Clay Looks Like: The Voice and Vision of Black Women Writers* (New York: Crown, 1994), p. 121.

49. Sonia Sanchez, "Memorial," in Erlene Stetson, ed., *Black Sister: Poetry by Black American Women, 1746–1980* (Bloomington: Indiana University Press, 1981), p. 244.

50. Daniel Patrick Moynihan's 1965 report "The Negro Family: The Case for National Ac-

tion" demonized Black women and pathologized Black families. Moynihan blamed the alleged strength of Black women for Black men's alleged inability to take the "normal" role as head of household. Many pro-Black and revolutionary Black men bought into the report and also began to blame Black women for what was "wrong" with Black families.

51. Sonia Sanchez, "Queen of the Universe," *Black Scholar* 1 (1970): 11.

52. Nikki Giovanni, "Woman Poem," in *Black Feeling, Black Talk, Black Judgement* (New York: Morrow Quill, 1979), p. 15.

53. Donald Bogle, *Toms, Coons, Mulattos, Mammies, and Bucks: An Interpretive History of Blacks in American Films* (New York: Viking, 1973), p. 251.

54. For works that take on the project of reconsidering Black feminism, see H. Carby, *Cultures in Babylon: Black Britain and African America* (New York: Verso, 1999); Collins, *Fighting Words;* James, *Shadow Boxing;* White, *Dark Continent of Our Bodies.*

55. Valerie Smith, *Not Just Race, Not Just Gender: Black Feminist Readings* (New York: Routledge, 1998), p. xv.

56. Ibid., p. xix.

57. Ibid., p. xiv.

58. Ibid., p. xxiii.

59. A very recent exception to this neglect is the self-published work of Adrienne Anderson, *Word: Rap, Politics, and Feminism* (Writers Club Press/iUniverse, 2003). The work is basically a compilation of the articles Anderson wrote while working for the now defunct Bay Area Hip-Hop magazine *4080*. The eighty-five-page book begins to chart some of the key issues surrounding Hip-Hop, gender, and Black feminism. The fact that Anderson self-published the work speaks volumes on a number of issues. The first issue is that existing publishing venues limit what we can read about women and Hip-Hop in much the same way that the record industry limits the number of female voices we are allowed to hear in rap music. With the exception of *Vibe Magazine's Hip Hop Divas* (New York: Three Rivers, 2001), Joan Morgan's *When Chickenheads Come Home to Roost: My Life as a Hip-Hop Feminist* (New York: Simon and Schuster, 1999), and now *Check It While I Wreck It,* where else can we get female voices and women as the subject matter? The second issue (and the one most crucial to my own project) is that she realizes the political potential of Hip-Hop culture. Therefore, she sees the urgency and spends her own money to get her message out there. She writes, "*Word* will course my travels with rap and the rap world. It will hopefully show how rap has the power to ignite, transform, and heal" (p. 1). While the compilation could use more development in spots, I think it is worth reading in conversation with *Check It While I Wreck It* in order to launch new and more expanded conversation about gender and feminism in Hip-Hop that will, I hope, evoke change.

60. Jacqueline Bobo, *Black Women as Cultural Readers* (New York: Columbia University Press, 1995), p. 22.

61. bell hooks, "Gangsta Culture—Sexism and Misogyny: Who Will Take the Rap?" in *Outlaw Culture: Resisting Representation* (New York: Routledge, 1994).

62. Michele Wallace, "When Black Feminism Faces the Music and the Music Is Rap," in Diana George and John Trimbur, eds., *Reading Culture: Context for Critical Reading and Writing* (New York: HarperCollins, 1995), pp. 23–25.

63. Eisa Davis, "Sexism and the Art of Feminist Hip-Hop Maintenance," in Rebecca Walker, ed., *To Be Real: Telling the Truth and Changing the Face of Feminism* (New York: Anchor Books, 1995), pp. 127–42.

64. For more detailed readings on Hip-Hop feminism see Shani Jamila, "Can I Get a Witness? Testimony from a Hip-Hop Feminist," in Daisy Hernandez and Bushra Rehman, eds.,

Notes to Pages 73–80

Colonize This! Young Women of Color on Today's Feminism (New York: Seal, 2002); Cheo Coker, dream hampton, and Tara Roberts, "A Hip-Hop Nation Divided," *Essence*, August 1994, pp. 62–64, 112–15; Tara Roberts and Eisa Nefertari Ulen, "Sisters Spin the Talk on Hip-Hop: Can the Music Be Saved?" *MS Magazine*, February/March 2000, pp. 70–74; Joan Morgan, *When Chickenheads Come Home to Roost: My Life as a Hip-Hop Feminist* (New York: Simon and Schuster, 1999); Gwendolyn Pough, "Do the Ladies Run This . . . ? Some Thoughts on Hip-Hop Feminism," in Rory Dicker and Alison Piepmeier, eds., *Catching a Wave: Reclaiming Feminism for the 21st Century* (Boston: Northeastern University Press, 2003); Gwendolyn Pough, "Love Feminism, But Where's My Hip-Hop? Shaping a Black Feminist Identity," in Daisy Hernandez and Bushra Rehman, eds., *Colonize This! Young Women of Color on Today's Feminism* (New York: Seal, 2002).

65. For more detailed discussion see M. Forman, " 'Movin' Closer to an Independent Funk': Black Feminist Theory, Standpoint, and Women in Rap," *Women's Studies* 23 (1994); K. Gaunt, "Translating Double-Dutch to Hip-Hop: The Musical Vernacular of Black Girls' Play," in J. Adjaye and A. Andrews, eds., *Languages, Rhythm, and Sound: Black Popular Cultures into the Twenty-first Century* (Pittsburgh: University of Pittsburgh Press, 1997); Guevara, Nancy, "Women Writin' Rappin' Breakin'," in William Eric Perkins, ed., *Droppin' Science: Critical Essays on Rap Music and Hip-Hop Culture* (Philadelphia: Temple University Press, 1996); Cheryl Keyes, " 'We're More than a Novelty, Boys': Strategies of Female Rappers in the Rap Music Tradition," in Joan Newlon Radner, ed., *Feminist Messages: Coding in Women's Folk Culture* (Urbana: University of Illinois Press, 1993); Cheryl Keyes, "Empowering Self, Making Choices, Creating Spaces: Black Female Identity via Rap Music Performance," *Journal of American Folklore* 113 (2000), 419, 255–69; Robin Roberts, " 'Ladies First': Queen Latifah's Afrocentric Feminist Music Video," *African American Review* 28 (1994); Tricia Rose, *Black Noise: Rap Music and Black Culture in Contemporary America* (Hanover: Wesleyan University Press, 1994).

CHAPTER 3

The title of this chapter is taken from Queen Latifah, "U.N.I.T.Y.," *Black Reign*, Motown, 1993.

1. Denise Troutman-Robinson, "The Tongue or the Sword: Which Is Master?" in Geneva Smitherman, ed., *African American Women Speak Out on Anita Hill–Clarence Thomas* (Detroit: Wayne State University Press, 1995), p. 214.

2. Geneva Smitherman, "Testifyin, Sermonizin, and Signifyin: Anita Hill, Clarence Thomas and the African American Verbal Tradition," in Geneva Smitherman, ed., *African American Women Speak Out on Anita Hill–Clarence Thomas* (Detroit: Wayne State University Press, 1995), p. 225.

3. Ibid., p. 240.

4. Ibid., p. 239.

5. Ibid., p. 241.

6. Alice Walker, *In Search of Our Mothers' Gardens: Womanist Prose* (New York: Harcourt Brace, 1983).

7. Paule Marshall, "The Making of a Writer: From the Poets in the Kitchen," in *Reena and Other Stories* (New York: The Feminist Press, 1983).

8. bell hooks, *Talking Back: Thinking Feminist, Thinking Black* (Boston: South End, 1989).

9. Faye Childs and Noreen Palmer, *Going Off: A Guide for Black Women Who've Just About Had Enough* (New York: St. Martin's, 1999), p. 5.

10. Ibid.

11. Ibid., p. 17.

12. Ibid.

13. Karla Holloway, *Codes of Conduct: Race, Ethics, and the Color of Our Character* (New Brunswick: Rutgers University Press, 1995), p. 1.

14. Jill Nelson, *Straight, No Chaser: How I Became a Grown-up Black Woman* (New York: G. P. Putnam's Sons, 1997), p. 201.

15. Ibid., p. 203.

16. Lisa Jones, *Bulletproof Diva: Tales of Race, Sex, and Hair* (New York: Anchor Books, 1994), p. 3.

17. Lauren Berlant, *The Queen of America Goes to Washington City: Essays on Sex and Citizenship* (Durham: Duke University Press, 1997), p. 223.

18. Nancy Guevara, "Women Writin' Rappin' Breakin'," in William Eric Perkins, ed., *Droppin' Science: Critical Essays on Rap Music and Hip-Hop Culture* (Philadelphia: Temple University Press, 1996), p. 51.

19. Christina Veran, "First Ladies: Fly Females Who Racked the Mike in the 70s and 80s," in *Vibe Magazine, Hip-Hop Divas* (New York: Three Rivers, 2001), p. 6.

20. For more detailed examinations, see V. Berry, "Feminine or Masculine: The Conflicting Nature of Female Images in Rap Music," in S. Cook and J. Tsou, eds., *Cecilia Reclaimed: Feminist Perspectives on Gender and Music* (Champaign: University of Illinois Press, 1994); Y. Bynoe, "Defining the Female Image Through Rap Music and Hip-Hop Culture," *Doula: The Journal of Rap Music and Hip Hop Culture* 1:2 (2001).

21. For more detailed examinations, see W. Porter, "Salt-N-Pepa, Lil' Kim, Foxy Brown, and Eve: The Politics of the Black Female Body," *Doula: The Journal of Rap Music and Hip Hop Culture* 1:1 (2000); T. Rose, "Bad Sistas: Black Women Rappers and Sexual Politics in Rap Music," in *Black Noise: Rap Music and Pop Culture in America* (Hanover: Wesleyan University Press, 1994); E. Watts, "The Female Voice in Hip Hop: An Exploration into the Potential of Erotic Appeal," in Marsha Houston, ed., *Centering Ourselves: African American Feminist and Womanist Studies of Discourse* (Cresskill: Hampton, 2002).

22. For more detailed discussion, see M. Forman, "'Movin' Closer to an Independent Funk': Black Feminist Theory, Standpoint, and Women in Rap," *Women's Studies* 23 (1994); R. Roberts, "'Ladies First': Queen Latifah's Afrocentric Feminist Music Video," *African American Review* 28 (1994).

23. See K. Gaunt, "Translating Double-Dutch to Hip-Hop: The Musical Vernacular of Black Girls' Play," in J. Adjaye and A. Andrews, eds., *Languages, Rhythm, and Sound: Black Popular Cultures into the Twenty-first Century* (Pittsburgh: University of Pittsburgh Press, 1997).

24. See C. Keyes, "Empowering Self, Making Choices, Creating Spaces: Black Female Identity via Rap Music Performance," *Journal of American Folklore* 113 (2000); C. Keyes, "'We're More Than a Novelty, Boys': Strategies of Female Rappers in the Rap Music Tradition," in J. Radner, ed., *Feminist Messages: Coding in Women's Folk Culture* (Urbana: University of Illinois Press, 1993).

25. Keyes, "'We're More than a Novelty, Boys,'" p. 204.

26. Ibid., p. 205.

27. Keyes, "Empowering Self, Making Choices, Creating Spaces," p. 256.

28. Berry, "Feminine or Masculine," p. 184.

29. Tricia Rose, *Black Noise: Rap Music and Black Culture in Contemporary America* (Hanover: Wesleyan University Press, 1994), p. 147.

30. Eric King Watts, "The Female Voice in Hip-Hop: An Exploration into the Potential of Erotic Appeal," in Marsha Houston and Olga I. Davis, eds., *Centering Ourselves: African American Feminist and Womanist Studies of Discourse* (Cresskill: Hampton, 2002).

31. Kyra Gaunt, "The Musical Vernacular of Black Girls' Play," in Joseph Adjaye and Adrianne Andrews, eds., *Language, Rhythm, and Sound: Black Popular Cultures into the Twenty-first Century* (Pittsburgh: University of Pittsburgh Press, 1997).

32. Bonz Malone, "Queen Latifah: Original Flavor," *The Source: The Magazine of Hip-Hop Music, Culture and Politics,* May 1994, p. 66.

33. Queen Latifah, "U.N.I.T.Y.," *Black Reign,* Motown, 1993.

34. Eve, "Love Is Blind," *Ruff Ryders' First Lady,* Ruff Ryders, 1999.

35. Margeaux Watson, "Eve Blows Our Mind," *Honey,* August 2002, p. 85.

36. Ryan Ford, "Eve: Material Girl," *The Source: The Magazine of Hip-Hop Music, Culture and Politics,* August 2002, p. 146.

37. Rebecca Walker, "Becoming the Third Wave," in Amy Kesselman, Lily D. McNair, and Nancy Schniedwind, eds., *Women, Images and Realities: A Multicultural Anthology* (Mountain View: Mayfield, 1999).

38. S. Craig Watkins, *Representing: Hip-Hop Culture and the Production of Black Cinema* (Chicago: University of Chicago Press, 1998), p. 6.

39. Ibid., p. 2.

40. Mary P. Ryan, "Gender and Public Access: Women's Politics in Nineteenth-Century America," in Craig Calhoun, ed., *Habermas and the Public Sphere* (Cambridge: Massachusetts Institute of Technology Press, 1996), p. 266.

41. Common Sense, "I Used to Love H.E.R.," *Resurrection,* Loud Records, 1994.

42. The Roots, "Act Too (The Love of My Life)," *Things Fall Apart,* MCA, 1999.

43. A Tribe Called Quest, "Bonita Applebum," *People's Instinctive Travels and the Paths of Rhythm,* Jive Records, 1990.

44. Jessica Care Moore, "I'm a Hip Hop Cheerleader," in Tony Medina and Louis Reyes Rivera, eds., *Bum Rush the Page: A Def Poetry Jam* (New York: Three Rivers, 2001).

45. Ibid.

46. Sarah Jones, "Your Revolution," http://www.africana.com/DailyArticles/index_20010830_1.htm (2001).

47. Sarah Jones, "Indecent Exposure," *Honey,* May 2002, p. 76.

48. Foxy Brown, "My Life," *Chyna Doll,* Def Jam, 1999.

CHAPTER 4

1. V. P. Franklin, *Living Our Stories, Telling Our Truths: Autobiography and the Making of the African-American Intellectual Tradition* (Oxford: Oxford University Press, 1995), p. 12.

2. Joanne Braxton, *Black Women Writing Autobiography: A Tradition Within a Tradition* (Philadelphia: Temple University Press, 1989), p. 2.

3. Maria Pia Lara, *Moral Textures: Feminist Narratives in the Public Sphere* (Berkeley: University of California Press, 1998), p. 71.

4. Ibid., p. 110.

5. Examples of these kinds of celebrity autobiographies can be seen in Gladys Knight, *Between Each Line of Pain and Glory: My Life Story* (Thorndike, Maine: G. K. Hall, 1998); Patti LaBelle, *Don't Block the Blessings: Revelations of a Lifetime* (Thorndike, Maine: G. K. Hall, 1997); Henry Louis Gates, *Colored People: A Memoir* (New York: Random House, 1994); bell hooks, *Bone Black: Memories of Black Girlhood* (New York: Henry Holt, 1996).

6. For examples of autobiographies written by people who were formally involved in the civil rights and Black Power movements, see Assata Shakur, *Assata: An Autobiography* (Chicago:

Lawrence Hill, 1988); Elaine Brown, *A Taste of Power: A Black Woman's Story* (New York: Pantheon, 1994); Geronimo Pratt and Jack Olsen, *Last Man Standing: The Tragedy and Triumph of Geronimo Pratt* (New York: Doubleday, 2000); Pauli Murray, *Pauli Murray: The Autobiography of a Black Activist, Feminist, Lawyer, Priest, and Poet* (Knoxville: University of Tennessee Press, 1989); Tananarive Due and Patricia Stephens Due, *Freedom in the Family: A Mother-Daughter Memoir of the Fight for Civil Rights* (New York: Ballantine Books, 2003); Earl Anthony, *Spitting in the Wind: The True Story Behind the Violent Legacy of the Black Panther Party* (Malibu: Rountable, 1990); David Hilliard, *This Side of Glory: The Autobiography of David Hilliard and the Story of the Black Panther Party* (Boston: Little, Brown, 1993).

7. See, for example, Bakari Kitwana, *The Hip-Hop Generation: Young Blacks and the Crisis of African-American Culture* (New York: Basic Civitas Books, 2002); Kevin Powell, *Keepin' It Real: Post-MTV Reflections on Race, Sex, and Politics* (New York: One World, 1997); Kevin Powell, *Who's Gonna Take the Weight? Manhood, Race, and Power in America* (New York: Three Rivers, 2003).

8. This section's subtitle is taken from the lyrics of Missy "Misdemeanor" Elliott's hit "The Rain (Supa Dupa Fly)" on the album *Supa Dupa Fly,* Elektra/Asylum, 1997.

9. Carter G. Woodson, *The Mis-Education of the Negro* (New York: AMS, 1933).

10. Christopher John Farley, "The Maverick: Lauryn Hill Does It Her Way," *Time,* February 8, 1999, p. 59.

11. Melissa Ewey, "Lauryn Hill: Hip-Hop's Hottest Star Balances Love, Motherhood and Fame," *Ebony,* May 1999, p. 64.

12. Monifa Young, "High on the Hill," *Essence,* June 1998, p. 76.

13. Ewey, "Lauryn Hill," p. 64.

14. Young, "High on the Hill," p. 160.

15. Yo Yo, "Black Pearl," *Black Pearl,* EastWest Records, 1992.

16. Kimberly Springer, "Third Wave Black Feminism?" *Signs: Journal of Women in Culture and Society* 27:4 (2002): 1060.

17. Sister Souljah, *No Disrespect* (New York: Vintage, 1994), p. x.

18. Ibid., p. xiv.

19. Queen Latifah and Karen Hunter, *Ladies First: Revelations of a Strong Woman* (New York: William Morrow, 1999).

20. Ibid., p. 2.

21. Ibid.

22. Souljah, *No Disrespect.*

23. It is not uncommon within various factions of Black communities to hear references made to the strong Black woman who does not need a man. This reference can be made as an insult or a compliment. For example, Black women who are viewed as deviant because they do not buy into normative restrictions of sexuality may find themselves being told: "Oh, you a strong Black woman. I guess you don't need a man." On the flip side, it is not uncommon for a Black women who wants to find a man but cannot for whatever reason to be told by her friends: "Oh girl, you know men are just scared of you [can't handle you] because you're a strong Black woman." In either case the strength of the Black woman is paired with their lack of a Black male mate.

24. Souljah, *No Disrespect,* p. 357.

25. Latifah, *Ladies First,* p. 125.

26. Ibid.

27. For more detailed discussion on lesbian baiting, see S. Pharr, *Homophobia: A Weapon of Sexism* (Berkeley: Chardon, 1997).

28. Ibid.

29. Veronica Chambers, *Mama's Girl* (New York: Riverhead, 1996), pp. 75–76.

30. Joan Morgan, *When Chickenheads Come Home to Roost: My Life as a Hip-Hop Feminist* (New York: Simon and Schuster, 1999), p. 87.

31. Houston Baker, "Generational Shifts and the Recent Criticism of Afro-American Literature," in Angelyn Mitchell, ed., *Within the Circle: An Anthology of African American Literary Criticism from the Harlem Renaissance to the Present* (Durham: Duke University Press, 1994). In this essay, Houston Baker defines "generational shifts" as "ideologically motivated movement overseen by young or newly emergent intellectuals who are dedicated to refuting the work of their intellectual predecessors and establishing a new framework of intellectual inquiry" (p. 282). For the purposes of this work, however, generational shifts represent the way Black women of the Hip-Hop generation (represented here by the title of Tupac's song "Dear Mama") build on and reject the images that historically and socially defined their mothers and foremothers (represented here by a phrase from Marvin Gaye's "What's Going On").

32. Jo Malin, *The Voice of the Mother: Embedded Maternal Narratives in Twentieth-Century Women's Autobiographies* (Carbondale: Southern Illinois University Press, 2000), p. 1.

33. Linked to the mothers' interwoven autobiographies in these texts are the stories of the fathers who either were not present or offered problematic examples of Black manhood. Much has been written by sociologists, Afrocentric critics, and Black nationalist scholars about the impact that the lack of a father or father figure in the homes has on young Black men growing up in urban American. However, until very recently little critical work has been done on the impact of absentee fathers on young Black women. The narratives of Queen Latifah, Sister Souljah, Joan Morgan, and Veronica Chambers all offer crucial personal stories and critical insight on the impact that fatherlessness has on young Black women. However, in terms of how these women talk about their own identity construction and coming of age, the relationship between themselves and their mothers has a larger impact.

34. Daniel Patrick Moynihan, *The Negro Family: The Case for National Action* (Washington, D.C.: U.S. Department of Labor, 1965).

35. Jawanza Kunjufu, "Turning Boys into Men," *Essence,* November 1988, p. 112.

36. Nelvia M. Brady's *This Mother's Daughter* (New York: St. Martin's, 2001) begins to give critical attention to the relationship between African American mothers and their daughters. She conducts interviews and gathers stories from twenty mother-daughter pairs in an attempt to begin to document what African-American mother-daughter relationships have been.

37. Souljah, *No Disrespect,* p. 50.

38. Chambers, *Mama's Girl,* pp. 25–26.

39. Morgan, *When Chickenheads Come Home to Roost,* p. 94.

40. Sheila Radford-Hill confirms and complicates the portrait of Black women of the 1970s raising their daughters to be strong Black women in "Keeping It Real: A Generational Commentary on Kimberly Springer's 'Third Wave Black Feminism?'" *Signs: Journal of Women in Culture and Society* 27:4 (2002). She notes, "As black mothers in the 1970s we were keenly aware of what we had faced as young adults. Although we hoped that our daughters would be spared the effects of racism and sexism, we feared otherwise, so we raised our daughters with the capacity to build a self-concept that could withstand male rejection, economic deprivation, crushing family responsibilities, and countless forms of discrimination. In our view, the most effective antidote to having our daughters' lives destroyed by their experiences with racism and sexism was to build an intact self. To develop such a self-concept required us to pass along a variation of the SBW absent, we thought, of the false promises and unrealistic expectations the image evoked in us" (p. 1086). Radford-Hill's words give voice to the Black mothers repre-

sented in the autobiographies and life stories discussed here. She confirms that Black mothers did raise their daughters to be strong. However, she also complicates the story by giving the very valid reasons why Black women felt they had to do so. Even though they hoped against hope that the disappointments in their own lives would not be replicated in their daughters' lives, they *had* to make sure that their daughters were prepared for whatever the world threw at them.

41. Ntozake Shange, *For Colored Girls Who Have Considered Suicide, When the Rainbow Is Enuf* (New York: Collier Books, 1975). "Reglar" as used here refers to Ntozake Shange's Lady in Red, who goes out of her way to adorn herself in sequins and sweet perfumes in an attempt to escape the pain and ordinariness of her life. All of her efforts, however, are washed away with a simple bath, and she becomes the "ordinary / brown braided woman / with big legs and full lips" (p. 34). She becomes, in fact, like any other regular Black woman.

42. Chambers, *Mama's Girl*, pp. 166–67.

43. Patricia Bell-Scott, "Telling Flat-footed Truths: An Introduction," in Patricia Bell-Scott with Juanita Johnson-Bailey, eds., *Flat-footed Truths: Telling Black Women's Lives* (New York: Henry Holt, 1998), p. xix.

44. Ibid.

CHAPTER 5

1. Lil' Bow Wow, "Ghetto Girl," *Beware of Dog,* Sony, 2000.

2. Christine A. Willis and Adrien Katherine Wing, "Sisters in the Hood: Beyond Bloods and Crips," in Adrien Katherine Wing, ed., *Critical Race Feminism: A Reader* (New York: New York University Press, 1997), p. 243.

3. Ibid.

4. Michele Wallace, *"Boyz 'N the Hood and Jungle Fever,"* in Gina Dent, ed., *Black Popular Culture* (Seattle: Bay, 1992), p. 123.

5. Ibid., p. 125.

6. For provocative analyses of Martin Lawrence's character She Nee Nee, see B. E. Smith-Shomade, *Shaded Lives: African American Women and Television* (New Brunswick: Rutgers University Press, 2002), and K. B. Zook, *Color by Fox: The Network and the Revolution in Black Television* (New York: Oxford University Press, 1999).

7. Alonzo Westbrook, *Hip Hoptionary: The Dictionary of Hip Hop Terminology* (New York: Harlem Moon, 2002), p. 55.

8. I use Hip-Hop terminology for these kinds of women throughout this chapter because it best captures the way these women are represented in the films and by extension the culture. Also, there are no better ways to convey the trio. It would mean a very different thing to say *teenage mother* as opposed to *baby mama,* or *Cinderella* instead of *tweener.* And even though the terms *hoochie* and *chickenhead* have derogatory implications in the music and the culture, to say *one of the guys* instead of *hoochie* or *gold digger* instead of *chickenhead* does not capture the roles that these women play in the films or in the culture. I use the terminology that is familiar to the culture because it best captures both the space and place of the ghetto.

9. Not everyone makes these kinds of distinctions between the hoochie and the chicken-head. For example, in the revised edition of *Black Feminist Thought* (New York: Routledge, 2000), Patricia Hill Collins sees the hoochie as the contemporary incarnation of the Jezebel and a continuation of white racist readings of the Black woman as sexually deviant. The difference between the hoochie and the Jezebel is that the hoochie has a Hip-Hop slant and Black men

are using it to exploit and denigrate Black womanhood (pp. 81–83). While I agree with most of what Collins has to say about the hoochie and the way hoochies have been represented as sexually promiscuous in Hip-Hop, I do feel that there are variations to the way the term gets used in the culture. For example, the term may be used to describe a girl in a gang, or to describe an average ghetto girl from the neighborhood, i.e., "She was a young South Central hooch." Even Collins notes the taxonomy of hoochies, which consists of "[p]lain hoochies or sexually assertive women who can be found across social classes. Women who wear sleazy clothes to clubs and dance in a 'slutty' fashion constitute 'club hoochies.' These women aim to attract men with money for a one-night stand. In contrast, the ambition of 'gold-digging hoochies' lies in establishing a long term relationship with a man with money. These gold digging hoochies often aim to snare a highly paid athlete and can do so by becoming pregnant. Finally, there is the 'hoochie-mama' popularized by 2 Live Crew, an image that links the hoochie image to poverty. As 2 Live Crew points out, the 'hoochie mama' is a 'hoodrat,' a 'ghetto hoochie' whose main purpose is to provide them sexual favors" (pp. 82–83). Where I differ with Collins is that I do not believe that the hoochie is always sexualized, whereas the chickenhead, because she is a gold digger performing sexual acts for material gain, is always linked to sex.

10. John Singleton and Veronica Chambers, *Poetic Justice: Filmmaking South Central Style* (New York: Delta, 1993), p. 6.

11. Ibid., p. 7.

12. Ibid.

13. The poetry, while beautiful and lyric, does not really give viewers a sense of Justice as a person. Even though Janet Jackson reads Maya Angelou's poetry—some of which was written for the film—as a voice over, there is a disconnect between the poetry and the character. Because we know so little about Justice it is hard to see the poetry as a part of her.

14. Singleton and Chambers, *Poetic Justice*, p. 81.

15. Ibid., p. 22.

16. Ibid., p. 92.

17. Ibid., p. 109.

18. Omar Tyree notes this goal in several interviews. See A. Jordan, "Interview with Omar Tyree," http://www.warhol.org/Andrea/interview.htm; The Urban Griot, "For Brothers Who Read, Write and Think," http://www.theurbangriot.com/links/interview.htm; L. Hubbard, "Why Men Don't Read: A Conversation with Omar Tyree," http://www/African.com/DailyArticles/index_20010910.htm.

19. Jordan, "Interview with Omar Tyree."

20. Omar Tyree, *Flyy Girl* (New York: Simon and Schuster, 1993), p. 408.

21. Sister Souljah, *The Coldest Winter Ever* (New York: Pocket Books, 2000), p. 193.

22. Ibid., p. 113.

23. Ibid., p. 155.

24. Ibid., pp. 405, 413.

25. Andre Willis, "A Womanist Turn on the Hip-Hop Theme: Leslie Harris's *Just Another Girl on the IRT*," in Joseph Adjaye and Adrianne Andrews, eds., *Language, Rhythm, and Sound: Black Popular Cultures into the Twenty-first Century* (Pittsburgh: University of Pittsburgh Press, 1997), p. 137.

26. Ibid., p. 136.

27. Paradise, "Hoochies Need Love Too," *Above the Rim*, Death Row Records, 1994.

28. Marilyn Frye, "Oppression," in *The Politics of Reality: Essays in Feminist Theory* (Trumansburg: Crossing Press, 1983), p. 4.

29. Willis and Wing, "Sisters in the Hood," p. 250.

30. Alice Walker, *Anything We Love Can Be Saved: A Writer's Activism* (New York: Random House, 1997).

CHAPTER 6

1. In addition, bell hooks has written several books on love in a series she calls "the love trilogy": *All About Love: New Visions* (New York: William Morrow, 2000), *Salvation: Black People and Love* (New York: William Morrow, 2001), and *Communion: The Female Search for Love* (New York: William Morrow, 2002).

2. bell hooks, "Love as a Practice of Freedom," in *Outlaw Culture: Resisting Representations* (New York: Routledge, 1994), p. 243.

3. As Paul Gilroy argues in "'After the Love Has Gone': Bio-Politics and Etho-Poetics in the Black Public Sphere," there is a lack of substantial analysis in relation to gender and sexuality in the scholarship on rap music, and the phenomenology of musical forms is not critiqued as much as the lyrics and video images are analyzed. He suggests that critics pay more attention to issues of gender and sexuality (in Black Public Sphere Collective, eds., *The Black Public Sphere: A Public Culture Book* [Chicago: University of Chicago Press, 1995], p. 56). I concur with Gilroy's suggestions for critics of Hip-Hop culture and rap. Both are rich with possibilities and open up spaces from which to interrogate issues of identity.

4. Sprite, known for its Hip-Hop-inspired commercials, had a string of Hip-Hop/kung fu commercials in the late 1990s that highlighted the female legacy in rap. Female MCs who were then new to rap, such as Eve and Mia X, fought men rappers karate-style, and their leader was pioneering female rapper Roxanne Shante. While true Hip-Hop fans appreciated the Sprite commercials paying homage to the legacy of women in rap, the "obey your thirst" drink took things to an entirely different level when they showed who the top leader of the group was in the last segment of the series, when the "Big Momma" ended up being Millie Jackson. Again Sprite's marketing department showed they knew a thing or two about Hip-Hop, particularly women's legacies.

5. William Eric Perkins, "The Rap Attack: An Introduction," in *Droppin' Science: Critical Essays on Rap Music and Hip-Hop Culture* (Philadelphia: Temple University Press, 1996), p. 4.

6. Angela Davis, *Blues Legacies and Black Feminism: Gertrude "Ma" Rainey, Bessie Smith, and Billie Holiday* (New York: Vintage, 1998), p. 20.

7. The word *dis* is Hip-Hop terminology for disrespect. These answer raps penned by women artists turned the dis around when men made records that disrespected women.

8. Hip-Hop culture has also expanded to include elements such as Hip-Hop soul, rapso (rap and calypso), gospel rap, and hip-house.

9. "Flip the script" is Hip-Hop terminology for the act of changing the agenda or evoking a different path than the one already set out.

10. Craig Calhoun notes Habermas's limited view on identity formation in his introduction to *Habermas and the Public Sphere* (Cambridge: Massachusetts Institute of Technology Press, 1996). He notes that Habermas weakens his own theory when he treats identities as if they were fully formed in the private world and equipped for the public realm based on that private formation. Calhoun offers an example from Habermas that contradicts the idea of identity being formed in the private sphere by looking at the way the literary public sphere and fiction enabled discussions about self-hood and subjectivity (p. 35).

11. Tricia Rose, *Black Noise: Rap Music and Black Culture in Contemporary America* (Hanover: Wesleyan University Press, 1994), p. 147.

12. Rappers such as Queen Latifah, MC Lyte, and Da Brat have all been accused of being lesbians because they have hard-core lyrics and rock the crowd better than some men rappers.

13. Laura Jamison, Laura. "A Feisty Female Rapper Breaks a Hip-Hop Taboo," *New York Times,* January 18, 1998, B34.

14. Queen Pen, "Girlfriend," *My Melody,* Lil' Man Records, 1997.

15. Jamison, "A Feisty Female Rapper."

16. For discussion of the various dialogues in which rap music participates, see Rose, *Black Noise;* R. Potter, *Spectacular Vernaculars: Hip-Hop and the Politics of Postmodernity* (Albany: State University of New York Press, 1995).

17. Alice Walker, *In Search of Our Mothers' Gardens: Womanist Prose* (New York: Harcourt Brace, 1983).

18. June Jordan, "Where Is the Love?" in *Civil Wars* (Boston: Beacon, 1981).

19. Lerone Bennett, *The Shaping of Black America: The Struggles and Triumphs of African-Americans, 1619 to the 1990s* (New York: Penguin, 1993), p. 156.

20. Kevin Powell, *Keepin' It Real: Post-MTV Reflection on Race, Sex, and Politics* (New York: Ballantine, 1997), p. 6.

21. Joan Morgan, *When Chickenheads Come Home to Roost: My Life as a Hip-Hop Feminist* (New York: Simon and Schuster, 1999), p. 72.

22. Sherley Anne Williams, "Some Implications of Womanist Theory," in Angelyn Mitchell, ed., *Within the Circle: An Anthology of African-American Literary Criticism from the Harlem Renaissance to the Present* (Durham: Duke University Press, 1994), p. 517.

23. For a discussion of rap music and sampling, see H. Baker, *Black Studies, Rap and the Academy* (Chicago: University of Chicago Press, 1993), N. George, *Hip Hop America* (New York: Viking, 1998); Potter, *Spectacular Vernacular;* Rose, *Black Noise.*

24. Dimitry Leger, "Hip-Hop/R&B Divas: The New 411," *The Source: Magazine of Hip-Hop Culture and Politics,* July 1995, p. 43.

25. See K. Chappell, "The New Mary J. Blige Tells How Drugs and Attitude Almost Ruined Her Sizzling Career," *Ebony,* January 1998; J. E. Davis, "Proud Mary," *Honey,* October 2001; d. hampton, "All Woman," *Vibe,* April 1997; C. Hancock Rux, "Mary Full of Grace," *Honey,* summer 1999; P. Johnson, "Mary J's Moment of Peace," *Essence,* July 1999; J. Morgan, "What You Never Knew About Mary," *Essence,* November 2001; J. Morgan, "Hail Mary," *Essence,* April 1997.

26. Morgan, "Hail Mary," p. 76.

27. Rux, "Mary Full of Grace," p. 56.

28. Morgan, "Hail Mary," p. 76.

29. Sister Souljah, "Mary's World: A Former Public Enemy Follows the Career of the Queen of Hip-Hop Soul," *New Yorker,* October 4, 1999, p. 58.

30. Johnson, "Mary J's Moment of Peace," p. 138.

31. Michael Eric Dyson, *Race Rules: Navigating the Color Line* (New York: Vintage, 1997), p. 130.

32. Morgan, "What You Never Knew about Mary," p. 135.

33. Mary J. Blige, "Real Love," *What's the 411?* Uptown MCA, 1992.

34. Mary J. Blige, "Be Happy," *My Life,* Uptown MCA, 1994.

35. Marita Golden, "Introduction" in *Wild Women Don't Wear No Blues: Black Women Writers on Love, Men and Sex* (New York: Anchor, 1993), p. xi.

36. I'm thinking specifically of Molefi Asante's notion of Afrocentricity and his discussion of love and romance in the African and African American novel. M. K. Asante, *The Afrocentric Idea* (Philadelphia: Temple University Press, 1987).

37. Lesley D. Thomas, "What's Love Got to Do with Hip-Hop? An Original Screenplay," *The Source: Magazine of Hip-Hop Culture and Politics,* February 1994, p. 54.

38. Cheo Coker, dream hampton, and Tara Roberts, "A Hip-Hop Nation Divided," *Essence,* August 1994, p. 115.

39. Morgan, *When Chickenheads Come Home to Roost,* p. 72.

40. The late Christopher Wallace went by several rap names: the Notorious B.I.G., Biggie Smalls, and Big Poppa. For the purpose of this chapter, I will use Biggie Smalls and the shorter Biggie.

41. The Notorious BIG, "Me and My Bitch," *Ready to Die,* Bad Boy, 1994.

42. Ibid.

43. Ibid.

44. Ibid.

45. Potter, *Spectacular Vernaculars,* p. 27.

46. The Notorious BIG, "One More Chance," *Ready to Die,* Bad Boy, 1994.

47. Ibid.

48. Ibid.

49. Ibid.

50. Method Man, "I'll Be There for You / You're All I Need to Get By," *Tical,* Def Jam, 1995.

51. Ibid.

52. Ibid.

53. *Mad* is Hip-Hop terminology for a lot or an enormous amount.

54. Lil' Kim, "We Don't Need It," *Hard Core,* Undeas, 1996.

55. Robert Marriott, "Blowin' Up," *Vibe,* June/July 2000, p. 132.

56. Lola Ogunnaike, "Hip-Hop's Glamour Girl," *USA Weekend,* June 28–30, 2002, p. 4.

57. Jaime Foster Browne, "Lil' Kim," *Pride,* April 2000, p. 69.

58. Foxy Brown, "(Holy Matrimony) Letter to the Firm," *Ill Na Na,* Def Jam, 1996.

59. Foxy Brown, "Get Me Home," *Ill Na Na,* Def Jam, 1996.

60. Michelle Burford and Chris Farley, "Foxy's Dilemma: Dignity or Dollars?" *Essence,* August 1999, p. 76.

61. Ibid.

62. Ibid.

63. Davis, *Blues Legacies and Black Feminism,* p. 32.

64. Joan Morgan, "The Bad Girls of Hip-Hop," *Essence,* March 1997, p. 134.

65. Ibid., p. 77.

66. Ibid.

67. Daniel Patrick Moynihan, *The Negro Family: The Case for National Action* (Washington, D.C.: U.S. Department of Labor, 1965).

68. Morgan, "The Bad Girls of Hip-Hop," p. 77.

69. Ja Rule featuring Charlie Baltimore, "Down Ass Bitch," *Pain Is Love,* Universal, 2001.

70. Smith Kemba as told to Stephanie Booth, "Pardon Me," *Honey,* September 2001, p. 86.

71. Ibid.

72. dream hampton, "Free the Girls; or, Why I Really Don't Believe There's Much of a Future for Hip-Hop, Let Alone Women in Hip Hop," in *Vibe Magazine, Hip Hop Divas* (New York: Three Rivers, 2001), p. 2.

73. Ibid.

74. Ibid.

75. Alicia Keys, in *Songs in A Minor,* J Records, 2001.

76. Morgan, "The Bad Girls of Hip-Hop," p. 134.

CHAPTER 7

1. Tricia Rose, *Black Noise: Rap Music and Black Culture in Contemporary America* (Hanover: Wesleyan University Press, 1994), p. 7. While I agree with this portrayal of rap's consumers to an extent, I believe that we will not be able to get a true and full account of rap's buying audience until we are able to track and monitor all the places where rap is sold. An accurate account of the consumer market for rap would necessarily have to include the people who do not buy their rap from suburban mall record stores or even mom-and-pop operations. It would have to include those who buy it from bootleg dealers who set up shop on street corners and operate out of car trunks. Questions of audience and even consumer issues are far more complicated than they appear.

2. Chuck D., "The Sound of Our Young World," *Time,* February 8, 1999, p. 66.

3. Angela Ards, "Rhyme and Resist: Organizing the Hip-Hop Generation," *The Nation,* July 26–August 2, 1999, pp. 11–20.

4. Rosa A. Eberly, Rosa A. "From Writers, Audiences and Communities to Publics: Writing Classrooms as Protopublic Spaces," *Rhetoric Review* 18:11 (1999): 167.

5. Ibid., p. 172.

6. Ibid., p. 174.

7. Ibid., p. 175.

8. Mark Costello and David Foster Wallace, *Signifying Rappers: Rap and Race in the Urban Present* (Hopewell: Ecco, 1990), p. 98.

9. Barbara Omolade, "Black Feminist Pedagogy," in *The Rising Song of African American Women* (New York: Routledge, 1994), p. 129.

10. Combahee River Collective, "A Black Feminist Statement," in Gloria T. Hull, Patricia Bell Scott, and Barbara Smith, eds., *All the Women Are White, All the Blacks Are Men, But Some of Us Are Brave: Black Women's Studies* (New York: Feminist Press, 1982), p. 18.

11. Anna Julia Cooper, *A Voice from the South* (Oxford: Oxford University Press, 1988 [1892]), p. 31.

12. Omolade, "Black Feminist Pedagogy."

13. This definition of "power moves" was taken from the description of the Power Moves Conference at the University of California, Los Angeles, May 14–15, 1999.

14. Since most students, no matter their class, color, sex, or creed, attend college to get a degree that will lead to a job and a secure living—usually a better job than their parents had, or the skills to run the family business, depending on privilege—it is not a giant step to assert that our students are making power moves when they take our classes as steps toward their degree. And it goes without saying that some students are a little more adept at making power moves than others. But they are all making power moves just the same.

15. Adrienne Rich, "Claiming an Education," in Amy Kesselman, Lily McNair, and Nancy Schiendewind, eds., *Women, Images and Realities: A Multicultural Anthology* (Mountain View: Mayfield, 1995), p. 18.

16. Cheryl Johnson, "Participatory Rhetoric and the Teacher as Racial/Gendered Subject," *College English* 56 (1994): 412.

17. Shirley Wilson Logan, "'When and Where I Enter': Race, Gender, and Composition Studies," in Susan C. Jarratt and Lynn Worsham, eds., *Feminism and Composition Studies: In Other Words* (New York: Modern Language Association, 1998), p. 46.

18. Ibid., p. 56.

19. Many times discussions and critiques of rap music ignore and erase the women rappers' presence and voice. In women's studies courses, this is not acceptable. A whole critique of the culture and the music is impossible without exploring women rappers.

20. Rose, *Black Noise*, p. 182.

21. bell hooks, *Teaching to Transgress: Education as the Practice of Freedom* (New York: Routledge, 1994), p. 202.

22. Ibid.

23. Ibid., p. 207.

24. Salt-N-Pepa, Foxy Brown, Lil' Kim, Queen Latifah, and Monie Love are all Black women rappers. In the continuum of women rappers Salt-N-Pepa would fall under the old school; they are the groundbreakers, the first woman rap group to go platinum. Salt-N-Pepa, along with Queen Latifah, have also been heralded as "feminist" and "pro-woman" rappers. Lil' Kim and Foxy Brown, on the other hand, have been charged with being "antifeminist" because they have sexually explicit lyrics and perform scantily clad.

25. Lil' Kim, "queen B@#$H," *Hard Core*, Undeas, 1996.

26. Mary Louise Pratt, "Arts of the Contact Zone," in *Profession 91* (New York: Modern Language Association, 1991), p. 444.

27. Ibid., p. 455.

28. In Hip-Hop culture "the battle" is a phrase that describes the lyrical back-and-forth that occurs between rappers when they attempt to see who is better at rapping and who is better at moving the crowd.

29. Susan Jarratt, "Feminism and Composition: The Case for Conflict," in Patricia Harkin and John Schilb, eds., *Contending With Words: Composition and Rhetoric in a Postmodern Age* (New York: Modern Language Association, 1991), p. 119.

30. Ibid., p. 121.

31. Eisa Davis, "Sexism and the Art of Feminist Hip-Hop Maintenance," in Rebecca Walker, ed., *To Be Real: Telling the Truth and Changing the Face of Feminism* (New York: Anchor Books, 1995), p. 131.

32. Ibid., pp. 131–32.

33. Throughout the course, we debated the issue of whether there is a third wave, and if so, when it began. Some believe that the third wave of feminism began when women of color and lesbians started to make their presence known. Others believe the third wave got started recently and can be traced to Rebecca Walker's groundbreaking essay "Becoming the Third Wave." Still others maintain that there cannot be a third wave because the second wave is still going on.

34. Costello and Wallace, *Signifying Rappers*, p. 98.

35. Russell Potter, *Spectacular Vernaculars: Hip-Hop and the Politics of Postmodernity* (Albany: State University of New York Press, 1995), pp. 154–55.

CONCLUSION

1. Arjun Appandurai, "Disjuncture and Difference in the Global Cultural Economy," in Bruce Robbins, ed., *The Phantom Public Sphere* (Minneapolis: University of Minnesota Press, 1993), p. 274.

2. Gloria Steinem, "Foreword," in Rebecca Walker, ed., *To Be Real: Telling the Truth and Changing the Face of Feminism* (New York: Anchor Books, 1995), p. xx.

3. Daniel Patrick Moynihan, *The Negro Family: The Case for National Action* (Washington, D.C.: U.S. Department of Labor, 1965).

4. Gil Scott-Heron, "The Revolution Will Not Be Televised," in *So Far, So Good* (Chicago: Third World, 1990).

5. Linda Villarosa, "The War on Girls: Our Girls in Crisis: What Every Woman Needs to Know About the Challenges of Being Young, Black and Female," *Essence,* January 2002.

6. Joan Morgan, "The War on Girls: Sex, Lies and Videos," *Essence,* June 2002.

7. Queen Latifah, "Lunch with Latifah: Seven Teens, One Queen and an Afternoon of Straight Talk: The War on Girls," *Essence,* October 2002.

8. Thomas C. Holt, "Afterword: Mapping the Black Public Sphere," in the Black Public Sphere Collective, eds., *The Black Public Sphere: A Public Culture Book* (Chicago: University of Chicago Press, 1995), p. 328.

Select Bibliography

BOOKS

Adjaye, Joseph K., and Adrianne R. Andrews, eds. *Language, Rhythm, and Sound: Black Popular Cultures into the Twenty-first Century.* Pittsburgh: University of Pittsburgh Press, 1997.

Anderson, Adrienne. *Word: Rap, Politics and Feminism.* New York: Writers Club, 2003.

Baker, Houston A., Jr. *Black Studies, Rap and the Academy.* Chicago: University of Chicago Press, 1993.

———. *Critical Memory: Public Sphere, African American Writing, and Black Fathers and Sons in America.* Athens: University of Georgia Press, 2001.

Bambara, Toni Cade, ed. *The Black Woman: An Anthology.* New York: New American Library, 1970.

Bell-Scott, Patricia, with Juanita Johnson-Bailey, eds. *Flat-footed Truths: Telling Black Women's Lives.* New York: Henry Holt, 1998.

Bennett, Lerone Jr. *The Shaping of Black America: The Struggles and Triumphs of African Americans, 1619 to the 1990s.* New York: Penguin, 1993.

Berlant, Lauren. *The Queen of America Goes to Washington City: Essays on Sex and Citizenship.* Durham: Duke University Press, 1997.

Black Public Sphere Collective. *The Black Public Sphere: A Public Culture Book.* Chicago: University of Chicago Press, 1995.

Bobo, Jacqueline. *Black Women as Cultural Readers.* New York: Columbia University Press, 1995.

Boyd, Todd. *Am I Black Enough For You? Popular Culture from the 'Hood and Beyond.* Indianapolis: Indiana University Press, 1997.

———. *The New H.N.I.C. (Head Niggas in Charge): The Death of Civil Rights and the Reign of Hip Hop.* New York: New York University Press, 2002.

Braxton, Joanne. *Black Women Writing Autobiography: A Tradition Within a Tradition.* Philadelphia: Temple University Press, 1989.

Calhoun, Craig, ed. *Habermas and the Public Sphere.* Cambridge: Massachusetts Institute of Technology Press, 1996.

Carby, Hazel V. *Cultures in Babylon: Black Britain and African America.* New York: Verso, 1999.

Carroll, Rebecca. *I Know What the Red Clay Looks Like: The Voice and Vision of Black Women Writers.* New York: Crown, 1994.

Chambers, Veronica. *Mama's Girl*. New York: Riverhead, 1996.

Childs, Faye, and Noreen Palmer. *Going Off: A Guide for Black Women Who've Just About Had Enough*. New York: St. Martin's, 1999.

Collins, Patricia Hill. *Black Feminist Thought: Knowledge, Consciousness, and the Politics of Empowerment,* 2nd edition. New York: Routledge, 2000.

———. *Fighting Words: Black Women and the Search for Justice*. Minneapolis: University of Minnesota Press, 1998.

Cooper, Anna Julia. *A Voice from the South*. Oxford: Oxford University Press, 1988.

Costello, Mark, and David Foster Wallace. *Signifying Rappers: Rap and Race in the Urban Present*. Hopewell: Ecco, 1990.

Davis, Angela. *Blues Legacies and Black Feminism: Gertrude "Ma" Rainey, Bessie Smith, and Billie Holiday*. New York: Vintage, 1998.

———. *Women, Culture, and Politics*. New York: Vintage, 1990.

DuCille, Ann. *Skin Trade*. Cambridge: Harvard University Press, 1996.

Dyson, Michael Eric. *Between God and Gangsta Rap: Bearing Witness to Black Culture*. New York: Oxford University Press, 1996.

———. *Race Rules: Navigating the Color Line*. New York: Vintage, 1997.

———. *Reflecting Black: African-American Cultural Criticism*. Minneapolis: University of Minnesota Press, 1993.

Fernando, S. H. Jr. *The New Black Beats: Exploring the Music, Culture, and Attitudes of Hip-Hop*. New York: Anchor Books, 1994.

Forman, Murray. *The Hood Comes First: Race, Space, and Place in Rap and Hip-Hop*. Middletown: Wesleyan University Press, 2002.

Franklin, V. P. *Living Our Stories, Telling Our Truths: Autobiography and the Making of the African-American Intellectual Tradition*. Oxford: Oxford University Press, 1995.

Fraser, Nancy. *Justice Interruptus: Critical Reflections on the "Postsocialist" Condition*. New York: Routledge, 1997.

George, Nelson. *Buppies, B-Boys, Baps, and Bohos: Notes on Post-Soul Black Culture*. New York: HarperCollins, 1992.

———. *Hip Hop America*. New York: Viking, 1998.

Giddings, Paula. *When and Where I Enter: The Impact of Black Women on Race and Sex in America*. New York: Bantam, 1984.

Golden, Marita. *Wild Women Don't Wear No Blues: Black Women Writers on Love, Men and Sex*. New York: Anchor Books, 1993.

Habermas, Jürgen. *The Structural Transformation of the Public Sphere: An Inquiry into a Category of Bourgeois Society,* trans. Thomas Burger. Cambridge: Massachusetts Institute of Technology Press, 1991.

Hine, Darlene Clark, and Kathleen Thompson. *A Shining Thread of Hope: The History of Black Women in America*. New York: Broadway, 1998.

Holloway, Karla. *Codes of Conduct: Race, Ethics, and the Color of Our Character*. New Brunswick: Rutgers University Press, 1995.

hooks, bell. *Black Looks: Race and Representation*. Boston: South End Press, 1992.

———. *Outlaw Culture: Resisting Representation*. New York: Routledge, 1994.

———. *Talking Back: Thinking Feminist, Thinking Black*. Boston: South End Press, 1989.

———. *Teaching to Transgress: Education as the Practice of Freedom*. New York: Routledge, 1994.

Jacobs, Harriet. *Incidents in the Life of a Slave Girl: Written by Herself*. Cambridge: Harvard University Press, 1987.

James, Joy. *Shadow Boxing: Representations of Black Feminist Politics.* New York: Palgrave, 1999.

Jones, K. Maurice. *Say It Loud: The Story of Rap Music.* Brookfield, Conn.: Millbrook, 1994.

Jones, Lisa. *Bulletproof Diva: Tales of Race, Sex, and Hair.* New York: Anchor Books, 1994.

Jordan, June. *Civil Wars.* Boston: Beacon, 1981.

Kelley, Robin. *Yo' Mama's Disfunktional: Fighting the Culture Wars in Urban America.* New York: Beacon, 1997.

Kitwana, Bakari. *The Hip Hop Generation: Young Blacks and the Crisis in African-American Culture.* New York: Basic Civitas Books, 2002.

———. *The Rap on Gangsta Rap.* Chicago: Third World, 1994.

Kluge, Alexander, and Oskar Negt. *Public Sphere and Experience: Toward an Analysis of Bourgeois and Proletarian Public Spheres.* Minneapolis: University of Minnesota Press, 1993.

Kunjufu, Jawanza. *Hip-Hop vs. MAAT: A Psycho/Social Analysis of Values.* Chicago: African American Images, 1993.

Landes, Joan. *Women and the Public Sphere in the Age of the French Revolution.* Ithaca: Cornell University Press, 1988.

Lara, María Pía. *Moral Textures: Feminist Narratives in the Public Sphere.* Berkeley: University of California Press, 1998.

Latifah, Queen, and Karen Hunter. *Ladies First: Revelations of a Strong Black Woman.* New York: William Morrow, 1999.

Light, Alan, ed. *The Vibe History of Hip-Hop.* New York: Three Rivers, 1999.

Logan, Shirley Wilson. *We Are Coming: The Persuasive Discourse of Nineteenth-Century Black Women.* Carbondale: Southern Illinois University Press, 1999.

———, ed. *With Pen and Voice: A Critical Anthology of Nineteenth-Century African-American Women.* Carbondale: Southern Illinois University Press, 1995.

Malin, Jo. *The Voice of the Mother: Embedded Maternal Narratives in Twentieth-Century Women's Autobiographies.* Carbondale: Southern Illinois University Press, 2000.

Mercer, Kobena. *Welcome to the Jungle: New Positions in Black Cultural Studies.* New York: Routledge, 1994.

Meehan, Johanna, ed. *Feminists Read Habermas: Gendering the Subject of Discourse.* New York: Routledge, 1995.

Morgan, Joan. *When Chickenheads Come Home to Roost: My Life as a Hip-Hop Feminist.* New York: Simon and Schuster, 1999.

Neal, Mark Anthony. *Soul Babies: Black Popular Culture and the Post-Soul Aesthetic.* New York: Routledge, 2002.

———. *What the Music Said: Black Popular Music and Black Public Culture.* New York: Routledge, 2002.

Nelson, Jill. *Straight, No Chaser: How I Became a Grown-up Black Woman.* New York: G. P. Putnam's Sons, 1997.

Omolade, Barbara. *The Rising Song of African American Women.* New York: Routledge, 1994.

Perkins, William Eric, ed. *Droppin' Science: Critical Essays on Rap Music and Hip-Hop Culture.* Philadelphia: Temple University Press, 1996.

Potter, Russell. *Spectacular Vernaculars: Hip-Hop and the Politics of Postmodernity.* Albany: State University of New York Press, 1995.

Powell, Kevin. *Keepin' It Real: Post-MTV Reflections on Race, Sex, and Politics.* New York: Ballantine, 1997.

Robbins, Bruce, ed. *The Phantom Public Sphere*. Minneapolis: University of Minnesota Press, 1993.

Rose, Tricia. *Black Noise: Rap Music and Black Culture in Contemporary America*. Hanover: Wesleyan University Press, 1994.

Royster, Jacqueline Jones, ed. *Southern Horrors and Other Writings: The Anti-Lynching Campaign of Ida B. Wells, 1892–1900*. Boston: Bedford, 1997.

———. *Traces of a Stream: Literacy and Social Change Among African American Women*. Pittsburgh: University of Pittsburgh Press, 2000.

Singleton, John, and Veronica Chambers. *Poetic Justice: Filmmaking South Central Style*. New York: Delta, 1993.

Smith, Valerie. *Not Just Race, Not Just Gender: Black Feminist Readings*. New York: Routledge, 1998.

Smitherman, Geneva. *Black Talk: Words and Phrases from the Hood to the Amen Corner*. New York: Houghton Mifflin, 1994.

Souljah, Sistah. *No Disrespect*. New York: Vintage, 1994.

———. *The Coldest Winter Ever*. New York: Pocket Books, 2000.

Tate, Greg. *Flyboy in the Buttermilk: Essays on Contemporary America*. New York: Fireside, 1992.

Toop, David. *The Rap Attack #3: African Rap to Global Hip-Hop,* 3rd edition. London: Serpent's Tail, 2000.

Tyree, Omar. *Flyy Girl*. New York: Simon and Schuster, 1993.

Vibe. Hip-Hop Divas. New York: Three Rivers, 2001.

Walker, Alice. *Anything We Love Can Be Saved: A Writer's Activism*. New York: Random House, 1997.

———. *In Search of Our Mothers' Gardens: Womanist Prose*. New York: Harcourt Brace, 1983.

Wallace, Michele. *Black Macho and the Myth of the Superwoman*. New York: Verso, 1991.

———. *Invisibility Blues: From Pop to Theory*. New York: Verso, 1990.

Watkins, S. Craig. *Representing: Hip-Hop Culture and the Production of Black Cinema*. Chicago: University of Chicago Press, 1998.

Westbrook, Alonzo. *Hip-Hoptionary: The Dictionary of Hip-Hop Terminology*. New York: Harlem Moon, 2002.

White, E. Frances. *Dark Continent of Our Bodies: Black Feminism and the Politics of Respectability*. Philadelphia: Temple University Press, 2002.

Wimsatt, William Upski. *Bomb the Suburbs*. Chicago: Subway and Elevated, 1994.

———. *No More Prisons*. Chicago: Subway and Elevated, 1999.

ARTICLES AND ESSAYS

Ards, Angela. "Rhyme and Resist: Organizing the Hip-Hop Generation." *The Nation,* July 26/August 2 1999, 11–20.

Berry, Venise. "Feminine or Masculine: The Conflicting Nature of Female Images in Rap Music." In Susan Cook and Judy Tsou, eds., *Cecilia Reclaimed: Feminist Perspectives on Gender and Music*, 183–201. Champaign: University of Illinois Press, 1994.

Brown, Elsa Barkley. "Negotiating and Transforming the Public Sphere: African American Political Life in the Transition from Slavery to Freedom." In Black Public

Sphere Collective, ed., *The Black Public Sphere: A Public Culture Book*, 111–50. Chicago: University of Chicago Press, 1995.

Bynoe, Yvonne. "Defining the Female Image Through Rap Music and Hip Hop Culture." *Doula: The Journal of Rap Music and Hip-Hop Culture* 1: 2 (2001): 20–25.

Carby, Hazel V. "Policing the Black Woman's Body in an Urban Context." *Critical Inquiry* 18 (1992): 738–55.

Chuck D. "The Sound of Our Young World." *Time,* February 8, 1999, 66.

Coker, Cheo, dream hampton, and Tara Roberts. "A Hip-Hop Nation Divided." *Essence,* August 1994, 62–64, 112–15.

Combahee River Collective. "A Black Feminist Statement." In Gloria T. Hull, Patricia Bell Scott, and Barbara Smith, eds., *All the Women Are White, All the Blacks Are Men, But Some of Us Are Brave: Black Women's Studies*, 13–22. New York: Feminist Press, 1982.

Davis, Eisa. "Sexism and the Art of Feminist Hip-Hop Maintenance." In Rebecca Walker, ed., *To Be Real: Telling the Truth and Changing the Face of Feminism*, 127–42. New York: Anchor Books, 1995.

Davidson, Jiton. "Embracing Our Confusion." In Michael Datcher and Kwame Alexander, eds., *Tough Love: The Life and Death of Tupac Shakur: Cultural Criticism and Familial Observations*, 117–23. Alexandria: Alexander, 1997.

Dawson, Michael. "A Black Counterpublic? Economic Earthquakes, Racial Agendas, and Black Politics." In Black Public Sphere Collective, eds., *The Black Public Sphere: A Public Culture Book*, 199–228. Chicago: University of Chicago Press, 1995.

Forman, Murray. "'Movin' Closer to an Independent Funk': Black Feminist Theory, Standpoint, and Women in Rap." *Women's Studies: An Interdisciplinary Journal* 23 (1994): 35–55.

Gaunt, Kyra. "The Musical Vernacular of Black Girls' Play." In Joseph K. Adjaye and Adrianne R. Andrews, eds., *Language, Rhythm, and Sound: Black Popular Cultures into the Twenty-first Century*, 146–63. Pittsburgh: University of Pittsburgh Press, 1997.

Gonzalez, Michael. "Lil' Kim and Foxy Brown: Mack Divas." *The Source: Magazine of Hip-Hop Culture and Politics,* February 1997, 62–67.

Guevara, Nancy. "Women Writin' Rappin' Breakin.'" In William Eric Perkins, ed., *Droppin' Science: Critical Essays on Rap Music and Hip-Hop Culture*, 49–62. Philadelphia: Temple University Press, 1996.

Habermas, Jürgen. "Further Reflections on the Public Sphere." In Craig Calhoun, ed., *Habermas and the Public Sphere*, 421–61. Cambridge: Massachusetts Institute of Technology Press, 1996.

hampton, dream. "Free the Girls: or, Why I Really Don't Believe There's Much of a Future for Hip-Hop, Let Alone Women in Hip-Hop." In *Vibe Magazine, Hip Hop Divas*, 1–3. New York: Three Rivers Press, 2001.

Height, Dorothy. "'We Wanted the Voice of a Woman to Be Heard': Black Women and the 1963 March on Washington." In Bettye Collier-Thomas and V. P. Franklin, eds., *Sisters in the Struggle: African American Women in the Civil Rights–Black Power Movement*, 83–92. New York: New York University Press, 2001.

Hine, Darlene Clark. "Rape and the Inner Lives of Black Women in the Middle West: Preliminary Thoughts on the Culture of Dissemblance." In Roger Lancaster and Micaela di Leonardo, eds., *The Gender and Sexuality Reader*, 434–39. New York: Routledge, 1997.

Holt, Thomas C. "Afterword: Mapping the Black Public Sphere." In Black Public Sphere Collective, ed., *The Black Public Sphere: A Public Culture Book,* 325–28. Chicago: University of Chicago Press, 1995.

hooks, bell. "Feminism as a Persistent Critique of History: What's Love Got to Do with It?" In Alan Reed, ed., *The Fact of Blackness: Frantz Fanon and Visual Representation,* 76–77. Seattle: Bay, 1996.

Jamison, Laura. "A Feisty Female Rapper Breaks a Hip-Hop Taboo." *New York Times,* January 18, 1998, B34.

Jarratt, Susan. "Feminism and Composition: The Case for Conflict." In Patricia Harkin and John Schilb, eds., *Contending With Words: Composition and Rhetoric in a Postmodern Age,* 105–23. New York: Modern Language Association, 1991.

Johnson, Cheryl. "Participatory Rhetoric and the Teacher as Racial/Gendered Subject." *College English* 56 (1994): 411–19.

Jones, Sarah. "Indecent Exposure." *Honey,* May 2002, 76.

Keyes, Cheryl. "Empowering Self, Making Choices, Creating Spaces: Black Female Identity via Rap Music Performance." *Journal of American Folklore* 113: 449 (2000): 255–69.

———. "'We're More Than a Novelty, Boys': Strategies of Female Rappers in the Rap Music Tradition." In Joan Newlon Radner, ed., *Feminist Messages: Coding in Women's Folk Culture,* 201–20. Urbana: University of Illinois Press, 1993.

Kunjufu, Jawanza. "Turning Boys into Men." *Essence,* November 1988, 112.

Lara, María Pía. "A Reply to My Critics." *Hypatia* 15: 3 (2000): 182–86.

Latifah, Queen. "Lunch with Latifah: Seven Teens, One Queen and an Afternoon of Straight Talk: The War on Girls," *Essence,* October 2002, 172–76, 237–39.

Leger, Dimitry. "Hip-Hop/R&B Divas: The New 411," *The Source: Magazine of Hip-Hop Culture and Politics,* July 1995, 43–46.

Logan, Shirley Wilson. "'When and Where I Enter': Race, Gender, and Composition Studies." In Susan C. Jarratt and Lynn Worsham, eds., *Feminism and Composition Studies: In Other Words,* 45–57. New York: Modern Language Association, 1998.

Morgan, Joan. "The Bad Girls of Hip-Hop." *Essence,* March 1997, 76–77, 132, 134.

———. "The War on Girls: Sex, Lies and Videos." *Essence,* June 2002, 120–24.

Parks, Rosa. "'Tired of Giving In': The Launching of the Montgomery Bus Boycott." In Bettye Collier-Thomas and V. P. Franklin, eds., *Sisters in the Struggle: African American Women in the Civil Rights–Black Power Movement,* 61–74. New York: New York University Press, 2001.

Porter, Wanda Renee. "Salt-N-Pepa, Lil' Kim, Foxy Brown and Eve: The Politics of the Black Female Body." *Doula: The Journal of Rap Music and Hip Hop Culture* 1: 1 (2001): 18–22.

Richardson, Elaine. "'To Protect and Serve': African American Female Literacies." *The Journal of the Conference on College Composition and Communication* 53: 4 (2002): 675–704.

Roberts, Robin. "'Ladies First': Queen Latifah's Afrocentric Feminist Music Video." *African American Review* 28: 2 (1994): 245–57.

Ryan, Mary P. "Gender and Public Access: Women's Politics in Nineteenth-Century America." In Craig Calhoun, ed., *Habermas and the Public Sphere,* 259–88. Cambridge: Massachusetts Institute of Technology Press, 1996.

Smith, Kemba, as told to Stephanie Booth. "Pardon Me." *Honey,* September 2001, 86.

Smitherman, Geneva. "Testifyin, Sermonizin, and Signifyin: Anita Hill, Clarence Thomas and the African American Verbal Tradition." In *African American Women Speak Out on Anita Hill–Clarence Thomas*, 224–42. Detroit: Wayne State University Press, 1995.

Springer, Kimberly. "Third Wave Black Feminism?" *Signs: Journal of Women in Culture and Society* 27: 4 (2002): 1059–82.

Thomas, Lesley D. "What's Love Got to Do with Hip-Hop? An Original Screenplay." *The Source: Magazine of Hip-Hop Culture and Politics,* February 1994, 54–58.

Troutman-Robinson, Denise. "The Tongue or the Sword: Which Is Master?" In Geneva Smitherman, ed., *African American Women Speak Out on Anita Hill–Clarence Thomas*, 208–23. Detroit: Wayne State University Press, 1995.

Veran, Christina. "First Ladies: Fly Females Who Rocked the Mike in the 70s and 80s." In *Vibe Magazine, Hip-Hop Divas,* 5–19. New York: Three Rivers, 2001.

Walker, Rebecca. "Becoming the Third Wave." In Amy Kesselman, Lily D. McNair, and Nancy Schniedewind, eds., *Women: Images and Realities: A Multicultural Anthology*, 532–33. Mountain View: Mayfield, 1999.

Wallace, Michele. "*Boyz 'N the Hood* and *Jungle Fever.*" In Gina Dent, ed., *Black Popular Culture*, 123–31. Seattle: Bay, 1992.

———. "When Black Feminism Faces the Music and the Music Is Rap." In Diana George and John Trimbur, eds., *Reading Culture: Context for Critical Reading and Writing*, 23–25. New York: HarperCollins, 1995.

Watts, Eric King. "The Female Voice in Hip-Hop: An Exploration into the Potential of Erotic Appeal." In Marsha Houston and Olga I. Davis, eds., *Centering Ourselves: African American Feminist and Womanist Studies of Discourse*, 187–213. Cresskill: Hampton, 2002.

Williams, Sherley Anne. "Some Implications of Womanist Theory." In Angelyn Mitchell, ed., *Within the Circle: An Anthology of African-American Literary Criticism from the Harlem Renaissance to the Present*, 515–21. Durham: Duke University Press, 1994.

Willis, Andre. "A Womanist Turn on the Hip-Hop Theme: Leslie Harris's *Just Another Girl on the IRT.*" In Joseph K. Adjaye and Adrianne R. Andrews, eds., *Language, Rhythm, and Sound: Black Popular Cultures into the Twenty-first Century*, 134–45. Pittsburgh: University of Pittsburgh Press, 1997.

Willis, Christine A., and Adrien Katherine Wing. "Sisters in the Hood: Beyond Bloods and Crips." In Adrien Katherine Wing, ed., *Critical Race Feminism: A Reader*, 243–54. New York: New York University Press, 1997.

Zook, Kristal Brent. "A Manifesto of Sorts for a Black Feminist Movement: When Mike Tyson's a Hero, Louis Farrakhan's a Leader and the Old Guard of Women Stands Silent, It's Left to a New Generation to Change the Rules." *New York Times Magazine,* November 12, 1995, 86–89.

MUSIC

Alicia Keys. *Songs in A Minor.* J Records, 2001.
Another Bad Creation. "Iesha." *Coolin' at the Playground Ya Know.* Motown, 1991.
Apache. "Gangsta Bitch." *Apache Ain't Shit.* Tommy Boy, 1991.
Beanie Sigel featuring Eve. "Remember Them Days." *The Truth.* Def Jam, 1999.
Common Sense. "I Used to Love H.E.R." *Resurrection.* Loud Records, 1994.

Erykah Badu. "On & On." *Baduizm*. Kedar, 1997.

Erykah Badu featuring Common. "Love of My Life (Ode to Hip Hop)." *Brown Sugar* [soundtrack]. MCA, 2002.

Eve. "Love Is Blind." *Let There Be Eve . . . Ruff Ryders' First Lady.* Interscope, 1999.

Foxy Brown. "Get Me Home." *Ill Na Na.* Def Jam, 1996.

———. "(Holy Matrimony) Letter to the Firm." *Ill Na Na.* Def Jam, 1996.

———. "My Life." *Chyna Doll.* Def Jam, 1998.

Fugees. *The Score.* Ruffhouse, 1996.

Gina Thompson featuring Missy Elliott. "The Things That You Do." *Nobody Does It Better.* Mercury, 1996.

Gladys Knight and the Pips. *The Very Best of Gladys Knight & the Pips.* Buddah Records, 1998.

Ja Rule featuring Charlie Baltimore. "Down Ass Bitch." *Pain Is Love.* Def Jam, 2001.

Ja Rule featuring Ashanti, Charlie Baltimore, and Vita. "Down 4 U." *Irv Gotti Presents— The Inc.* Def Jam, 2002.

Lauryn Hill. *The Miseducation of Lauryn Hill,* Ruffhouse, 1998.

Leschea. "Hip-Hop." *Rhythm & Beats.* Warner Brothers, 1996.

Lil' Bow Wow. "Ghetto Girls." *Beware of Dog.* So So Def, 2000.

Lil' Kim. "Queen B@$#H." *Hard Core.* Undeas, 1996.

———. "We Don't Need It." *Hard Core.* Undeas, 1996.

LL Cool J. "Around the Way Girl." *Mama Said Knock You Out.* Def Jam, 1990.

———. "I Need Love." *Bigger and Deffer.* Def Jam, 1987.

Mary J. Blige. "Be Happy." *My Life.* Uptown MCA, 1994.

———. "My Life." *My Life.* Uptown MCA, 1994.

———. "Real Love." *What's the 411?* Uptown MCA, 1992.

Method Man. "I'll Be There for You/You're All I Need to Get By." *Tical.* Def Jam, 1994.

Missy "Misdemeanor" Elliott. "The Rain (Supa Dupa Fly)." *Supa Dupa Fly.* Elektra, 1997.

Notorious B.I.G. "Me and My Bitch." *Ready to Die.* Bad Boy, 1994.

———. "One More Chance." *Ready to Die.* Bad Boy, 1994.

Paradise. "Hoochies Need Love Too." *Above the Rim.* Death Row Records, 1994.

Queen Latifah. "Just Another Day." *Black Reign.* Motown, 1993.

———. "Ladies First." *All Hail the Queen.* Tommy Boy, 1989.

———. "U.N.I.T.Y." *Black Reign.* Motown, 1993.

Queen Pen. "Girlfriend." *My Melody.* Lil'Man Records, 1997.

Roxanne Shante. "Roxanne's Revenge." *Fat Beats & Bra Straps: Battle Rhymes & Posse.* Rhino, 1998.

Super Nature [early incarnation of Salt-N-Pepa]. "The Show Stoppa (Is Stupid Fresh)." *Fat Beats & Bra Straps: Battle Rhymes & Posse.* Rhino, 1998.

Sugar Hill Gang. "Rapper's Delight." Sugar Hill Records, 1979.

The Roots. "Act Too (Love of My Life)." *Things Fall Apart.* MCA, 1999.

A Tribe Called Quest. "Bonita Applebum." *People's Instinctive Travels and the Paths of Rhythm.* Jive Records, 1990.

Trina. "Mama." *Da Baddest B***h.* Slip N Slide Records, 2000.

Yo-Yo. "Black Pearl." *Black Pearl.* EastWest Records, 1992.

FILMS

Above the Rim, dir. Jeff Pollack, 1994.

Beat Street, dir. Stan Lathan, 1984.

Boyz 'N the Hood, dir. John Singleton, 1991.

Breakin', dir. Joel Silberg, 1984.

Brown Sugar, dir. Rick Famuyiwa, 2002.

Do the Right Thing, dir. Spike Lee, 1989.

Don't Be a Menace to South Central While Drinking Your Juice in the Hood, dir. Paris Barclay, 1996.

Friday, dir. F. Gary Gray, 1995.

Jason's Lyric, dir. Doug McHenry, 1994.

Juice, dir. Ernest Dickerson, 1992.

Just Another Girl on the IRT, dir. Leslie Harris, 1993.

Menace II Society, dir. Albert Hughes and Allen Hughes, 1993.

New Jersey Drive, dir. Nick Gomez and Howard McMaster, 1995.

Nobody Knows My Name, dir. Rachel Raimist, 1999.

A Place of Rage, dir. Pratibka Parmar, 1991.

Poetic Justice, dir. John Singleton, 1993.

Race, Identity, and the Politics of Gangsta Rap, dir. Sut Jhalley, 1995.

Rhyme & Reason, dir. Peter Spirer, 1997.

Set It Off, dir. F. Gary Gray, 1996.

The Show, dir. Brian Robbins, 1995.

Straight Outta Brooklyn, dir. Matty Rich, 1991.

Waiting to Exhale, dir. Forest Whitaker, 1995.

Wild Style, dir. Charlie Ahearn, 1982.

Index

Black Fire (ed. Neal and Jones), 65
Black Liberation Army, 61
Black Macho and the Myth of the Superwoman (Wallace), 75, 115
Black men/manhood: Black public sphere and, 36, 39, 75–76; fathers, absenteeism of, 141, 143, 185, 235n.33; ghetto girl as threat to, 135–36; lack of, and strong Black woman, 234n.23. *See also* men rappers
Black mothers: narratives of, 120–25, 235–36n.40; relationship with daughters, 235–36n.40, 235n.36; single, demonization of, 130–31, 229n.39; stereotypes of, 63–64, 122–25, 217; as threat to Black manhood, 139, 229–30n.50
Black nationalism, 166, 225n.10
Black Panther Party: media criticism of, 226n.28; and pussy power, 60–61, 229n.46; and representation, 22–23; and spectacle, 20, 25–27, 225n.10
"Black Pearl" (Yo Yo), 110
Black popular culture, Black feminism and, 70–71
Black Power movement, 65–66, 99, 187
Black public sphere: and American public sphere, 16–17, 18; and Black public culture, 36; Black women and, 36–40, 41–42, 44–47, 60, 75–77; blaxploitation movies, 65–68; blues culture as, 57–58; civil rights movement as, 58–60; as counterpublic, 35–36; defined, 16, 34; Habermas and, 34; male dominance of, 36, 39, 75–76; as space of critique/transformation, 221
Black Public Sphere Collective, 16
Black Public Sphere, The, 34–35
Black Sister (ed. Stetson), 65
Black Thought, 96
Black Woman, The (ed. Bambara), 63, 65
Black women: and American public sphere, 6, 18; and Black community, concern for, 49, 51–52; and Black public sphere, 36–40, 41–42, 44–47; and fairy tale, 176–77, 178; fatherlessness and, 235n.33; and gangs, 129–30; gangsta bitch image and, 89–90; and Hip-Hop, 8–11, 19, 224n.15; Hip-Hop symbolized as, 92–97; misrepresentation of, in male rap, 97–101; oppression of, 158–61; in precolonial Africa, 47; in prison, 188–92; rap and, 188–92; and sass, 49–50; slavery and, 50–51; spectacle/representation used by, 22–24, 217; as teachers in white classrooms, 198; vindication of, as theme, 49, 50–51, 53–56, 89; war on girls, 220–21;

White male desire for, 67. *See also* Black mothers; Black women, expressive cultures of; Black women, Hip-Hop-generation; Black women, sexuality of; Black women, stereotypes of; ghetto girl, in film/literature; women rappers
Black Women as Cultural Readers (Bobo), 70–71
Black women, expressive cultures of, 47; adaptability of, 43–44; Black Arts movement, 61–65; blues women and, 57–58; cipher and, 41–42, 44; civil rights movement and, 58–60; clubwomen and, 52–53, 59; common themes in, 49, 52; feminism and, 45–47; and illocutionary force, 44–45; intellectual/activist traditions of, 47–56, 69; lineage of, 42–44; overlapping/continuations in traditions, 56–57; rhetorical tools of, 48–50, 77–83
Black women, Hip-Hop-generation: autobiographies of, 111–20; and Black public sphere, 75–77; generational shifts of, 235n.31; and misrepresentation in male rap, 97–101; mothers of, 120–25, 235–36n.40; and rap, 83–92; and rap as autobiography, 106–11; and representation, 92–97; rhetoric of, 77–83; soul divas and, 175
Black women, sexuality of, 49; Black Arts movement and, 62–63; in blaxploitation movies, 66–68; blues women and, 57–58; clubwomen and, 52–56; and culture of dissemblance, 23, 50; men rappers and, 186–87; spoken-word poetry and, 99; stereotypes of, 152, 187–88, 236–37n.9; women rappers and, 182–92, 201–5
Black women, stereotypes of: of Black mothers, 63–64, 122–25; Black Power movement and, 63–64; blues women and, 57; early activism against, 47–48; female responsibility for perpetuation of, 204; Hip-Hop generation women and, 87–88; men rappers and, 73–74; representation and, 217; strong Black woman, 234n.23, 235–36n.40; subversion of, in film, 66–68, 149–51; women rappers and, 186–88. *See also* ghetto girl, in film/literature; *specific stereotype*
Blackstreet, 166
blaxploitation films, 26, 65–68, 130, 183
Blige, Mary J., 8, 106–7, 172–76, 180, 181, 182
blues, 36, 37, 39, 57–58
boasting rap, 180
Bobo, Jacqueline, 70–71
body: exploitation of, 67–68; policing of, 58
Bogle, Donald, 66